Special Purpose Computers

This is Volume 5 in
COMPUTATIONAL TECHNIQUES
Edited by Berni J. Alder and Sidney Fernbach
A list of titles in this series appears at the end of this volume.

Special Purpose Computers

Edited by

BERNI J. ALDER

Lawrence Livermore National Laboratory
Livermore, California

ACADEMIC PRESS, INC.

Harcourt Brace Jovanovich, Publishers
Boston   San Diego   New York
Berkeley   London   Sydney
Tokyo   Toronto

ACADEMIC PRESS, INC.
1250 Sixth Avenue, San Diego, CA 92101

United Kingdom Edition published by
ACADEMIC PRESS INC. (LONDON) LTD.
24–28 Oval Road, London NW1 7DX

Library of Congress Cataloging-in-Publication Data

Special purpose computers / edited by Berni J. Alder.
    p.   cm. — (Computational techniques : v. 5)
  Bibliography: p.
  Includes index.
  ISBN 0-12-049260-1
  1. Electronic digital computers.   I. Alder, B. J.   II. Series.
QA76.5.S6588 1988   87-28914
004 — dc19   CIP

Printed in the United States of America
88 89 90 91   9 8 7 6 5 4 3 2 1

Contents

Contributors   *vii*
Introduction   *ix*

Chapter 1   **The Hypercube and the Caltech Concurrent Computation Program: A Microcosm of Parallel Computing**   1
                   Geoffrey C. Fox

Chapter 2   **The QCD Machine**   41
                   Anthony E. Terrano

Chapter 3   **Geometry-Defining Processors for Partial Differential Equations**   67
                   D. Dewey and A. T. Patera

Chapter 4   **Navier-Stokes Computer**   97
                   Daniel M. Nosenchuck, William Flannery, and Ehtesham Hayder

Chapter 5   **Parallel Processing with the Loosely Coupled Array of Processors System**   135
                   E. Clementi and D. Logan

Chapter 6   **Design and Implementation of the Delft Molecular-Dynamics Processor**   183
                   A. F. Bakker and C. Bruin

Chapter 7   **The Delft Ising System Processor**   233
                   A. Hoogland, A. Compagner, and H. W. J. Blöte

Contributors

Numbers in parentheses refer to the pages on which the authors' contributions begin.

A. F. Bakker (183), *University of Technology, Laboratory of Applied Physics, Lorentzweg 1, 2628 CJ Delft, The Netherlands*

H. W. J. Blöte (233), *University of Technology, Laboratory of Applied Physics, Lorentzweg 1, 2628 CJ Delft, The Netherlands*

C. Bruin (183), *University of Technology, Laboratory of Applied Physics, Lorentzweg 1, 2628 CJ Delft, The Netherlands*

E. Clementi (135), *IBM Corporation, Data Systems Division, Department 48 B, MS 428, PO Box 100, Neighborhood Road, Kingston, New York 12401*

A. Compagner (233), *University of Technology, Laboratory of Applied Physics, Lorentzweg 1, 2628 CJ Delft, The Netherlands*

Daniel Dewey (67), *Department of Mechanical Engineering, Massachusetts Institute of Technology, 77 Massachusetts Avenue, Cambridge, Massachusetts 02139*

William Flannery (97), *School of Engineering and Applied Science, Department of Mechanical and Aerospace Engineering, D 323, Princeton University, Princeton, New Jersey 08544*

Geoffrey C. Fox (1), *Concurrent Computing Group, Mail Code 0 15-79, California Institute of Technology, Pasadena, California 91125*

Ehtesham Hayder (97), *School of Engineering and Applied Science, Department of Mechanical and Aerospace Engineering, D 323, Princeton University, Princeton, New Jersey 08544*

A. Hoogland (233), *University of Technology, Laboratory of Applied Physics, Lorentzweg 1, 2628 CJ Delft, The Netherlands*

D. Logan (135), *IBM Corporation, Data Systems Division, Department 48 B, MS 428, PO Box 100, Neighborhood Road, Kingston, New York 12401*

D. Nosenchuck (97), *School of Engineering and Applied Science, Department of Mechanical and Aerospace Engineering, D 323, Princeton University, Princeton, New Jersey 08544*

Anthony Patera (67), *Department of Mechanical Engineering, Massachusetts Institute of Technology, 77 Massachusetts Avenue, Cambridge, Massachusetts 02139*

Anthony E. Terrano (41), *Department of Electrical and Computer Engineering, School of Engineering, Rutgers University, Piscataway, New Jersey 08854*

Introduction

General purpose computers are designed to run a large variety of application programs. Since different problems make different demands on a computer, compromises are made in the design that will limit the efficiency of running any individual program. In contrast, if the computer is specifically designed to solve a particular problem, every feature of this computer can be tuned to the problem at hand. For this reason, problems can be solved orders of magnitude faster on special purpose computers.

The purpose of this book is to describe such computers, which were especially designed and built to solve particular scientific problems and to compare them to general purpose computers, in both speed and cost. This is for the benefit of others who might contemplate similar endeavors.

Drawbacks to the special purpose computer approach are that the designing and building of such computers is more expensive and time consuming than developing programs for general purpose computers. Moreover, special purpose computers can rarely be adapted to solve other problems or be modified to exploit algorithmic improvements. Hence, it is not advisable to freeze a particular numerical approach into hardware unless the algorithm is both planned to be used for a long time and also well established, since as much efficiency can be gained by searching for better numerical techniques as by better arrangement of the computer components.

There are many scientific problems that are inherently too complex to be solved on any general purpose computer available in the foreseeable future. One such case described in this book is the lattice gauge calculation. Since the very foundation of high energy physics depends on a numerical validation of these equations, several special purpose computers have been built for solving that problem. One such special purpose computer (the hypercube) interestingly enough has turned out to be useful for a variety of other scientific applications. This is a good example of how the building of a special purpose computer with a different architecture stimulated the design of a new class of more general purpose computers. On the other hand, some new computer architectures are built without specific purposes in mind, although they turn out to be particularly suitable for solving certain classes of problems. One such example is the connection machine that solves Ising, cellular automata, and neural networks problems very efficiently.

The computers that were designed for the efficient solution of long established algorithms described in this book are Navier–Stokes hydrodynamic solvers, classical molecular dynamic machines, and Ising model computers. The hope is that the documentation of the experiences of building those devices will advance the process of numerically solving scientific problems.

—Berni J. Alder
Series Editor

1

The Hypercube and the Caltech Concurrent Computation Program: A Microcosm of Parallel Computing

GEOFFREY C. FOX[†]

California Institute of Technology
Pasadena, California

I. Original Motivation and Historical Overview

The CalTech Concurrent Computation Program. An evolution from computational high energy physics to a supercomputer initiative.

A. Introduction

This article is a personal impression of the research of the Caltech Concurrent Computation Program. Its autobiographical slant allows me to paint issues as black and white that when averaged over others' outlooks would

† Research supported by the Department of Energy grant, DE-FG03-85ER25009, the Parsons Foundation, the Systems Development Foundation, and the office of the program manager of the Joint Tactical Fusion Office.

1

be muddied and unclear. I should note that I am very grateful to my many collaborators, but they should not be held responsible for opinions expressed here; these opinions are my own. We will chronicle the progress of our research with the purpose of clarifying the lessons learned—from detailed computer architecture issues to such global points as the trade-offs between inhouse and commercial development.

The progress of the Caltech Concurrent Computation Program can be divided into four stages. Birth and early struggles to survive occupied 1981–1983. Carefree youth and unblemished success lasted from mid-1983 to the end of 1984. Middle age with difficult bittersweet choices was successfully weathered in 1985 and 1986. In the current stage, we look to fresh beginnings with new initiatives starting in 1986 and 1987. We give an overview of these four stages in the remainder of this section.

In Sections II and IV respectively, we describe two particular areas— hardware and software—where our project, like others, has had successes but also difficulties. In each case, we discuss the plusses and minuses of inhouse versus commercial development. We break up these logistic sections by a description in Section III of the major result of our research— namely, that a hypercube can be a general purpose supercomputer—and of how we were led to this conclusion. In the final section, we turn to the future, where we see a growing interest not in showing that particular parallel machines are usable but in comparing and evaluating the different architectures.

This paper is, of course, not complete. We refer to our last annual report [1] for a programmatic description of our research. Another subjective and historical account will be found in [2] which covers more issues but in less depth.

B. The Beginning

We can trace the origins of our research to the work, led by Chris Cole and Stephen Wolfram, in developing the Symbolic Manipulation Program (SMP). This work required us to bring up UNIX on our new VAX11/780, the first time this had been done at Caltech. This endeavor established our first ties with the Caltech Computer Science department and I can still remember Carver Mead urging us to get back with them if we had insoluble large-scale computational needs. However, these events just provided the ambiance; the real conception of C^3P, the Caltech Concurrent Computation Program, occurred in May 1981 when Carver Mead gave a Physics Colloquium on VLSI, very large scale integration, and the opportunities it opened up. By that time, I had switched my interest from symbolic to numerical computation techniques for QCD, Quantum Chromodynamics. It had become apparent that (symbolic) evaluation of perturbation series for QCD missed the point, and only approaches that included nonperturbative effects would allow realistic predictions for a range of observables. Thus, my approach had changed from SMP to numerical computations which ran for many days (weeks) on the long-suffering VAX. At Carver's colloquium, I realized that our QCD calculations could be performed concurrently and that his VLSI revolution would lead to cost-effective concurrent computers for this problem.

During the summer of 1981, my research group, especially Eugene Brooks and Steve Otto, showed that effective concurrent algorithms could be developed, and we presented our conclusion to the Caltech Computer Scientists. This presentation led to the plans, described in more detail in Section II, to produce the first hypercube, with Chuck Seitz and his student Erik DeBenedictis developing the hardware and my group the QCD software. My group did not understand what a hypercube was at that stage, but agreed with the computer scientists because the planned six-dimensional hypercube was isomorphic to a $4 \times 4 \times 4$ three-dimensional mesh, a topology whose relevance a physicist could appreciate. With the generous help of the computer scientists, we gradually came to understand the hypercube topology with its general advantage (maximum distance between nodes is $\log_2 N$) and its specific feature of including a rich variety of mesh topologies. Here N is the total number of nodes in the concurrent computer. We should emphasize that our understanding of the relevance of concurrency to QCD was not particularly novel; it followed from ideas already known from earlier concurrent machines such as the Illiac IV. We were, however, fortunate to investigate the issues at a time when microprocessor technology (in particular the INTEL 8086/8087) allowed one to build large (in terms of number of nodes) cost-effective concurrent computers with interesting performance levels. The QCD problem was also important in helping ensure that the initial Cosmic Cube was built with sensible design choices; we were fortunate that in choosing parameters, such as memory size, appropriate for QCD, we also realized a machine of general capability.

From the start, we realized that the Cosmic Cube was too small and that we needed a much larger system for decisive QCD calculations. My initial attempts to raise money to support this were certainly naive, but I was fortunate that my conversations with potential funding agencies, especially Don Austin at DOE and Charles Smith at Systems Development Foundations, forced me to understand the issues more deeply and to develop some ideas that were perhaps novel. These developed during 1982 while we used a small four-node test system to develop our QCD applications. I used this time to explore other applications of the Cosmic Cube as I wandered around first Campus and then JPL (the Jet Propulsion Laboratory) and tried to understand the "reason" why many groups were dissatisfied with

VAX-class computing and needed more computational power. This led to one major qualitative discovery: namely, the Cosmic Cube seemed suitable for many other applications besides its original high-energy physics and computer science motivation. I was also able to develop a rather quantitative speedup analysis which was later borne out experimentally and is described in Section III. In early 1983, we put together our first significant proposals to INTEL, DOE, and the Parsons and Systems Development Foundations. This started the next phase of the project, since we were funded to investigate the hypercube as a relatively general-purpose computer for scientific and engineering problems.

C. Carefree Youth

In August 1983, or in reality in the fall quarter of 1983–84, we started our next phase. The late spring and summer had been full of worry. Would we get funded? Could we make commitments to key people like my graduating student S. Otto? Would the Cosmic Cube be finished in a timely fashion and would it run reliably? How should one organize such a complicated cross-disciplinary project?

In fact, all the issues were answered satisfactorily, and the year or so beginning in August 1983 was in retrospect the most enjoyable period of our project. The project was still relatively small and we made some interesting discoveries that were well received by our peers. The term C^3P was coined at this time and the initial collaboration included C. Seitz (computer science), myself (high-energy physics), R. Clayton and B. Hager (geophysics), A. Kuppermann (chemistry) and H. Keller and P. Saffman (applied mathematics). We also involved the Jet Propulsion Laboratory at this stage as a professional engineering team to construct our future hypercube hardware and software.

Our major achievement during 1984 was, I believe, to experimentally verify the basic assertion of our proposals: yes, the hypercube is a generally usable concurrent computer. We ran the initial Cosmic Cube for 2500 hours on a QCD calculation of the $\bar{q}q$ potential; this was at the time better than the competitive CRAY and CDC-205 calculations. Further, we were able to develop 10 programs that actually ran on the hypercube and "solved real problems with real hardware using real software"—still the underlying motif of our research. These programs also verified the simple speedup model that I had developed earlier and this success allowed one to extrapolate their performance to larger systems.

These 10 initial applications are recorded for posterity in [3], an internal document which we should have published as a collection of papers. Mistakenly, we decided to write a book, a good but time-consuming idea which did not replace the immediate publication of the reprints. Our 10 pioneers were:

Table 1. The Ten Pioneer Hypercube Applications

Dynamics of sand grains	B. Werner, P. Haff
Lattice gauge theory	S. Otto
Sorting	E. Felten, S. Karlin
Travelling salesman by simulated annealing	S. Otto
Coulomb gas Monte Carlo	F. Fucito, S. Solomon
Melting of a two-dimensional solid	M. Johnson
Evolution of the universe	J. Salmon
Two-dimensional hydrodynamics	D. Meier
Acoustic wave equation	R. Clayton
Matrix inversion for chemical reaction studies	P. Hipes, A. Kuppermann

We were a success and achieved flattering attention from the outside, but now we entered a new stage.

D. Middle Age — Crisis of Identity and Purpose

Our work in 1984 established a solid framework on which we were able to build and expand our work in ways that continued to be important and successful. For instance, our high-energy physics calculations on the hypercube have, so far, led to a total of 16 publications. Further, some 20 different groups at Caltech have now used the hypercube and as shown in Table 2, these span a wide variety of disciplines. This confirms and reinforces our assertion that hypercubes are not specialized processors; they are

Table 2. Representative Users of Concurrent Computers at Caltech (Scientists are Caltech faculty unless otherwise indicated)

General Field	Associated Scientists	Topic
Applied Math & Computer Science	A. Barr	Computer graphics
	J. Goldsmith (JPL)	
	B. Beckman (JPL)	Time-warp event-driven simulation
	D. Jefferson (UCLA)	
	M. Buehler (JPL)	Computer-aided design
	G. Fox	Matrix algorithms
	W. Furmanski	Load-balancing algorithms
		Optimization
		Computer chess
	H. Keller	Parallel shooting
	P. Saffman	Multigrid adaptive meshes
	C. Seitz	Mathematics and logic
		Computer-aided design

Table 2. Representative Users of Concurrent Computers at Caltech
(Scientists are Caltech faculty unless otherwise indicated) *(Continued)*

General Field	Associated Scientists	Topic
Biology	J. Bower J. Hopfield C. Koch W. Furmanski	Modelling of cortex and applied neural networks
Chemistry and Chemical Engineering	J. Brady W. Goddard A. Kuppermann	Flow of porous media Protein dynamics Chemical reaction dynamics
Engineering	N. Corngold R. Gould P. Liewer (JPL) J. Hall W. Johnson A. Leonard B. Sturtevant R. McEliece E. Posner F. Pollara (JPL) J. Solomon (JPL)	Turbulence (strange attractors) Plasma physics (PIC) Finite-element analysis of earthquake engineering Condensed matter simulations for material science Fluid turbulence in computational aerodynamics Convolution decoding Image processing
Geophysics	R. Clayton B. Hager T. Tanimoto	Seismic waves tomography Geodynamics Normal modes of earth
Physics	R. Blandford D. Meier (JPL) M. Cross G. Fox T. Gottschalk S. Koonin A. Readhead T. Prince T. Tombrello	Fluid jets in astrophysics Condensed matter Two-dimensional melting High-energy physics Lattice gauge theory Tracking, Kalman filters Nuclear matter Astronomical data analysis Granular physics Molecular dynamics

general-purpose computers applicable to the vast majority of large scientific and engineering problems.

However, this very success brought with it difficulties that were compounded by other outside influences. In 1985 and 1986, we were faced with difficult issues such as

- What do we do for an encore, since our very success has led to some 100 commercial hypercubes sold (as of early 1987), and counting Caltech applications can no longer be considered a measure of success?
- Caltech is at its best in blazing new trails; we are not the best place for programmatic research that dots i's and crosses t's.
- My group started off as computational physicists. What are we now? Certainly, much of our research is outside a conventionally defined physics program.
- How do we disseminate the results of our research?
- Our research was originally motivated by the solution of real problems on the hypercube. However, the new NSF Supercomputer Centers have made more computer time available to Caltech researchers than is possible on the older 8086/80286-based hypercubes.
- What is our relation to the several commercial hypercube projects? This is a flattering development that could, however, stifle our research, especially as the initial commercial offerings offered other researchers test machines without offering us an interesting computer.
- Should we have in-house hardware and systems software efforts or should we rely on commercial developments?

As you see, these issues were not due to failure in a conventional sense; in fact, during this period the hypercube-related research at Caltech grew rapidly and currently involves some 100 people at Campus and JPL. However, as we found, success was a mixed blessing. In fact, I have often thought that we and indeed the world would have been better served if we could have delayed our perceived success and the commercial developments by a year or so. This would have allowed us to present our initial results in a more orderly fashion and would have resulted in more effective commercial endeavors which paid quantitative and not just qualitative attention to our research.

Sections II and IV discuss how we evolved hardware and software within the context of the issues listed above. Here we will skip over these logistic problems and rather discuss the resolution of our mid-life identity crisis.

E. A New Beginning?

Over the last year (1986–1987), we have made two important decisions at Caltech that will inevitably change the course of our research. The latest of these decisions is the clearest: our research makes little sense unless we focus it on supercomputers or more precisely concurrent computers with supercomputer performance. This decision is necessitated by the growing availability of conventional supercomputers (DOE and NSF CRAY class machines) and our focus on solving real computational problems. Thus, we have returned, in some sense, to our original goal—build/acquire a large concurrent computer to solve QCD but with the amplification of the project to develop a concurrent supercomputer capable of addressing the majority of Caltech scientific and engineering problems. This rationale lies behind our new "Concurrent Supercomputing Initiative at Caltech" (CSIC). We also believe that we should consider a broader range of architectures; it is now generally agreed that parallel computers "work," and we now need to find out which works best. Again, I have studied the hypercube for five years, and now is a good time to branch out and consider concurrent supercomputers without prejudice to the architecture. So we find two new logistic thrusts of research:

- Concentration on parallel machines with supercomputer performance;
- Evaluation and comparison of various architectures. In particular, future machines at Caltech may well not be hypercubes; we will also consider shared-memory, fine-grain, neural-network or dataflow machines. May the best architecture win!

A second development at Caltech is less obvious. Our provost, Robbie Vogt, recognized that several faculty members at Caltech had related interests in computation which were not well served by the existing academic groupings. Thus, a small working group led by John Hopfield proposed the new Computation and Neural Systems (CNS) Ph.D. program at Caltech, which cut across traditional boundaries since it united biology, computer science, and physics. My original interest in CNS stemmed from the following question:

- We now understand rather well scientific and engineering applications on the hypercube; what about artificial intelligence?

Actually, I now believe that the most promising approach to intelligent or better-phrased autonomous computers is not LISP/PROLOG on parallel machines but rather the use of neural networks. The hypercube is an excellent simulator of neural networks which are themselves distributed memory "computers." In fact, neural networks are really similar to many other scientific systems and can be addressed on the hypercube by techniques developed for matrices and circuit simulation [4].

I believe that CNS will be a growing focus of my research both in terms of neural networks for intelligent computers and also for biological simulations and the study of complex systems [5]. The latter is an off-beat field studied by Wolfram, Gell-Mann, and Hopfield, to name a distinguished company. I have found complex systems to be a good framework for classifying problems and computers; it is a convenient way of quantifying studies of computer architecture.

We have come a long way in five years and each year we find ourselves doing things that we could not and did not predict even a year ahead. I cannot, therefore, have any useful idea as to what the future holds. I hope it is fun and useful to the world.

II. Hypercube Hardware

Trials and tribulations. The in-house machine compared to working with industry.

Hypercube concurrent processors have one of the simpler architectures; namely, these are "just"

A collection of "ordinary computers" (called nodes) connected by a set of communication channels.

There is no shared memory, and the nodes communicate via messages. Each node runs asynchronously with, in general, a separate clock.

Commentators have often said, sometimes in jest and sometimes seriously, that this is little more than a bunch of PCs or SUN Workstations connected by Ethernet. Actually, a collection of networked workstations can certainly be considered as a distributed memory coarse-grain-size concurrent computer; the complete interconnect provided by the Ethernet can be used to emulate the hypercube or indeed any topology. This idea is the basis of our SURFcube system, which allows a group of PCs (currently AT or XT) connected by RS-232 links to run the identical software to the hypercubes [6]. This SURFcube system is a good learning environment since each node of the SURFcube can be equipped with a graphics monitor, whereas a real hypercube is lucky to have one graphics device for the full system. However, such systems are not competitive in performance with hypercubes designed from scratch, because one needs high bandwidth channels between the nodes. As described in Section III, it is sufficient to build the hardware so that

$$\tau = \frac{t_{comm}}{t_{calc}} \sim 1. \tag{1}$$

Here t_{comm} is a typical time taken to communicate a 32-bit word between two nodes and t_{calc} is typical time to complete a calculation within a node. In our original hardware (the Cosmic Cube or Mark I and the Mark II) [7]

$$t_{comm} \sim 60 \ \mu s,$$
$$t_{calc} \sim 25 \ \mu s, \tag{2}$$

and

$$\tau \sim 2.$$

A 9600 kbaud RS232 line has

$$t_{comm} \sim 3000 \; \mu s,$$

which is unacceptably slow for many applications.

We have taken this diversion to explain why it is not trivial to build hypercubes. One cannot take CPU nodes designed for other purposes and easily adapt them for a hypercube. In fact, all current hypercubes have node boards that have been designed from scratch. This point is illustrated in Figure 1 which shows the node board for the Mark II hypercube. The bottom half of the board implements the eight high-speed communication channels, while the top half is a conventional computer which is of course comparable to an IBM PC in power.

The original Cosmic Cube was designed by Chuck Seitz and his student Erik DeBenedictis at the end of 1981. Each node contained:

8086 microprocessor

8087 floating point co-processor

128K bytes memory

6 communication channels

In spite of various logistic problems, we were using prototype 4-node systems in 1982 and had completed 8- and 64-node (3- and 6-dimensional hypercubes) by October 1983. My student, Mark Johnson, played a major role in debugging the systems during summer of 1983 so that they ran reliably.

As described in Section I, the project had modest scope in these early days, but during 1983 we obtained the funding to really open up the project as a discipline-wide investigation of the hypercube in a variety of scientific and engineering fields. We decided that this required a different approach to hardware, and we involved Caltech's Jet Propulsion Laboratory (JPL) in the design and construction. JPL is a division of Caltech and therefore responsive to the needs of the Campus; the repute of its professional engineering skill is reemphasized every time Voyager flies by another planet. We had tried to raise funds in mid-1983 to build a really large (1024-node) hypercube; we understood that this was desirable both to test the scaling of algorithms with number of nodes and to provide good peak performance. The latter was correctly considered crucial because in our approach the hypercube acted as a carrot to computational scientists. Thus, we were asking scientists to invest the time in developing concurrent algorithms and benchmarking experimental machines; in exchange, we wanted to offer the use of high-performance machines which could perform major calculations. However, probably wisely, our funding agencies decided that both the microprocessor technology and the concurrent algorithm field were developing so rapidly that it was inappropriate to build a

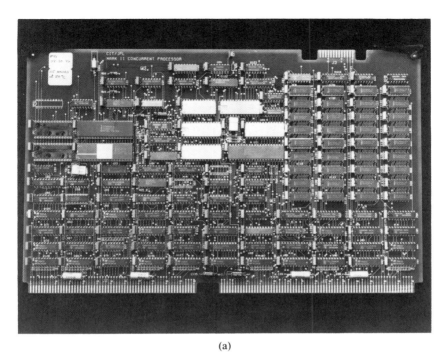

(a)

Mark II Node Board

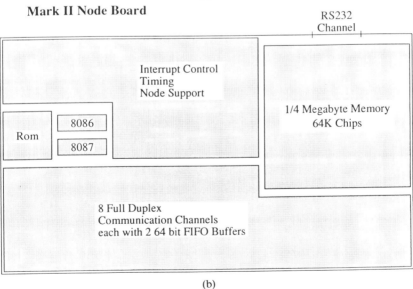

RS232
Channel

Interrupt Control
Timing
Node Support

1/4 Megabyte Memory
64K Chips

Rom

8086

8087

8 Full Duplex
Communication Channels
each with 2 64 bit FIFO Buffers

(b)

Figure 1. (a) Node board for the Mark II hypercube designed and constructed at JPL in 1983–84.

(b) The block diagram shows the division into processor, memory and communication channels.

large machine. We were able to mount a modest program, and after toying with use of new processors and new 8086/80186/80286 designs, we decided correctly that the initial step was the production of a new machine with only minor changes from the original Mark I or Cosmic Cube. Thus, the Mark II systems shown in Figures 1 and 2 were born. Each node consisted of:

8086 microprocessor
8087 floating point unit
256K bytes memory
8 communication channels

We did not upgrade to the 80286 processor, since our applications were dominated by floating point calculation and the 80287 is not faster than the 8087. We increased the memory because the applications clearly needed it — our first machine was designed to QCD calculations that were state-of-the-art in 1981; it was already too small on its completion in October 1983. We corrected one minor miscue on the Mark I and allowed every node to have an extra channel to the outside world (with eight channels on the node, allowing seven internal channels). In the original Cosmic Cube, the node that connected to the outside world was a special design with an extra channel.

The Mark II design was complete in 1984 and the first systems were running in the fall of 1984, one year after the Cosmic Cube. We built a total of 256 active nodes of the Mark II which were initially configured as

One 128 node and

Four 32 node systems,

although some of the 32-node machines were later broken down into two 16-node systems. These machines were the workhorse of the hypercube research at Caltech and JPL through 1985 and 1986. The 128-node is still an interesting computer, with 32 megabytes of directly accessible memory and a performance equivalent to about 25 times the VAX11/780 (i.e., about 5 megaflops). It is clearly more powerful than the current top-of-the-line of the DEC VAX family — the 8800 — and this performance by an essentially obsolete hypercube illustrates the advantages of the concurrent approach.

While the Mark II systems were still being assembled, we made a difficult and perhaps incorrect decision. What should we do for the future? The Mark II was interim and was nowhere near a supercomputer; furthermore, the 8086 is not the most pleasant processor to work with! During early 1984, we conceptually designed the third generation machine targeting:

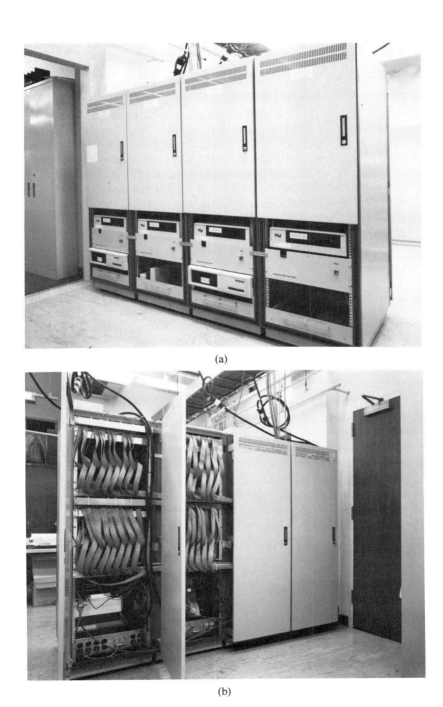

(a)

(b)

Figure 2. The 128-node Mark II system at Caltech (a) showing, in the back view (b), the cabling that implements the hypercube interconnect.

- Larger memory, higher performance nodes
- Improved communication capability with a separate processor handling it

We considered INTEL, NATIONAL, and MOTOROLA processors, but when the schedule of the 68020 became clear in mid-1984 we decided that the new Mark III should be based around the MOTOROLA 68020. This decision was also motivated by MOTOROLA's generous offer to help us with technical help and equipment donations.

Let us return to previous times and note that INTEL had supported the project since early 1983 with chips for both the Mark I and II. The review team that INTEL sent down in early 1983 included John Palmer, who with colleagues later set up a startup company NCUBE to produce commercial hypercubes. INTEL monitored our progress with a second visit in January 1984, where Justin Rattner replaced Palmer on the review team. In the next months, INTEL decided to produce hypercubes in a new independent business unit "Intel Scientific." This illustrates graphically the possible gains for commercial support of university research; I am certain that INTEL had no expectation of such direct commercial spin-off when it originally agreed to the donations.

However, the situation in the fall of 1984 was complicated. There were potentially at least three commercial hypercubes, AMETEK, INTEL, and NCUBE. Should we continue the in-house hardware effort and proceed with the Mark III? It was a more ambitious effort than the Mark II, and we would need increased funding to bring it off. The very existence of the commercial projects made it hard to fund our in-house machines even though we could correctly point out clear technical advantages of the Mark III over the commercial machines. Eventually, we made probably the easiest decision; we continued the in-house effort. We obtained adequate funding through the tireless efforts of Carl Kukkonen and the generous support of DOE, NSA, JTF, USAF, NASA, and other DOD agencies. However, the project was always handicapped by funding problems and did not, I feel, proceed anywhere near as well as it could. I see this as illustrating an important point. What is the correct relation of university and commercial development? With all due respect to my friends in AMETEK, FPS, INTEL, and NCUBE—the current commercial hypercube vendors—all the initial commercial machines were rather scruffy and had problems in some areas. For instance, INTEL had poor internode communication, NCUBE had modest software, and FPS had difficult-to-use WEITEK and transputer chips. Hypercube technology would have benefited either from a delay in the commercial development or more realistically from keeping the university effort fully funded during the initial stages of commercial development. It is worth noting that one normally associates commercial machines with issues like improved support and better systems packaging. Actually, our in-house machines have proved to be just as reliable as the commercial offerings, and I see our in-house effort as having faltered in two different areas. One is the time it takes to build large systems; we appear to be able to design and build prototypes competitively with industry. However, it takes an in-house effort a long time to come from working prototypes to large systems, e.g., from the first 32-node to the full 128-node machine. Secondly, the commercial efforts involve more people and are able, as in the INTEL line, to offer a broader range of hardware and software.

After this soul-searching, let us return to the Mark III, shown in Figure 3. Each node consists of:

Two 68020 microprocessors—one for calculation and one to control communication

68881 floating point co-processor to be replaced by 68882

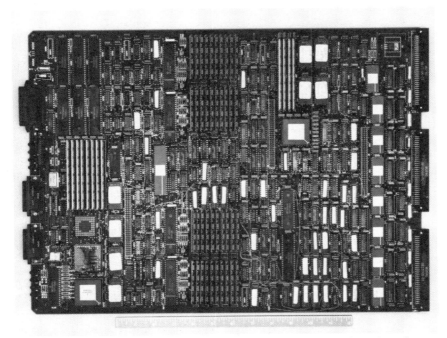

Figure 3. Node board for the Mark III hypercube designed and constructed at JPL in 1984–86.

68851 memory management unit

4 megabytes of memory shared by two 68020s

We currently have funds to build a 128-node Mark IIIfp where each node will be augmented with a WEITEK-based floating point unit. This will use WEITEK's new XL chip set which is expected to be much easier to use than older WEITEK-based systems. The 128-node Mark IIIfp will be our first in-house hypercube supercomputer with gigaflop peak performance. It is also worth noting that it has ½ gigabyte of directly addressable memory. It is well suited to large scientific calculations.

In Figure 4, we show the first INTEL hypercube, illustrating that the packaging is neater than the Mark II. Each node contains:

80286 microprocessor

80287 floating print co-processor

one-half megabyte memory

8 communication channels

The smaller size of the iPSC node is partly due to use of Ethernet chips to control serial communication channels. Unfortunately, these chips introduce substantial latency (startup) time into the message transmission. Our original hypercubes had little latency and excellent ratio of t_{comm}/t_{calc}. The later machines have been troubled in this area. Even the JPL-built Mark III had difficulties; we added a second 68020 to offload the message processing from the main processor. However, this introduced latency since we did not put in fast enough hardware to allow the two 68020's on a single board to speedily communicate with each other! Great care is needed in the design of these machines to work through real software to see that there are no hidden overheads. All current machines have had much slower communication than the designers expected!

In Figure 5, we show the very different NCUBE philosophy. Each node is now seven chips:

One integrated chip with CPU/floating point unit/11 communication channels

6 memory chips leading to ½ megabyte memory per node with 1 megabit chips

The physically small node allows NCUBE to scale to large systems (they offer up to 1024 nodes) and offer small systems with from 4 to 16 nodes available as a PC-addon.

The NCUBE can be considered as a supercomputer with 1024 nodes capable of about 100 megaflops. Currently, we see that the major difficulty with this design is the host or controller for the large systems; we may have

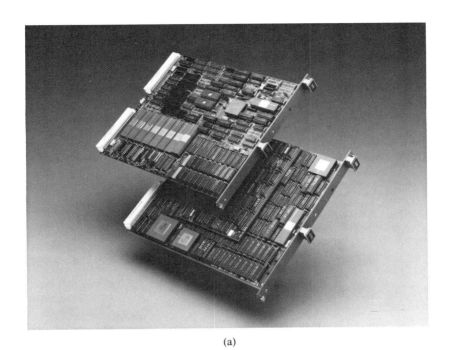

(a)

(b)

Figure 4. (a) The INTEL iPSC node board and (b) packaging into a 32-node system.

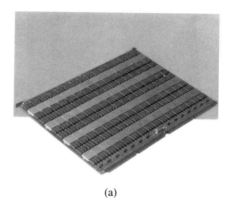

(a)

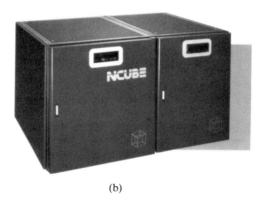

(b)

Figure 5. (a) The NCUBE board containing 64 nodes with (b) the packaging for 1024-node system.

100 megaflops on the hypercube, but the controller is little better than a PC-AT with rather flaky software. This contrasts with CRAYs of comparable performance to the NCUBE but which might use a big IBM mainframe as the controller.

Future systems, including both back-end disk systems (available from NCUBE now) and the front-end user interface (both graphics and the general user connections), will clearly address the I/O question in a better fashion.

I believe it is unlikely that Caltech will build future general-purpose hypercubes—i.e., the Mark IV. We expect that the commercial world will be the best source of the next generation. We do expect to work closely with the hardware vendors and perhaps have a viable, more special-purpose, local hardware effort. Maybe JPL will produce space-qualified supercomputers?

Actually, some still see the in-house effort as crucial since they believe that the commercial sector will NOT address the high-end concurrent supercomputers — there is more money to be made on PC power boosters and VAX beaters, $0.5M superminicomputers. However, as described in Sections III and V, we at Caltech are interested in hypercubes and indeed other architectures with only one constraint: we wish to use the concurrent supercomputer with highest performance on a wide variety of scientific problems. We must wait to see if industry will be motivated to build such large systems.

We would like to note that, in spite of the usual arguments against in-house machines, Caltech has successfully built three distinct hypercubes in five years. They have all worked reliably and have no serious design flaws. So one should not reject out of hand, as some do, this mode of operation! Our success is a tribute to the skill and professionalism of both Caltech's Computer Science department and the Jet Propulsion Laboratory.

III. Domain Decomposition and the Hypercube as a General-Purpose Supercomputer

How to use the hypercube and why it is general purpose. Comparison with other architectures and the theory of complex systems.

One initially disappointing feature of parallel computing is that, in some sense, it is trivial. Namely, there is essentially only one way of using such machines, as is illustrated in Figure 6. We can view problems as an algorithm applied to a dataset. Concurrency is achieved by decomposing the dataset into parts or subdomains and acting concurrently on each part. We call each part a *grain* and the feature of the hypercube is its *large grain* size; each node contains enough memory to hold quite large subdomains. Each grain is made of atomic entities we call *members;* the smallest allowable grain size would contain a single member.

In Figure 6, we show the decomposition of four problems that we have implemented on the hypercube and illustrated for the case of a simple two-dimensional, 4-node machine. The small machine size is chosen to allow a reasonable illustration and not for any algorithmic limit.

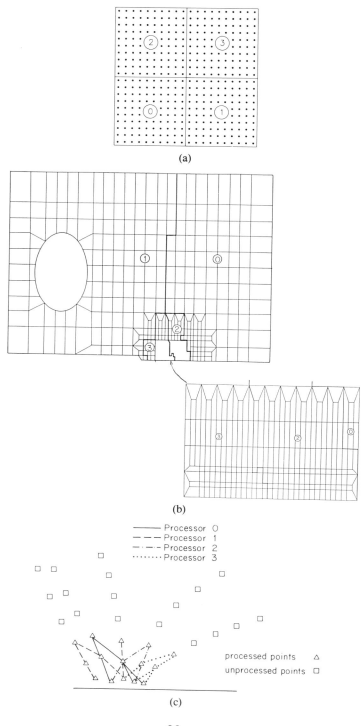

(a)

(b)

Processor 0
Processor 1
Processor 2
Processor 3

processed points △
unprocessed points □

(c)

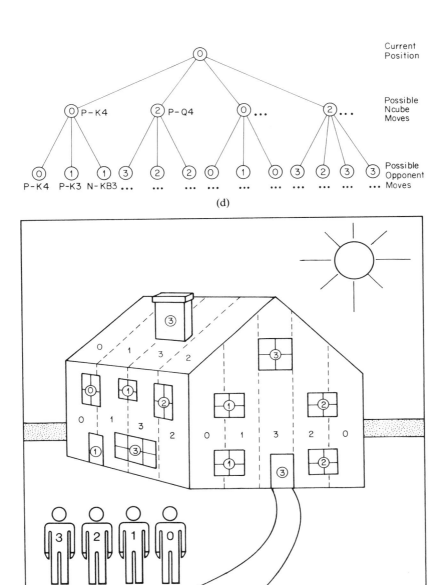

Figure 6. Decomposition in a variety of problems:
  (a) Two-dimensional finite difference;
  (b) Irregular geometry finite element mesh;
  (c) Sensor data recording tracks of multiple objects;
  (d) Game tree associated with computer chess;
  (e) Construction of a house with a four-member construction
       team.
In each case, we show the breakup onto a 4-node processor.

21

Two-Dimensional Finite Difference [8].   Here we have a regular grid broken into four equal area subdomains. This respects load balancing, and the local nature of the Laplacian operator mandates a 2×2 two-dimensional processor topology.

Irregular Two-Dimensional Finite Element [9].   Here we illustrate an irregular mesh and show how load balancing of the nodes has concentrated them in the region near a developing crack, where the mesh points are finest. This decomposition was found by techniques that minimize internode communication.

Missile Tracking [10].   Here we are solving the pattern recognition problem of interpreting data from a sensor observing many missiles. Now the *members* are the missiles or more precisely the candidate tracks, and these are decomposed over the nodes of the hypercube which concurrently apply Kalman filters to each track.

Computer Chess [11].   Here the data domain is more abstract, since it is generated by the computer as it traverses down the tree of possible moves; each board position represents a *member* of the domain.

Finally, Figure 6(e) illustrates that *domain decomposition* is a well-known concept in society and the traditional approach to large engineering projects [8]. Although domain decomposition is the universal technique, we see wide variety in the underlying domain and members. Further, this decomposition is by no means always static; the decomposed chess game tree is changing very rapidly and particle-dynamics problems are illustrative of a slower varying decomposition.

The simplicity of the concept of domain decomposition is very important because it allows one to extrapolate with confidence to larger future machines. If it required a very detailed mathematical proof to show the effectiveness of current machines, such a proof would be very unlikely to survive extrapolation in machine technology and problem class.

We have been able to quantify the intuitive ideas described above. The basic formalism relies on the idea of a *complex system* [5]. This is a collection of interconnected *members* which do something or other. As shown in Tables 3 and 4, such systems vary from the collection of galaxies forming the universe to the wires and switches that form the world's telephone system. In this formalism, the map of one complex system onto (into) another is crucial. In fact, modelling can be thought of as mapping some aspect of the real world onto some theoretical idealization. Most of my life has been spent in phenomenology, which is the map of the quantum field theory forming the interacting particles onto a hodge-podge complex system formed from quarks and gluons, interacting by perturbation theory and connected by adhoc rules into the observed hadrons. Parallel computing is concerned with the map of an initial complex

Table 3. Various Disciplines as Complex Systems

Field	Problem	Algorithm	World	Member or Degree of Freedom	Connection
Biology	Intelligence	Unknown	Brain	Neuron	Axon, Dendrite
Computer Science	PC board layout	Optimization	PC board	Chip	Trace Wire
Physics (Cosmology)	BIG BANG	Einstein's Equations	Universe	Galaxy	Gravity
Mathematics	Differential equation	Finite Difference	R^n	$f(x)$	Differential operator
Communications	SDI battle management	Message Routing	Earth	Satellite and ground links	Microwaves Lasers etc.
Social Science	Society	Unknown	Earth	Person	Conversation Roads Telephones
Construction	Building house	Bricklaying	Wall	Bricks	Mortar

Table 4. Various Problems as Complex Systems

Field	Problem	Algorithm	World	Member or Degree of Freedom	Connection
Structural Analysis	Stress calculation	Finite element	Building	Nodal points	Next-to-nearest neighbor
Condensed Matter	2D melting	Monte Carlo	2D solid or liquid	Molecules	Forces
High-Energy Physics	Lattice gauge theory	Monte Carlo	4D world $\approx$ proton	Quark and gluon field values	Local Lagrangian
Granular Physics	Formation of ripples in sand	Time evolution	Desert	Sand grain	Contact
Data Analysis	Image processing	Convolution	2D pixel space	Pixel	Defined by convolution
Defense	War games	Event-driven simulation	Battle of Hasting	Archers Arrows Knights	Movement Launch of weapons
AI	Computer algebra	Simplification	Expression	Variables Coefficients	Laws of arithmetic

system—the *complex problem*—onto a final one—the *complex computer*. The latter is an appropriate term because any large concurrent machine has enough structure that it should be considered as a complex system. The *domain decompositions* illustrated in Figure 6 are just particular maps of certain complex systems onto a 4-node complex computer. In this sense, the statement that one uses domain decomposition is almost tautological; this is, in fact, just another phrase for a *map of a complex problem onto a complex computer.*

Let us consider the three hardware architectures that currently can provide relatively general purpose parallel architectures of high (supercomputer) performance. These are

1. Distributed Memory, Large Grain Size, MIMD.
    This is typified by the hypercube and in Europe by transputer arrays.
2. Shared Memory, Large Grain Size, MIMD.
    This architecture is currently dominant commercially and is represented by multiheaded CRAYs, ALLIANT, BUTTERFLY, ELXSI, ENCORE, and SEQUENT, among others. The CEDAR and RP3 are major research machines in this class.
3. Distributed Memory, Small Grain Size, SIMD.
    The above two classes involved asynchronous (MIMD) nodes, but with small-sized computing elements one is more or less forced to synchronous (SIMD) operation. Three examples of such machines are the ICL, DAP, GOODYEAR MPP, and the Connection Machine from Thinking Machines.

We can see that these classes form systems with differing interconnects (from buses to meshes to hypercubes) and with different sized nodes. If the complex computer is built from small nodes, one will only be able to map one or a few members (degrees of freedom) of the complex problem into each computer node. Thus, the node must match the member in computational capability and interconnect (topology) with its neighbors. On the other hand, in classes 1) and 2) each node will hold many (100–10000, say) members, and so the node is not required to match very precisely the nature of individual members.

Understanding domain decomposition requires a theory of the structure of the grains or subdomains into which the complex problem is divided. Such grains wash out the properties of individual members and so large-grain-size machines are much more generally applicable than those of small grain size. On the other hand, for cases where complex problems and computers match well, the small-grain-size machine offers the best performance. This is illustrated in Figure 7. The large-grain-size machine works well in both c) and e) but is typically out-performed by the small-

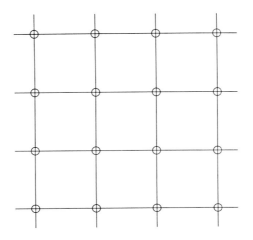

○ Fundamental Entities

── Connection Between Entities

(a)

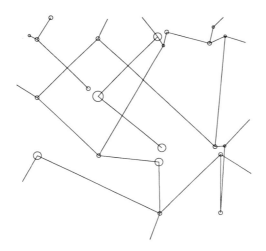

○ Fundamental Entities
     Size Proportional to Calculation Complexity

── Connection Between Entities

(b)

Figure 7 a, b

Figure 7. (a) Part of graph defining a regular problem
        (b) Part of graph defining an irregular problem showing fundamental entities and their connections.

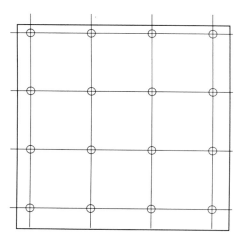

○   Fundamental Entities

──   Connection Between Entities

•   Communication Mismatch = *Edge/Area* is reduced by

a factor of $\left[\dfrac{1}{(\text{Grain Size})^{1/dimension}}\right]$

•   Load Balancing by user as MIMD and reduced statistically
by large grain size $\left[\dfrac{1}{\sqrt{\text{Grain Size}}}\right]$

(c)

○   Fundamental Entities

──   Connection Between Entities

(d)

Figure 7 c, d

(c)   Part of a regular problem decomposed onto a node of a large-grain-size machine.

(d)   Part of a regular problem decomposed onto several nodes of a small-grain-size machine.

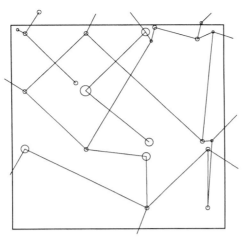

○ Fundamental Entities
    Size Proportional to Calculational Complexity
── Connection Between Entities
• Communication Mismatch = $Edge/Area$ is reduced by

a factor of $\left[\dfrac{1}{(\text{Grain Size})^{1/dimension}}\right]$

• Load Balancing by software as MIMD and reduced statistically
by large grain size. $\left[\dfrac{1}{\sqrt{\text{Grain Size}}}\right]$

(e)

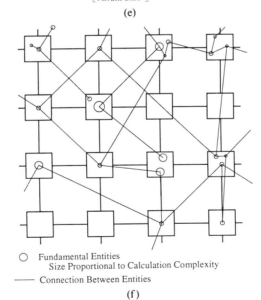

○ Fundamental Entities
    Size Proportional to Calculation Complexity
── Connection Between Entities

(f)

Figure 7 e, f

(e) Part of an irregular problem decomposed onto a node of a
large-grain-size machine.

(f) Part of an irregular problem with a poor decomposition
onto a small-grain-size machine.

grain-size machine in d). The latter will perform poorly in f). In each case, we show the complex system form of the problem as interconnected members; the size of the members in Figure 7 is a measure of their varying (in b), d) and f)) calculational complexity. Figure 8 summarizes the characteristics of the three architectures and indicates that, at least in an algorithmic sense, classes 1) and 2), with either distributed or shared memory, are really very similar.

We have tried to quantify some aspects of a complex system and the properties of its grains by the definition of its (in general fractional) *system dimension d* given by

$$
\left[\begin{array}{c} \text{Information (Connections)} \\ \text{Flowing Out of Grain} \end{array} \right] \alpha \left[\begin{array}{c} \text{Information} \\ \text{(Calculational Complexity)} \\ \text{Inside Grain} \end{array} \right]^{1-1/d}. \quad (3)
$$

Equation (3) generalizes the relation between surface and volume for geometric structures.

This definition is only interesting if d has some universality independent of grain size and position of grain in the system. This does seem to be true in several examples [5, 8] and we are able to summarize all our early results in the hypercube by the following formulae for the *efficiency* ϵ. This is defined as the ratio of the *speedup S* on a concurrent machine to the number of nodes N. Consider a complex problem of system dimension d_p and a complex computer of dimension d_c. Then, we find:

(a)   If $d_c \geq d_p$,

$$
\epsilon = 1 - \frac{\text{const}}{n^{1/d_p}} \frac{t_{\text{comm}}}{t_{\text{calc}}}, \quad (4)
$$

where each grain contains n members. Here t_{comm} and t_{calc} are the fundamental hardware parameters introduced in Section II.

(b)   If the computer has lower dimension than the problem, $d_c < d_p$, then

$$
\epsilon = 1 - \frac{\text{const}}{n^{1/d_p}} N^{[1/d_c - 1/d_p]} \frac{t_{\text{comm}}}{t_{\text{calc}}}, \quad (5)
$$

where the complex computer has N nodes. Equations (4), (5) express an important feature of the hypercube; it has a large dimension $d_c = \log_2 N$, and so the result (Equation (4)) describes the majority of hypercube applications. With values of the hardware ratio $t_{\text{comm}}/t_{\text{calc}} \lesssim 2$ as in the Caltech machines, one can expect to find high efficiencies, and nearly all our implementations have efficiencies near 1, or to be precise, we find efficiencies $\epsilon \gtrsim 0.8$.

It is more relevant to discuss the speedup S, since this is the real measure

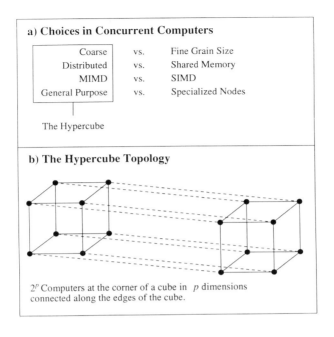

a) Choices in Concurrent Computers

Coarse	vs.	Fine Grain Size
Distributed	vs.	Shared Memory
MIMD	vs.	SIMD
General Purpose	vs.	Specialized Nodes

The Hypercube

b) The Hypercube Topology

2^p Computers at the corner of a cube in p dimensions connected along the edges of the cube.

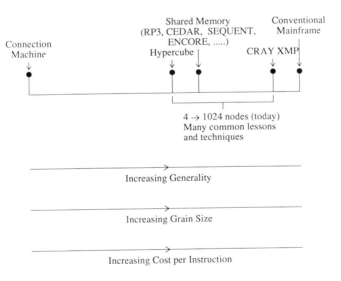

Connection Machine

Shared Memory (RP3, CEDAR, SEQUENT, ENCORE, ...)

Hypercube

Conventional Mainframe

CRAY XMP

$4 \rightarrow 1024$ nodes (today)
Many common lessons and techniques

Increasing Generality

Increasing Grain Size

Increasing Cost per Instruction

c) An Approximate Classification
of Concurrent Computers

Figure 8. Comparison of classes of concurrent machines.

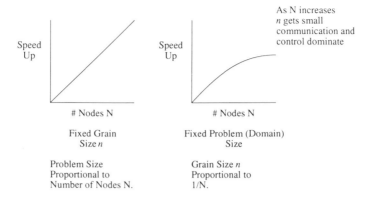

Figure 9. A plot of the speedup S as a function of number of nodes N for two cases: (a) Fixed grain size n (b) Fixed problem size nN

of the performance. Equation (4) and Figure 9 show that one can expect linear (in N) speedup as long as one keeps n fixed, i.e. as long as one uses the larger machine (more nodes N) to solve a larger problem whose size is itself linear in N. We believe that this shows clearly that the only practical constraint on the use of parallel machines is that we use them to solve large problems. The results in Equations (4), (5) quantify what one means by large for particular values of n, N, t_{comm}, and t_{calc}. This is explained in great detail in [5, 8, 12, 13].

The reader may be surprised that we waxed eloquent for so long without discussing any detailed applications. This has been explained in the introduction. Our project produced hypercubes which had good but not supercomputer performance. Thus, much of our research was devoted not to detailed computations in any one field but to exploring the issues and to developing codes to be run on future machines. We also emphasize that most of our lessons at the algorithmic level are independent of the details of the concurrent computer. Our discussion would be qualitatively the same for the three rather different classes of concurrent computers discussed above. We will find more differences between the machines when we consider software in the next section.

In spite of a preoccupation with general techniques, the hypercubes have performed many interesting calculations as is illustrated in two recent Caltech Ph.D. theses, one by Jon Flower in lattice gauge theory [14] and one by Brad Werner in granular physics or in particular a study of the wind-driven motion of sand [15]. In both cases, the hypercube was the major computational tool and produced world-class results, even considering the competition of many large CRAY calculations in lattice gauge theory. We probably used the hypercubes for an integrated total of three years on the lattice calculations, and the result of some 2000 hours on the 128-node Mark II is shown in Figure 10, which improves on the original Cosmic Cube calculation reported in [16] and [17]. The wealth of different lattice calculations, some 20 in all [1], testifies to the comparative ease of use of the hypercube. We benefited from the ability to use conventional high-level languages, C and FORTRAN, to program the machines.

We now believe that we need to refocus our research onto its original goals, namely, major scientific and engineering calculations. Thus, we have set up the "Concurrent Supercomputing Initiative at Caltech" and intend to concentrate on concurrent supercomputers in the future. Our focus during the last five years was not, in any sense, a mistake. It was certainly not what I expected when I started in 1981, but it has been a very exciting

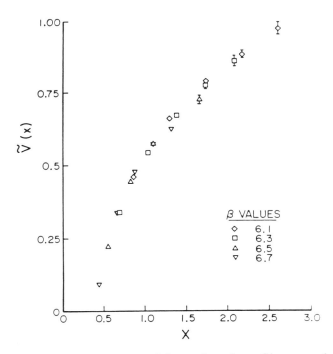

Figure 10. A plot of the $\bar{q}q$ potential as a function of interquark distance calculated from 20^4 lattice on the 128-node Mark II hypercube [14].

and intellectually stimulating experience. I have learned about a wide range of computer science and computational science issues. Now, I believe that we have the intellectual and technological tools to do what we set out to do in 1981: acquire concurrent machines that outperform any sequential computers, and with these machines make major scientific breakthroughs.

IV. Software for the Hypercube

Trade-offs between performance, flexibility, and portability. How does a small research group produce codes for the outside world? How can we set up standards to facilitate application software development?

In the previous section, we introduced three classes of concurrent super-computers and found many similarities in the algorithmic issues. They can differ quite significantly in the software area, for we should extend our complex-system description from a map of

$$\text{Complex Problem} \rightarrow \text{Complex Computer} \qquad (6)$$

to a two-stage process,

$$\text{Complex Problem} \rightarrow \text{Complex Code} \rightarrow \text{Complex Computer}, \qquad (7)$$

where by *complex code* we denote the software which implements the problem onto the concurrent machine. Clearly, the complex code is a dynamic complex system consisting of an irregularly connected set of machine instructions and storage locations.

In fact, we can compare distributed- and shared-memory systems as follows. If we consider the structure of the complex problem, a shared memory is rarely important; distributed memory is usually natural. However, the complex code typically maps more easily into shared- rather than distributed-memory machines. In other words, algorithms naturally suggest distributed memory; however, shared-memory machines are expected to be easier to program. This conventional wisdom has, in fact, not really been proven because the distributed-memory DAP and hypercubes were available before the large shared-memory machines; there is more code written for the machines that are meant to be harder to program! There is also good reason to believe that getting good performance out of shared-memory machines leads you to exactly the same issues and difficulties one finds in programming distributed-memory computers [27].

The basic programming model for the hypercube can be termed LAPMP or large asynchronous processes communicating with message passing. In general, one would have several processes within each node of the hypercube, but the vast majority of current work has used exactly one process within each node. LAPMP has been implemented in many ways by the different research groups and the different commercial companies. A lot of our work has used the so-called *crystalline operating system* [18] which stems from original ideas by Eugene Brooks. The latest version, CrOS III, has proven to be quite robust and capable of implementation on many different hypercubes including both the in-house and commercial machines. CrOS provides a *synchronous* communication system, which may seem peculiar since the nodes are intrinsically asynchronous. However, CrOS only uses what we call *loose synchronization* [8] — in other words, the problem can be arranged so that all the processes compute away and there is some time when they all expect to send, forward and receive messages. In our applications, this loose synchronization is provided either by time or iteration count within a simulation. Within CrOS both the calculation and communication can be spatially very irregular as long as they are synchronized in time. We have found CrOS much more general than one might have first thought.

Most hypercube communication systems support asynchronous operation, which although more general is not needed for most of our applications (as defined by Table 2, for example). Generality usually comes at the cost of performance. CrOS is much faster in both throughput and latency than current asynchronous systems. We have had a recent revelation that allows us the best of both worlds. Firstly, we note that CrOS is a communications library supporting message passing between nodes, and it is not an operating system. Secondly, we note that a true operating system has to support both the user and his problem. The problems may be synchronous as we explained above, but surely the user, drinking coffee and reading the debugger manual, is not. A plausible environment is built around an asynchronous system providing the conventional user environment. This system will support high performance and possibly specialized communication systems like CrOS that allow the problems to perform well on the hypercube, i.e., for t_{comm} in Equations (3) and (4) to be as small as possible. We have built preliminary versions of this hybrid system on the INTEL and NCUBE commercial hypercubes combining the commercial asynchronous system with our own fast CrOS communication system.

An interesting and important enhancement was CUBIX, developed by John Salmon [20]. At first sight, this seems rather trivial as it "just" provides conventional UNIX I/O and system calls from within the nodes of the hypercube. However, in fact, it changes an essential feature of the programming model. Before Salmon's work, we had regarded the hypercube as an "attached" processor controlled by some master or "intermediate host" (IH) computer. This model is embodied in all the current commercial systems. It requires the user typically to write two programs, one for the IH and one for the node. The IH program contains most control and I/O functions with the node performing the basic calculations. In CUBIX, one need only write a single program for the node and the IH just acts as a network and disk controller and has no user-specific code. In this model, the hypercube (CUBIX) program is very similar to sequential codes, and in fact we have successfully written several codes which run on either the hypercube or a conventional sequential machine with appropriate values for flags. In the simpler examples, one can say that the "only" difference between sequential and hypercube codes lies in

- Geometry Section — a typical hypercube code has to address the data in a single grain, i.e., a subdomain. The sequential code must address the geometry of the full domain.
- Boundary Value Section — often interprocessor communication is associated with the boundaries of the grains stored in a given node. Correspondingly, one can deal with node-to-node communication as a generalized boundary value.

Thus, software written in a modular fashion with, say, well-defined boundary value and geometry modules can be transported between concurrent and sequential machines. In fact, hypercube code is usually straightforward to implement on shared-memory machines, and so one finds the possibility of developing software that is portable between sequential and large-grain-size distributed- and shared-memory machines.

CUBIX also offers the possibility of removing the sequential bottleneck caused by the IH in current hypercube implementations. As we mentioned in Section II, current IHs are inadequate to handle the necessary interface between a variety of users and a supercomputer-performance hypercube. CUBIX allows one to develop a distributed environment with functions distributed over the nodes of the hypercube and over user workstations networked to the cube.

An important development is the concept of automatic decomposers or load balancers [9]. These have been studied in the context of the theory of complex systems [5, 21] and reviewed in [22, 23]. We now understand how to perform the map (6) of problem onto computer by several methods, especially simulated annealing [9], neural networks [24] and graphical methods [25]. These methods divide up the data domain of the complex problem in such a way as to minimize communication and balance the load on the nodes of the concurrent computer. Although our methods were developed for the hypercube, they can certainly be used on other architectures and for other similar resource allocation problems [23]. Some examples are given in Table 5. The simulated annealing and neural network decomposers are particularly attractive, since they can easily be implemented as concurrent algorithms and conveniently run on the hypercube itself. This is particularly important in cases such as particle dynamics and adaptive meshes when the decomposition is dynamic and needs to change as the problem runs on the hypercube. Our software model is based on an object-oriented approach. The complex problem is decomposed into fixed *granules* or subdomains such that the number of granules is much larger ($N_{granule} \sim 10\ N_{nodes}$) than the number of nodes in the concurrent computer [22]. The map (6) is obtained by optimizing the decomposition of granules onto the computer. This method makes the details of the decompositions transparent to the user who writes code to control a granule.

Table 5. 10 Optimization Problems Which Can Use Similar Techniques [23]

1.	Decomposing graphs (problems) onto hypercube
2.	Coarse graining: finding medium-grain objects for object-oriented approach
3.	Fine-grain dataflow assignment
4.	Use of "caches" on shared-memory concurrent machines and sequential computers
5.	Optimizing compilers
6.	Optimal adaptive meshes and determination of cells for "particle in the cell" problems
7.	Controlling the nation's defense system
8.	Designing the nation's defense system
9.	Controlling AT&T's phone network
10.	Designing AT&T's phone network

The system places granules optimally in the nodes and routes messages between them. This optimization is performed by a neural network running concurrently as a separate set of processes decomposed onto the hypercube. It would be more direct and accurate to manipulate the fundamental entities of the complex problem, but it is hard to implement this in a fashion that does not intimately involve the user in the dynamic decomposition.

The picture described above appears quite straightforward to implement but needs the solution of several difficult technical problems. Currently, we are working on the necessary underlying multitasking system, MOOSE, for the hypercube [26].

The above picture is very attractive, but one should emphasize that direct user decomposition has been the heart of our project so far, and I expect this to continue. I believe that the vast majority of applications can use simple decomposition techniques and do not need computer-generated and dynamic decompositions. It should also be noted that there are some problems such as computer chess and the trickier matrix algorithms for which our current version of the automatic decomposer will not work. In the chess case, which typifies a class of tree-based algorithms, we load-balance by treating the nodes as a pool of workers to which computation (analysis of a particular position) is assigned as it becomes available. The matrix algorithms require subtle and very time-dependent decompositions [19].

However, the automatic decomposition will be successful for a broad range of irregular simulations including particle dynamics, adaptive meshes, and real-life simulations including some "war games." However, even in this case, one only addresses the map (6) of problem onto computer and one leaves aside the question of the actual code. This implies that the user must still write the software to manipulate the individual granule or object. There is some reason to believe that one can extend our ideas to include the full map (7). Rather than decomposing the problem, one can divide up, as in the manner of an optimizing compiler, the sequential code for a given problem and assign it to the nodes of the concurrent computer [24]. Preliminary work in this area is underway.

Actually, although the above load-balancing research is important, it is not the pacing item. Software is the limiting aspect to concurrent computing, but the main problems are

1. The primitive nature of the user interface to hypercubes in the area of I/O, graphics, debugging, multiuser capability, etc.
2. Lack of commercial quality application software.

The second issue is clearly the main difficulty, since it implies that hypercubes and other concurrent machines can only be installed in experimental and research establishments. For large parallel machines to compete in the major computer markets, we need to develop some fraction of the sequential software produced over the last 30 years. For instance, engineers need parallel versions of programs like NASTRAN and banks need parallel machines to support transaction analysis compatibly with that on current sequential machines.

Unfortunately, there is a chicken and egg situation: the hardware sales will not grow until the software is available; it is not attractive financially to develop the software until there is a large hardware base. . . .

Still, I believe that huge amounts of useful software will be developed both in universities and industry, and that in a three-to-five-year time frame one will see a dramatic change with a rich variety of parallel software. I do believe that research at Caltech and elsewhere has in fact shown that the majority of important commercial applications that need powerful computers are amenable to parallel processing. We "only" need to implement the "proofs in principle" from current research.

I expect that software development will be greatly enhanced if we can establish some simple standards to encourage the development of portable code. There is a wealth of computer architectures and clearly no agreement as to the nature of future systems. These facts will clearly cramp parallel software development unless one can be ensured that standard environments will be supported over a range of machines. I hope that Caltech can play a role in setting up such common software environments.

V. The Future

The hypercube and our research in perspective. New programmatic and intellectual directions

We have already reviewed some of our new initiatives at the end of Section I. In concurrent computation, we are coming to the end of the exploratory stage. We must concentrate on supercomputing and the translation of our model and demonstration projects into day-to-day use of concurrent supercomputers as a scientific tool. We need to examine and contrast a variety of differing architectures. The development of both attractive and reasonably general (across architectures) supercomputer software environments is clearly crucial. Only this will motivate both the general use of such machines by university researchers and provide the framework for commercial application software. We expect the future to see less emphasis on in-house hardware but perhaps more emphasis on software. In any case, we need to work closely with commercial hardware and software developers.

I see the new Computation and Neural Systems option at Caltech as key to extending our understanding of concurrent implementations for conventional scientific algorithms to those associated with intelligence. It is likely that distinct architectures will be needed for these very different applications.

Finally, we speculate on the importance of the theory of complex systems. We have found it useful in classifying complex problems. Can we extend this to the more general map (7), i.e. to understand the structure of software? More importantly, we expect that the theory will be applicable to real-life situations and should be helpful in designing a variety of complex systems including communication and military applications.

References

1. C^3P-290B "Caltech Concurrent Computation Program Annual Report for 1985–86," CALT-68-1404, G. C. Fox, October 13, 1986. Published in proceeding of 1986 Hypercube Conference in Knoxville, edited by M. T. Heath, SIAM, 1987.
2. C^3P-288 "Questions and Unexpected Answers in Concurrent Computation," CALT-68-1403, G. C. Fox, June 16, 1986. Published in *Experimental Parallel Comput-*

ing Architectures, J. J. Dongarra (ed.), Elsevier Science Publishers B. V. (North-Holland), 1987.

3. C^3P-166B "Annual Report 1983–1984 and Recent Documentation-Applications," Caltech/JPL Concurrent Computation Project. Collection of reports by G. Fox.

4. C^3P-404 "Piriform (Olfactory) Cortex Model on the Hypercube," J. M. Bower, M. E. Nelson, M. A. Wilson, G. C. Fox, W. Furmanski, February 1987.
   C^3P-405 "Hypercube Communication for Neural Network Algorithms," G. C. Fox, W. Furmanski, February 1987.

5. C^3P-255 "Concurrent Computation and Theory of Complex Systems," G. C. Fox, S. W. Otto, March 3, 1986. Published in proceedings of 1985 Hypercube Conference in Knoxville, August 1985, edited by M. T. Heath, SIAM, 1986.

6. C^3P-374 "SURFcube: The Development of a Small Hypercube for Personal Computers," M. Breaden, D. Chang, S. Chen, J. O'Dea, October 1986, published in proceedings of 1986 hypercube conference edited by M. T. Heath, SIAM, 1987.

7. C^3P-254 "Performance of the Mark II and INTEL Hypercubes," A. Kolawa, S. Otto, February 25, 1986. Published in proceedings of 1985 Hypercube Conference in Knoxville, August 1985, edited by M. T. Heath, SIAM, 1986.

8. *Solving Problems on Concurrent Processors,* G. C. Fox, M. A. Johnson, G. A. Lyzenga, S. W. Otto, J. K. Salmon, D. W. Walker, Prentice Hall, March 1988.

9. C^3P-292 "A Preprocessor for Irregular Finite Element Problems," CALT-68-1405, J. W. Flower, S. W. Otto, M. C. Salama, June 1986.

10. C^3P-398 "Multiple-Target Track Initiation on a Hypercube," T. D. Gottschalk, January 1987. Presented as the Second International Conference on Supercomputing. Published by International Supercomputing Institute Inc., St. Petersburg, Florida, 1987.

11. C^3P-383 "Chess on the Hypercube," E. Felten, R. Morison, S. Otto, K. Barish, R. Fatland, F. Ho, November 1986. Published in 1986 Knoxville Conference, edited by M. T. Heath, SIAM, 1987.

12. C^3P-161 "The Performance of the Caltech Hypercube in Scientific Calculations: A Preliminary Analysis," G. Fox, April 1985. Invited Talk at Symposium on "Algorithms, Architectures and the Future of Scientific Computation," Austin, Texas, March 18-20, 1985. Published in "Supercomputers—Algorithms, Architectures and Scientific Computation," F. A. Matsen and T. Tajima (eds.), University of Texas Press, Austin, 1985.

13. C^3P-391 "The Hypercube as a Supercomputer," G. C. Fox, January 7, 1987. Presented at the Second International Conference on Supercomputing. Published by International Supercomputing Institute Inc., St. Petersburg, Florida, 1987.

14. "Lattice Gauge Theory on a Parallel Computer, J. W. Flower, March 1987. Ph.D. Thesis, Caltech.

15. "A Physical Model of Wind-Blown Sand Transport," B. T. Werner, April 1987. Ph.D. Thesis, Caltech.

16. C^3P-65 "Pure Gauge SU(3) Lattice Theory on an Array of Computers," Preprint CALT-68-1112, E. Brooks, G. Fox, M. Johnson, S. Otto, P. Stolorz, W. Athas, E. DeBenedictis, R. Faucette, C. Seitz, J. Stack, March 1984. *Phys. Rev. Letters* **52,** 2324(1984).

17. C^3P-67 "The SU(3) Heavy Quark Potential with High Statistics," CALT-68-1113, S. Otto, J. Stack, April 1984. *Phys. Rev. Letters* **52,** 2328(1984).

18. C^3P-268 "Concurrent Computation and its Application to the Study of Melting in Two Dimensions," M. A. Johnson, May 9, 1986. Ph.D. Thesis, Caltech.

19. C^3P-314 "Optimal Communication Algorithms on the Hypercube," G. C. Fox, W. Furmanski, July 8, 1986.
   C^3P-329 "Communication Algorithms for Regular Convolutions on the Hypercube," G. C. Fox, W. Furmanski, September 1, 1986. Published in 1986 Hypercube Conference in Knoxville, edited by M. T. Heath, SIAM, 1987.

20. C^3P-378 "CUBIX — Programming Hypercubes Without Programming Hosts," J. Salmon. Published in the Proceedings of Second Knoxville Conference on Hypercube Multiprocessors, September 1986, edited by M. T. Heath, SIAM, 1987.

21. C^3P-214 "Monte Carlo Physics on a Concurrent Processor," CALT 68-1315, G. C. Fox, S. W. Otto, E. A. Umland, Nov 6, 1985. Published in the Proceedings of "Frontiers of Quantum Monte Carlo" Conference at Los Alamos, September 6, 1985. Published in special issue of *Journal of Statistical Physics,* Vol. 43, p. 1209, Plenum Press, 1986.

22. C^3P-328 "The Implementation of a Dynamic Load Balancer," G. C. Fox, R. Williams, November 1986. Published in proceedings of 1986 Hypercube Conference in Knoxville, edited by M. T. Heath, SIAM, 1987.

23. C^3P-385 "A Review of Automatic Load Balancing and Decomposition Methods for the Hypercube," G. C. Fox, November 1986. To be published in proceedings of IMA Workshop, Minnesota, November 1986.

24. C^3P-363 "Load Balancing by a Neural Network," CALT-68-1408, G. C. Fox, W. Furmanski, September 1986.

25. C^3P-327B "A Graphical Approach to Load Balancing and Sparse Matrix Vector Multiplication on the Hypercube," G. C. Fox, December 5, 1986. To be published in proceedings of IMA Workshop, Minnesota, November 1986.

26. C^3P-427 "A MOOSE Status Report," J. Salmon, S. Callahan, J. Flower, A. Kolawa, May 6, 1987.

27. C^3P-392 "Domain Decomposition in Distributed and Shared Memory Environments," G. C. Fox, June 8, 1987, published in proceedings of ICS 87, International Conference in Supercomputing, June 8 – 12, 87, Athens, Greece; a Springer-Verlag Lecture Note in Computer Science, edited by C. Polychronopoulos.

2   The QCD Machine

ANTHONY E. TERRANO

Department of Electrical and Computer Engineering
Rutgers University
Piscataway, New Jersey

I. Introduction

The task of designing and building a computer that has been optimized for solving a particular problem is formidable. But if the problem is important, has a sufficiently regular structure, and requires computing resources on a scale that cannot be realized by conventional means, then the effort required to "build your own" can be justified. The numerical solution of the lattice QCD problem that arises in particle physics is such a problem.

In this chapter, I will describe the QCD Machine, a special-purpose parallel supercomputer that was designed and built to solve the lattice QCD problem. I will begin with a statement of the problem and its importance. Following this is a discussion of the numerical techniques used to attack the problem. The next section presents the architecture of the QCD Machine and relates important features of its design to properties of the problem it was built to solve. I then discuss the issues involved in programming the computer. A section presenting the details of the actual implementation follows. In a concluding section, measurements of the computer's performance and its construction history are presented.

II. Background

A. Description of the Lattice QCD Problem

The central activities within the discipline of high-energy physics are the discovery of the basic constituents of matter and the description of the interactions between them. For more than a decade, a paradoxical situation has prevailed in our understanding of the nature of the strong interaction between the nucleons and other hadrons. On the one hand, there is a universally accepted theory of the properties of these particles. It is known that the proton, for instance, is composed of more fundamental particles called quarks, that the quarks interact by exchanging another type of fundamental particles called gluons, that the quarks and gluons carry a strong-interaction charge called color, and that the system of quarks and gluons is described by a Lagrangian, which is a generalization of the Lagrangian of electrodynamics. This theory is called quantum chromodynamics, or QCD.

On the other hand, the only quantitative predictions of the theory concern the behavior of high-energy collisions of nucleons. However, derivations of low-energy phenomena, such as a demonstration that the bound states of quarks corresponding to the observed nucleons exist, have yet to be made, despite the efforts of many physicists over more than a decade. It is of great importance to be able to demonstrate that QCD predicts the existence of the proton and to calculate its properties. The lattice formulation of QCD provides a basis for carrying out these calculations numerically.

As with the simulation of most continuous systems, the numerical analysis of QCD begins with the formulation of a discrete version of the theory. Since the calculations intrinsically involve time as well as space, the lattice version of QCD is defined on a four-dimensional grid. However, unlike other continuum simulations, the degrees of freedom are associated with the edges of the grid as well as with the vertices (Figure 1). In the original formulation of the theory [1], the quark field is represented by assigning a twelve-component complex vector to each vertex in the lattice, and the

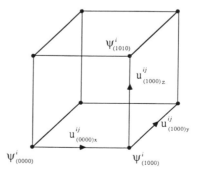

Figure   1. Geometry of lattice QCD problem. $\psi^i_{(xyzt)} \equiv$ Site Variable; $u^{ij}_{(xyzt)l} \equiv$ Link Variable.

gluon field is represented by associating a three-by-three complex matrix with each edge connecting adjacent vertices.

By employing the Feynman path integral formulation of field theory [2], the calculation of any physical quantity can be reduced to an integration:

$$\langle \mathcal{O} \rangle = \int \prod_{\text{links}} dU \prod_{\text{sites}} dq \; \mathcal{O}(U, q) \exp(-S(U, q)). \tag{1}$$

Here $\mathcal{O}$ is the operator corresponding to the quantity in question, and the value of the integral is the expectation value of $\mathcal{O}$. The integration is performed over all possible values of *each* of the quark vectors q and gluon matrices U. A particular complete choice of vectors and matrices is called a configuration and represents a unique quark and gluon field. The integration is thus an integration over all possible configurations. The integrand consists of two factors. The first is the operator representing the physical quantity being evaluated. The second is a universal weight function, which determines the relative importance of a given configuration, and is given by the exponential of minus the action of the configuration. The action is in turn composed of two pieces. The contribution of the gluons is given by

$$\sum_{\square} \text{Tr}(U \cdot V \cdot W^{\dagger} \cdot X^{\dagger}), \tag{2}$$

where the sum is over the smallest planar closed loops or plaquettes, and the summands are the traces of the product of the gluon matrices around the plaquettes (Figure 1). The contribution of the quarks can be integrated analytically and yields a factor given by the determinant of a matrix whose dimension is equal to the number of quark degrees of freedom, or $12 \times$ the number of sites in the lattice. For a more extensive elementary description of the formulation of lattice QCD, see [3].

Having expressed the calculation as a numerical integration, the solution can now be obtained using standard methods of numerical integration. Since the integration is over a very large number of variables and since the integrand is exponentially peaked, it is desirable to employ a statistical or importance sampling technique, such as Monte-Carlo, in order to perform the integration efficiently. An ensemble of configurations is generated, with the relative probability of the occurrence of a configuration given by the weight function $\exp(-S(U, q))$. For each configuration, the value of $\mathcal{O}$ is calculated, and the results are then averaged to get the final expectation value. Note that several different observables can be calculated at once from a single ensemble, since the importance sampling does not depend on the operator $\mathcal{O}$ in Equation (1). The ensemble of configurations is produced by cycling through the link matrices one at a time, generating a random candidate updated value and accepting or rejecting it according to a statistical technique.

B. *Computing Resources Needed to Solve the Problem*

In order for a calculation to yield realistic answers, several conditions must be met. The first is that the distance between lattice points must be small enough that the discretization of the problem doesn't introduce spurious effects in the simulations. This condition can be formulated precisely, and empirical evidence suggests that lattices with at least 20 sites on a side must be employed [4] to satisfy it. A calculation on such a lattice involves 7×10^6 degrees of freedom. Furthermore, the quark matrix whose determinant must be evaluated for each update is almost 2×10^6-dimensional. Approximate techniques for evaluating the determinant have been devised that rely upon the sparseness of the matrix, the fact that only one link matrix is being changed at a time, and the fact that the change is usually small. With these techniques, the amount of work required to evaluate the determinant becomes comparable to the computation required to evaluate the change in the gluonic action (Equation (2)).

Since the precision of the result is statistical, reducing the error in a measurement by a factor of N requires that N^2 times as much data must be taken. This condition assumes that all the measurements are independent, which is not true for an importance sampling technique like a Monte-Carlo. Again, experience indicates that hundreds of thousands of update sweeps through a lattice are required to obtain accuracies on the order of 10%.

Finally, the calculation involves two parameters and must be repeated several times for several values of each to permit an extrapolation of the results in order to yield a physically meaningful answer. When these effects are combined, the estimates of the time required to calculate the proton mass to an accuracy of a few percent range from 10 [5] to 10^6 gigaflop years! [6]

III. Architecture

A. *Properties of the Problem that Can Be Exploited in the Design of a Dedicated Machine*

The lattice QCD problem is particularly well suited for solving with a dedicated computer. To begin with, the amount of computation to be carried out is great enough to justify the considerable effort involved in building a custom computer: even a computer with peak performance in the multigigaflop range would need to run for several years to complete the calculation. Furthermore, since the calculation consists of running essentially a single program, varying only a few parameters, it is not necessary to develop a complete programming environment. The program can be written in assembly language, and the programming effort will be amortized along with the hardware design effort.

The lattice QCD calculation has a number of properties that can be directly translated into architectural features of a special-purpose machine. First, the problem is homogeneous, with the same set of operations carried out for each variable throughout the lattice. As a result, the problem is suitable for solution on a parallel computer, in particular one with a SIMD architecture.

Second, the calculation is built out of local operations. The two fundamental operations on the field variables are (see Figure 2)

1. Multiply each of the three-component vectors at a vertex with the matrix associated with one of the edges emerging from the vertex;
2. Multiply the matrix on an edge by the matrix associated with one of the contiguous edges.

With this constraint on the data usage, a distributed-memory parallel architecture is appropriate. In particular, since the data references are nearest–neighbor on the lattice of the problem, the natural topology for a dedicated QCD Machine is also a grid, or torus, since the calculations can be performed with periodic boundary conditions. The dimensionality of the torus should not exceed that of the lattice (i.e., four).

Third, the calculation is dominated by complex floating-point arithmetic. In particular, both of the fundamental field operations just described can be reduced to taking a series of vector inner products between vectors

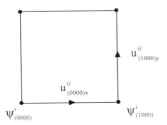

Figure 2. Fundamental operations in lattice QCD calculation. $\phi^i_{(1000)} = \Sigma_j \, u^{ij}_{(0000)x} \psi^j_{(0000)}$; $M^{ik}_{(1100)} = \Sigma_j \, u^{ij}_{(1000)y} u^{jk}_{(0000)x}$.

with three complex components. A computer that performs this operation efficiently will be able to carry out the entire calculation efficiently.

Fourth, the calculation does not require high-precision arithmetic. The accuracy of the final results is statistical and arises from averaging together many separate calculations. A low-precision, compact data type can be used, reducing both the amount of memory required and the interprocessor communication load. Furthermore, the time required to complete a floating-point operation increases with the length of the floating-point number; with short floats, the fastest possible clock can be used.

B. Global Organization of the QCD Machine

By exploiting these properties, the QCD Machine [7, 8] is able to provide a cost-effective, high-performance dedicated computation engine for solving the lattice QCD problem. The machine is organized as a two-dimensional torus network of high-speed computational nodes. As was mentioned earlier, a torus of dimension four or less would be suitable. The actual dimension chosen is determined by the interplay between the maximum size of the problem and of the machine, and the implementation complexity. As mentioned earlier, the maximum problem size ranges up to about 30 sites along each axis. For reasons of reliability, the maximum practical machine size is several hundred processing elements. And clearly the difficulty of implementing a torus network grows as the dimensionality becomes larger. The smallest dimension allowing a 32^4 lattice to be mapped onto a torus with hundreds of processors is two; a 16×16 torus contains 256 processors. The computation lattice is mapped into the grid of the machine through a simple projection. The machine grid corresponds to one of the coordinate planes of the problem, conventionally the $x-y$ plane. Lattice points are then assigned to memory nodes by their x and y coordinates—all of the z and t coordinates for a given (x, y) pair are assigned to the same memory node.

It is conventional to try to classify parallel computers as either SIMD (single instruction–multiple data) or MIMD (multiple instruction–multiple data). A SIMD machine has a single clock and a single instruction stream that each processor executes simultaneously. A MIMD machine has independent clocks and independent instruction streams that are coordinated by an explicit mechanism, either in hardware or software. However, the QCD Machine does not fit comfortably into either class, since it combines a single global clock with independent programs in each processing element.

Rather than thinking of the QCD Machine as a network of computers, it is more convenient to regard it as a grid of memory nodes, with the processors providing the interconnections between them. In particular, for each pair of nearest-neighbor memory nodes, there is a unique processor, which can access data contained in both memory nodes. As far as the processor is concerned, both of the memory nodes lie in a single linear address space, and operations can be performed directly on data lying in either or both of the memories. Since the computation is local, this interconnection guarantees that there is a processor that can carry out both of the elementary operations without requiring any noncomputational data transfer steps.

Viewed from the processor's perspective (Figure 3), the complete implementation of a two-dimensional torus network requires that each processor node has direct access to three distinct memory nodes. All three memory nodes lie in the same linear address space. Of course, this implies that there are three processors with direct access to each memory node. In general, in a MIMD mode of operation, with each processor executing different programs, contention for access to a memory node will arise between different processors. However, no provision is made in the hardware to resolve such possible conflicts. Instead, a programming constraint is imposed: whenever a program is being executed that requires free access to a processor's entire data memory address space, the entire machine must be operated strictly in a SIMD fashion.

More specifically, for each processor, one of the memory nodes is designated to be local. The remaining two nodes are distant, with one lying in the $+x$ direction and the other in the $+y$ direction. When a program only

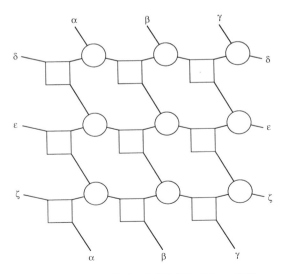

Figure 3. Global organization of the QCD Machine. ○ Processor; □ Memory.

uses data contained in the local memories, different programs may be executed on each procesor; then the QCD Machine is a true MIMD computer, but the interconnection network is unavailable. In order to execute code that requires access to the data lying in the distant memories, the computer must be operated in SIMD mode, with each processor executing the same instruction in a given clock cycle. To switch from MIMD mode to SIMD mode, the system must be synchronized. A simple controller performs this function: when an individual processor reaches the end of its MIMD code, it raises a synchronization request flag on the controller, stores the starting address of the SIMD code to be executed next, and then halts. When all of the flags have been set, the controller issues a global reset command and each of the processors begins executing the SIMD code in lockstep.

Two final remarks complete the architectural specification of the QCD Machine. Since the computer has a (restricted) MIMD mode of operation, there is no provision for broadcasting instructions. The only global control mechanism provided is the synchronization procedure just described. Finally, the entire machine is run as an attached processor to a host computer, which provides the facilities for program development and off-line data storage.

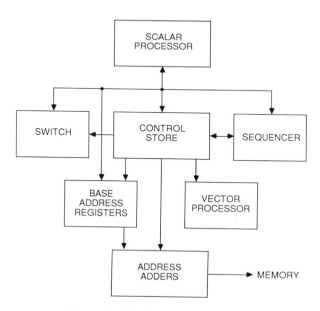

Figure 4. Scalar and control unit.

C. *Organization of the Processing Elements*

A processor, together with its local data memory node, consists of a single-board implementation of a general-purpose computer combined with an attached floating-point vector processor. Each circuit board contains four principal functional units:

1. Microprocessor-based computer for scalar operations and control
2. Floating point multiplier accumulator
3. Data memory doubling as a large vector register
4. Switch implementing the interconnection network

The scalar and control unit is a complete serial computer (Figure 4). In

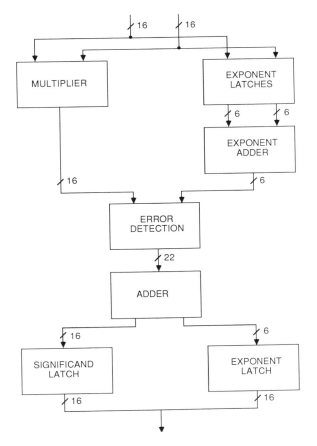

Figure 5. Vector processor.

addition to the microprocessor, the CPU includes a high-precision but unpipelined floating-point processor. A program memory, which is not directly connected to the network and can be accessed while the data memories are in use, is provided to support the MIMD execution mode. The microprocessor also provides an interface to a standard bus, permitting bulk data storage and access to a host computer.

The floating-point vector processor (Figure 5) is organized as a single pipeline, with a multiplier followed by an accumulator. The pipeline has a cycle time of 125 ns, giving a peak computational speed of 16 megaflops per second. The vector processor is completely microcoded, with the microcode stored in RAM so that it can be tailored to the specific application.

The data memory is accessed through the switch (Figure 6) and can be accessed by both the scalar and the vector units. To the scalar unit, it appears to be a single linearly addressed random access memory. To the vector unit, it is organized as two independently addressable register files. Within each file, there is no constraint placed on the addresses of sequential accesses.

The switch determines which register file is connected to each input of the vector processor. In addition, one of the register files may be located on the neighboring board lying in the $+x$ or $+y$ direction.

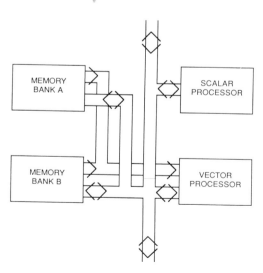

Figure 6. Data memories and switch.

IV. Programming

A. Programming Model

The QCD Machine adds two distinct types of parallel program execution to the conventional serial programming model. One arises from the use of multiple processing elements. This is a *coarse-grained* parallelism, involving coordination of multiple subroutines or even complete programs. The other source of parallel program execution arises from the use of pipelined arithmetic units. This is a *fine-grained* parallelism and involves the simultaneous execution of individual arithmetic operations.

Both sources of parallelism give rise to programming problems that do not arise in the conventional serial case. However, for lattice QCD calculations, both types of problems are amenable to quasimechanical solutions that can be implemented in an automatic fashion. We describe these techniques by beginning with the standard serial version of a program and describing the steps taken to transform it into a parallel, vectorized program.

As described earlier, one of the algorithms for updating the link matrices in a lattice consists of the following steps:

1. Select a link U to update;
2. Calculation of the contribution of U to the energy of the system. This requires the calculation of the plaquette variable for each of the six plaquettes that contain U;
3. Select a candidate update value V for U. This involves the generation of a random $SU(3)$ matrix;
4. Accept or reject V according to the Monte-Carlo procedure. This step also involves the use of random numbers, as well as conditional or data-dependent program execution.

There are many refinements of this basic algorithm, but implementing them will involve only minor modifications of this program.

B. Decomposition of the Problem for Parallel Solution

The most straightforward approach for decomposing the lattice QCD calculation is simultaneously updating different links with different processors. The first step in implementing this scheme is the separation of the SIMD parts of the program from the MIMD parts. Steps three and four in the algorithm presented earlier naturally involve MIMD execution. Even though the program on each processor will be the same (i.e., a conventional serial link update program), the sequence of random numbers generated by each processor must be different—each processor is given a different seed for the random number generator—so different random matrices will be generated, different conditional choices will be made by each processor, and the actual instructions being executed at any given time will be different on different processors.

The first two steps can be carried out in SIMD mode. The sequence of operations performed in the evaluation of the contribution to the energy of a single link is completely deterministic and involves no random numbers or data-dependent choices. Furthermore, it does not depend on the location of the link, but only on its orientation. Thus, the natural decomposition of the problem consists of a regular partition of the lattice into identical sublattices, one for each processor. Since the QCD machine has a two-dimensional interconnection topology, we can associate it with one of the coordinate planes of the problem, the $x-y$ plane by convention. We then assign identical regions in the $x-y$ plane to each processor, and associate all points with x and y coordinates in a region with the processor. For a 16^4 lattice and a 16 (4×4) processor QCD machine, each processor will be responsible for updating a $4 \times 4 \times 16 \times 16$ site lattice.

With this decomposition, the plaquettes associated with the sites in a given sublattice fall into three classes (Figure 7):

1. All of the link matrices lie within the sublattice;
2. One of the link matrices lies in a neighboring sublattice;
3. Two of the link matrices lie in a neighboring sublattice.

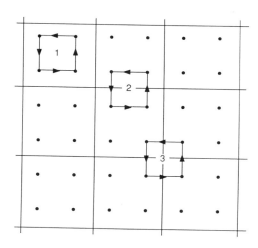

Figure 7. Plaquette classes. The solid lines indicate the node boundaries.

The evaluation of plaquettes in the first class is the same as for a serial program. For the second two classes, provision must be made for receipt of the off-board link matrices. A simple programming protocol eliminates the need for explicit, noncomputational communication operations. The evaluation of a plaquette variable involves the multiplication of a series of matrices lying along a continuous curve through the lattice. Each multiplication is associated with a step from the current site to a new site at the other end of a link. The product must be written in the memory that contains the new site. This protocol guarantees that the intermediate result is in either the same memory node as the next matrix to be multiplied or in one adjoining it. It further guarantees that the speedup of N processors over a single one will be N-fold.

The implementation of this protocol turns out to be surprisingly simple. It is most easily described by construction. Begin by writing a conventional serial Monte–Carlo for a single sublattice, using periodic boundary conditions *for the sublattice*. The program will maintain a current site and a current matrix product in a temporary storage location. As a new link matrix is multiplied, the coordinate of the current site corresponding to the link direction is incremented (or decremented, depending on the direction in which the link was traversed). The periodic boundary conditions are implemented by performing this addition or subtraction modulo the lattice size in the given direction.

This program will serve as the basis for the node program for a calculation on the full lattice. To convert it, the treatment of the periodic boundary conditions must be modified: after detecting a lattice edge, the result is written to the temporary storage location in the neighboring memory in the link direction. The value of the current site is updated as before, and the contents of the *local* temporary storage location are used for the next operation. The effect is for a processor to work on whatever product curve is crossing it at a given moment and to hand off a curve to a neighboring processor whenever the curve reaches the edge of the sublattice. The crucial aspect of this technique is that it is trivial to implement. The program can be developed and debugged as a conventional serial program on the host, taking advantage of all the programming tools available on a commercial general-purpose computer. The translation of the program can then be done mechanically by another program without introducing any bugs.

C. Vectorizing the Calculation

The second programming issue to be addressed is the efficient use of the vector arithmetic unit. For most calculations and vector CPUs, the task of vectorization is formidable, and vectorizing compilers are of only moderate usefulness. However, vectorizing lattice QCD for the QCD Machine is fairly simple. As was stressed earlier, the basic operations needed to carry out the calculation are matrix–matrix and matrix–vector multiplications. Each of the operations reduces in turn to a series of accumulations of products. Such sequences of operations can be efficiently carried out by a single arithmetic pipeline consisting of a multiplier followed by an adder, provided that the number of stages in the pipeline is not too large. No provision is made in hardware for the efficient execution of arbitrary sequences of operations. This implies that the usual programming difficulty of ordering instructions to keep the pipeline full doesn't arise. In fact, the efficiency of the vector unit for taking the product of two matrices is nearly 70% of the theoretical maximum.

Given this situation, the problem of vectorization is transformed from one of reorganizing the entire calculation to one of adding a small number of customized machine instructions to the system. If U and V represent matrices and x and y represent vectors, then the instructions needed are $U \cdot V$, $U \cdot V^\dagger$, $U^\dagger \cdot V$, $U \pm V$, $U \pm V^\dagger$, $U \cdot x$, $x \cdot U^\dagger$ and $x \pm y$. In the conventional serial version of the program, these operations are implemented as subroutines to be called as needed. The process of vectorization then consists of simply converting the subroutines into microcoded instructions, which can be called by the microprocessor. The control interface between the microprocessor and the vector processor, described in detail later, provides a direct hardware implementation of the standard FORTRAN subroutine calling convention.

V. Implementation

A. Host Interface

The QCD Machine is operated in a single-user, batch-job mode. It is connected to a host computer through a parallel DMA interface. In our case, a DR-11W interface is attached to a VAX-780 host. The DMA channel terminates on the controller in a buffer memory. The controller board is installed in one of the processor's cardcages, and the buffer memory is accessible over the Multibus. A bucket-brigade program contained in the boot PROMs on the processor boards permits the delivery of the contents of the buffer memory to an arbitrary location in the register file on any board. Conversely, the buffer memory can be filled with data contained in any of the register files and then transferred back to the host over the DMA channel. All the program development as well as the final data analysis is carried out on the host computer.

Since the QCD Machine is operated only in a single-user, batch-job mode, there is no need for a resident operating system. Two control signals, system reset and the '286 nonmaskable interrupt, suffice to control the operation of the machine. These signals are sent by the host to the controller, which then broadcasts them simultaneously to all the processors. A single job is downloaded from the host computer and execution is initiated. When program execution has been completed, a signal is sent by each processor to the controller, which sets a flag in a status register. This flag can be read by the host computer. The transfer of the results of the calculation to the host computer is then initiated by the host.

B. Node Specifications

The scalar and control unit is built around an Intel 80286 microprocessor running at eight megahertz. It is coupled with an Intel 80287 floating point numeric processor. The program memory consists of 32 kilobytes of 55 ns static RAM. A Multibus interface is implemented with the 8288 bus controller, and one edge of the circuit board contains a standard Multibus connector. Each node board is installed in a separate Multibus cardcage. For the 16-processor prototype, the standard configuration of the machine included one megabyte of DRAM in each cardcage, providing sufficient data storage for lattices with up to 16^4 vertices.

The local data memory consists of 128 kilobytes of 55 ns static RAM, broken into two independent banks of 64 kilobytes each. All the data buses are 16 bits wide to match the data bus of the '286. Similarly, the address buses are 20 bits wide. The off-board buses are implemented with twisted-pair ribbon cable. Since the nonlocal memory references are permitted only in SIMD mode, only the off-board data needs to be transferred. No addresses are exported. Instead, each processor addresses its local memory, but the data is read by a neighboring processor.

The array processor is a pipelined, microcoded multiplier accumulator built around the TRW 1022 22-bit floating-point ALU and a companion floating-point multiplier based on the TRW 16MPYHJ 16-bit integer multiplier. The floating-point format is highly nonstandard. The significand is represented as a 16-bit, 2's-complement fractional integer, and the exponent is represented as a 6-bit 2's-complement integer. A single floating-point number is stored in two consecutive words, with the significand in the first word and the exponent in the lower byte of the second word. A complex floating-point number is stored in three consecutive words. The first word contains the real significand. The real exponent and the imaginary exponent are stored in separate bytes in the second word. The third word contains the imaginary significand.

The pipeline contains nine stages. The first stage begins with the issuing of the register file addresses for the two operands that are to be multiplied.

At the end of the first cycle, the operands that have been read from the memory are latched into pipeline registers at the beginning of the switch. In the second stage, the operands traverse the switch and are latched into the inputs of the multiplier. The multiplier chip is itself pipelined, with the result being available at the beginning of the third cycle after the data is clocked in. Thus, the third and fourth pipeline stages are internal to the multiplier chip. During the fourth cycle, the exponents of the two operands are added, so that at the beginning of the fifth cycle, the complete floating point result is available. Error detection and treatment of special cases are performed during the fifth stage, and the 22-bit result is loaded into the ALU.

The ALU is also pipelined, with two internal stages. It has a single external input, two internal inputs, and an internal data path connecting the output to one of the internal inputs. It is also programmable, allowing the data on the external input to be loaded into one of the internal input registers, added to the data already contained in one of the internal input registers, or accumulated with the data emerging from the ALU on that cycle. In addition, the sign of any of the arguments can be changed for any of these instructions. The sixth and seventh pipeline stages are the internal ALU stages. The eighth stage consists of latching the 22-bit result from the ALU into a pair of 16-bit latches, separating the exponent from the significand. The ninth and final stage consists of writing the contents of a latch back into one of the register files. Since the actual write occurs at the end of

cycle	A data	B data	product
1	x(2)		
2			
3	x(1)	y(1)	
4	x(3)	y(2)	real(x)*real(y)
5		y(3)	imag(x)*real(y)
6	x(1)		imag(x)*imag(y)
7			real(x)*imag(y)

Figure 8. Memory accesses during a pipelined complex multiplication. x and y are complex numbers, with x stored in memory A and y stored in memory B. Both x and y are three words long, with the real significand stored in the first word, both of the exponents stored in the second word, and the imaginary significand stored in the third word. The cycle column counts clock cycles; the data columns show the data being transferred during the second pipeline stage; and the product column indicates which real multiplication is being initiated in the third pipeline stage. Note that $x(1)$ is fetched twice.

the cycle, the data can traverse the switch and be written into the memory in a single cycle.

An important consequence of the compact representation of complex numbers is the fact that no temporary storage registers are needed in the vector unit. A complex multiplication requires four real multiplications and therefore needs at least four cycles to initiate. However, only three cycles are required to fetch a complex number is stored in three words. A complex multiplication can be performed by holding both exponents when they are fetched and using the extra bus cycle to fetch one of the real significands twice (Figure 8).

The address space of the microprocessor showing the location of the memories and control latches is shown in Figure 9.

C. Vector Processor Control

The operation of the vector processor is entirely under microcode control. To initiate the execution of a microcode subroutine, the microprocessor must

1. Transfer the addresses of the arguments;
2. Set the configuration of the switch;
3. Check for completion of the last microcode subroutine;
4. Transfer the starting address of the microcode subroutine;
5. Initiate subroutine execution.

The addresses of the arguments are stored in latches, which are mapped into the microprocessor's address space. Four 16-bit addresses may be stored for each of the register files. The actual data address issued in a given cycle of a microcode subroutine is determined by selecting one of these base addresses and adding to it an 8-bit offset contained in the microcode instruction. With this technique, any location within 512 words of one of the base addresses can be reached in a given cycle. (Note that a 3×3 complex matrix is only 56 words long.)

A switch configuration is determined by loading three bits into the memory control latch. The output of the latch determines the state of the various latches and multiplexors that make up the switch. The memory control latch can store two switch configurations at once, allowing different configurations to be used for reading and writing operations.

No provision is made for program execution flow control in the microcode. The microcode sequencer is a simple counter, with the consequence that a microcode subroutine can contain only a simple list of instructions to be executed in order. There can be no looping, iterations, or conditional branching.

fc0000 – ffffff	EPROM containing the bootstrap and resynchronization programs.
f40000 – fbffff	Multibus address.
fc000 – ffffff	EPROM containing the bootstrap and resynchronization programs.
e0000 – fc000	Decoded address lines used for control signals.
d0000 – dffff	bank B) Local data memory.
c0000 – cffff	bank A) ''
b0000 – bfffff	bank B) Offboard data memory
a0000 – affff	bank A) in the y direction.
90000 – 9ffff	bank B) Offboard data memory
80000 – 8ffff	bank A) in the x direction.
66000 – 66fff	Microcode bits 30-37)
64000 – 65fff	Microcode bits 20-2f) Microcode
62000 – 63fff	Microcode bits 10-1f) memory
60000 – 61fff	Microcode bits 0-f)
24000 – 25fff	Vector processor startup signal and transfer address.
20000 – 24000	Decoded address lines used for control signals.
0 – 7fff	Microprocessor program memory.

Figure 9. Address space of the microprocessor.

58

```
subroutine mxm(m1,m2,ans)
complex m1(3,3),m2(3,3),ans(3,3)
ans(1,1) = m1(1,1)*m2(1,1) + m1(1,2)*m2(2,1) + m1(1,3)*m2(3,1)
ans(1,2) = m1(1,1)*m2(1,2) + m1(1,2)*m2(2,2) + m1(1,3)*m2(3,2)
ans(1,3) = m1(1,1)*m2(1,3) + m1(1,2)*m2(2,3) + m1(1,3)*m2(3,3)
ans(2,1) = m1(2,1)*m2(1,1) + m1(2,2)*m2(2,1) + m1(2,3)*m2(3,1)
ans(2,2) = m1(2,1)*m2(1,2) + m1(2,2)*m2(2,2) + m1(2,3)*m2(3,2)
ans(2,3) = m1(2,1)*m2(1,3) + m1(2,2)*m2(2,3) + m1(2,3)*m2(3,3)
ans(3,1) = m1(3,1)*m2(1,1) + m1(3,2)*m2(2,1) + m1(3,3)*m2(3,1)
ans(3,2) = m1(3,1)*m2(1,2) + m1(3,2)*m2(2,2) + m1(3,3)*m2(3,2)
ans(3,3) = m1(3,1)*m2(1,3) + m1(3,2)*m2(2,3) + m1(3,3)*m2(3,3)
return
end

var m1    complex a 0  ;declare complex array m1,  in memory a
var m2    complex b 0  ;declare complex array m2,  in memory b
var ans   complex a 0  ;declare complex array ans, in memory a

; ans(1,1) = m1(1,1)*m2(1,1) + m1(1,2)*m2(2,1) + m1(1,2)*m2(3,1)
xpi   m1 0 m2 0        ;initialize pipe and multiply m1(0) by m2(0)
xp    m1 1 m2 3        ;accumulate m1(1)*m2(3)
xpf   m1 2 m2 6        ;accumulate m1(2)*m2(6)  and flush pipe
xs    ans 0            ;store result in ans(0)
```

Figure 10. Vectorized matrix multiplication.

```
; ans(1,2) = m1(1,1)*m2(1,2) + m1(1,2)*m2(2,2) + m1(1,3)*m2(3,2)
xpi    m1 0    m2 1
xp     m1 1    m2 4
xpf    m1 2    m2 7
xs     ans 1

; ans(1,3) = m1(1,1)*m2(1,3) + m1(1,2)*m2(2,3) + m1(1,3)*m2(3,3)
xpi    m1 0    m2 2
xp     m1 1    m2 5
xpf    m1 2    m2 8
xs     ans 2

; ans(2,1) = m1(2,1)*m2(1,1) + m1(2,2)*m2(2,1) + m1(2,3)*m2(3,1)
xpi    m1 3    m2 0
xp     m1 4    m2 3
xpf    m1 5    m2 6
xs     ans 3

; ans(2,2) = m1(2,1)*m2(1,2) + m1(2,2)*m2(2,2) + m1(2,3)*m2(3,2)
xpi    m1 3    m2 1
xp     m1 4    m2 4
xpf    m1 5    m2 7
xs     ans 4
```

Figure 10. (Continued)

```
;  ans(2,3) = m1(2,1)*m2(1,3) + m1(2,2)*m2(2,3) + m1(2,3)*m2(3,3)
xpi    m1 3    m2 2
xp     m1 4    m2 5
xpf    m1 5    m2 8
xs     ans 5

;  ans(3,1) = m1(3,1)*m2(1,1) + m1(3,2)*m2(2,1) + m1(3,3)*m2(3,1)
xpi    m1 6    m2 0
xp     m1 7    m2 3
xpf    m1 8    m2 6
xs     ans 6

;  ans(3,2) = m1(3,1)*m2(1,2) + m1(3,2)*m2(2,2) + m1(3,3)*m2(3,2)
xpi    m1 6    m2 1
xp     m1 7    m2 4
xpf    m1 8    m2 7
xs     ans 7

;  ans(3,3) = m1(3,1)*m2(1,3) + m1(3,2)*m2(2,3) + m1(3,3)*m2(3,3)
xpi    m1 6    m2 2
xp     m1 7    m2 5
xpf    m1 8    m2 8
xs     ans 8
end
```

Figure 10. (Continued)

61

```
mtm:    mov  si,[bx+2]      ;load the pointer to the first
        mov  ax,lind[si]    ;matrix into ball, a base
        mov  ball,ax        ;address latch for the B memory.

        mov  ax,[bx+4]      ;load the pointer to the second
        mov  aal1,ax        ;matrix into aal1, a base
                            ;address latch for A the memory.

        mov  ax,[bx+6]      ;load the pointer to the destination
        mov  aal3,ax        ;matrix into aal3, a base
                            ;address latch for A the memory.
        mov  ax,0d0c0h      ;load the intended contents of the
                            ;memory control latch into ax.

        add  bx,8           ;set bx to point to the next
                            ;routine.
        mov  vwait,ax       ;wait until the vector processor
                            ;has finished the previous operation.
        mov  svp+mu_mtm,ax  ;load the memory control latch (at
                            ;address svp) and start the vector
                            ;processor. The lower bits of the
                            ;address (mu_mtm) determine the
                            ;microcode program being started.

        jmp  tab[bx]        ;jump to next portion of code
                            ;selected by bx which starts up
                            ;the next microcode program.
```

Figure 11. Microcode subroutine call linkage.

D. *Programming Tools for Vectorization*

The principal difficulty in programming a pipelined processor is the need to control all of the stages synchronously. For a pipeline with nine stages, the programmer must control nine separate calculations, each in a different degree of completion, in each line of microcode. Further, by reordering the sequence of operations, it may prove possible to minimize flushing and reloading the pipeline, resulting in faster program execution. Vectorizing compilers have had only limited success in transforming and optimizing most programs. However, the simplicity of the pipelined vector unit in the QCD Machine allowed the development of two tools: an arithmetic assembly language and an optimizer.

With an arithmetic assembly language, two operations are specified for a pair of arguments. These operations completely determine the manipulations to be performed on the operands as they move through the pipeline. The first operation must be a multiplication. The only options are whether the operands are real or complex numbers. The second operation can be any one of the ALU operations described in the earlier discussion of node specifications. The result is either written into the output latch of the vector unit or held in the last stage of the ALU for further use.

The instruction set is orthogonal and (somewhat) mnemonic. Each instruction begins with a field indicating the data type: x for complex and f for real. Next follows a field indicating whether the sign of the product is to be preserved or changed when it is clocked into the adder: p adds the result, m subtracts it. An optional final field determines whether the pipeline is being initiated or flushed. An example of a matrix multiplication subroutine in FORTRAN and assembler is shown in Figure 10, and the '286 assembly language to implement the subroutine call linkage is shown in Figure 11.

Each of the assembler instructions corresponds to a two-dimensional template of microcode bits, where the horizontal axis corresponds to the different control signals and the vertical axis corresponds to time. Since there is only one pipeline, the only possible optimization is to minimize the delay between instructions. This can be accomplished automatically by translating a sequence of instructions into a series of templates and then pushing the templates as close together as possible without overlapping them.

VI. Experience

A. *Performance Measurements*

Since the QCD Machine is a special-purpose computer dedicated to a single calculation, it isn't reasonable to measure its performance with

Table 1. Measured Performance of the QCD Machine and the Cray–I

	Nominal Peak Speed	3 × 3 Complex Matrix Mult	Link Update Time
16-node QCD machine	256 Mflop/s	160 Mflop/s	100 μs.
Cray–I	160 Mflop/s	100 Mflop/s	70 μs.

standard benchmarks. However, two interesting performance measurements can be made by comparing it to lattice QCD programs that have been written to run on the Cray-I. These programs were written by physicists who were trying to make efficient use of a precious resource and are probably fairly well optimized.

The first benchmark (see Table 1) is the time required to perform one of the elementary operations: the multiplication of a pair of 3 × 3 complex matrices. This benchmark measures the overhead of the pipeline for short vectors.

The second benchmark is the time required to update one link matrix using a given algorithm. This is a complete benchmark in the sense that it involves a mixture of scalar and vector operations, and measures the performance that can be achieved in a complete calculation.

B. Chronology of Design, Implementation, and Use

- January 1983: Initial architectural design
- May 1983: Detailed electrical and software design
- January 1984: Construction of first prototype board
- February 1984: Vectorization of first application program
- June 1984: Construction of 16-processor prototype
- July 1984: Parallelization of first application program
- September 1984: Debugging of 16-processor prototype
- March 1985: Beginning of first calculation
- September 1985: Completion of first calculation. [4]

References

1. Wilson, K. G. (1974). "Confinement of quarks," *Physical Review,* **D10,** 2455.
2. Feynman, R., and Hibbs, A. (1965). *Path Integrals and Quantum Mechanics.* Addison Wesley.
3. Rebbi, Claudio (1983). "The lattice theory of quark confinement," *Scientific American.* **248,** 54.

4. Christ, N. H., and Terrano, A. E. (1986). "The deconfining phase transition in lattice QCD," *Physical Review Letters.* **56,** 111.
5. Weingarten, D. (1985). Technical Report, IBM T. J. Watson Research Center.
6. Wilson, K. G. (1986). *Brookhaven Conference.*
7. Christ, N. H., and Terrano, A. E. (1984). "A very fast parallel processor," *IEEE Transactions on Computers.* **C-33,** 344.
8. Christ, N. H., and Terrano, A. E. "A micro-based supercomputer," *BYTE.* April 1986, 145–160.

3 Geometry–Defining Processors for Partial Differential Equations

D. DEWEY AND A. T. PATERA

Department of Mechanical Engineering
Massachusetts Institute of Technology
Cambridge, MA

I. Introduction

A great many computational tasks in engineering and scientific analysis involve extensive processing of geometry. For instance, in the computer-aided design of mechanical and electrical systems, the efficient manipulation of geometric objects is a critical prerequisite for effective system analysis and simulation. Similarly, in investigations of the physics of continua, geometry input and mesh generation is an all-important preprocessing step necessary for subsequent numerical solution of the governing partial differential equations. In both of these applications, the success of the overall simulation procedure is strongly dependent on the ability to efficiently represent and manipulate geometric and geometry-based entities.

The importance of geometry processing has led to the development of special-purpose processors and peripherals optimized for precisely this purpose. An example of such a device is the graphics tablet, which is now widely used as a peripheral for inputting two-dimensional curves directly from graphical representations. The success of the graphics tablet derives from the fact that the geometric relations that are self-evident to the user in two-dimensional physical space are directly translated by the device into a symbolic representation that can then be used for further processing. In essence, the function of the graphics tablet is critically tied to its particular physical embodiment.

The ubiquity of peripherals such as the graphics tablet suggests that similar, but more sophisticated, devices be constructed for three-dimensional processing, and furthermore, that such devices be capable not only of sensing and communicating geometry, but also of performing calculations on the basis of intrinsic geometric connectivity. In this paper we describe such a class of processors, which we have denoted Geometry-Defining Processors, or GDPs. GDPs are microprocessors which are housed in *manually reconfigurable physical geometric packages,* and which are capable of communicating intrinsic geometric information, as well as numerical data, to nearest neighbors in a GDP assembly. By virtue of physical proximity and fidelity to geometric relations, GDP assemblies are able to automatically generate symbolic representations of three-dimensional solids, as well as perform parallel computations on the associated connection topology.

The motivation for Geometry-Defining Processors is best understood in terms of the solution of partial differential equations (PDEs), and we therefore begin our discussion by reviewing in Section II the role of geometry and parallelism in the finite-element simulation of continuous systems. In Section III we introduce the basic features of Geometry-Defining Processors, and describe the architectures of both individual GDPs and GDP assemblies. Section IV addresses the application of GDPs to geometry input and mesh generation for PDE solvers, while Section V discusses the parallel solution of PDEs using GDP assemblies. In Section VI, we present prototype hardware mesh-generator Geometry-Defining Processors that illustrate some of the basic features of the GDP concept. Finally, in Section VII we discuss the design and expected performance of first-generation computational GDPs.

II. The Finite-Element Method: Geometry and Parallelism

A large number of problems in continuum physics are mathematically described by mixed initial/boundary value problems of the form,

$$\partial_t u = \mathcal{L}u + f(\vec{x}) \qquad \text{in } D, \tag{1}$$

where D is the spatial domain of interest, u is the dependent variable, $f(\vec{x})$ is the forcing term, t and $\vec{x}$ are time and space, respectively, and $\mathcal{L}$ is a spatial differential operator defined on the domain D. Examples of physical phenomena which can be described by equations of this form are heat conduction, the mechanics of solids and fluids, electromagnetism, and quantum mechanics.

For the purpose of making our discussion somewhat more concrete, we consider two (related) special cases of (1),

$$\partial_t u = \nabla^2 u + f(\vec{x}) \qquad \text{in } D, \tag{2}$$

$$0 = \nabla^2 u + f(\vec{x}) \qquad \text{in } D, \tag{3}$$

the former corresponding, for example, to unsteady conduction heat flow, and the latter corresponding to steady-state conduction heat transfer. In most cases the time-asymptotic (t → ∞) solution of (2) also solves the steady equation (3); however this time-accurate approach to a steady-state does not lead to efficient numerical procedures, and we therefore consider the unsteady and steady equations as distinct problems. Although Equations (2) and (3) may appear too simple to be representative of real problems of interest, this is, in fact, not the case. For instance, numerical algorithms for the Navier–Stokes equations for incompressible fluid flow can be constructed out of equation sets only slightly more complicated than (2)–(3) [1].

For problems on general domains with arbitrary nonhomogeneities, analytical solution of (2)–(3) is not possible, and a numerical treatment is required. There are two distinct, but related, difficulties associated with numerical solution of partial differential equations in arbitrary three-di-

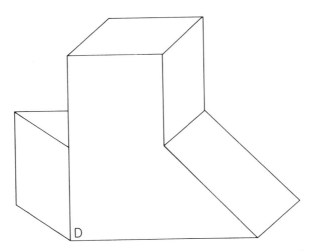

Figure 1. Example of a three-dimensional spatial domain D in which the solution of a partial differential equation is sought.

mensional domains: the first is the "interface" problem of geometry input, mesh generation, and subsequent discrete equation generation; the second is the "computational" problem of solution of the resulting set of algebraic equations.

To illustrate the interface and computational problems described above, we consider the finite-element solution [2] of (2)–(3) on the representative domain D depicted in Figure 1. We begin by considering the purely spatial problem given by (3), since this also corresponds to the right-hand side of the time-dependent problem (2). For simplicity we choose finite-element discretization by cubes and triangular prisms, for which an illustrative mesh is shown in Figure 2.

The finite-element method proceeds by first considering a given element

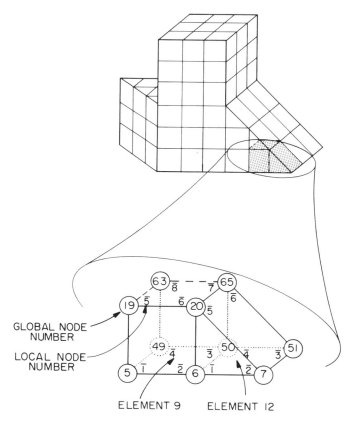

Figure 2. Illustrative finite element discretization of the spatial domain D shown in Fig. 1.

k, in which the discrete approximation of the Laplacian is generated by a variational projection operator,

$$(\nabla^2 u)_{\bar{i}}^k \rightarrow \sum_{\bar{j}} \overline{A}_{\bar{i}\bar{j}}^k u_{\bar{j}}^k. \tag{4}$$

Here the $u_{\bar{j}}^k$ are the nodal unknowns, with superscript k referring to element, and barred subscripts denoting local nodes (e.g., $\bar{j} = 1, \ldots, 8$ for cubical elements). To generate the global system equations from the elemental components, we sum all contributions (4) that correspond to the same (i.e., physically coincident) global node i,

$$(\nabla^2 u)_i = \sum_j A_{ij} u_j = \sum_k{}' (\nabla^2 u)_{\bar{i}}^k, \tag{5a}$$

$$A_{g_{\bar{i}}^k g_{\bar{j}}^k} = \sum_k{}' \overline{A}_{\bar{i}\bar{j}}^k, \tag{5b}$$

where $g_{\bar{i}}^k$ is the local-to-global transformation which maps the local node numbers $\bar{i}$ of a given element k to their corresponding (unique) global identities $g_{\bar{i}}^k$. Unbarred subscripts refer to global nodes, and Σ' refers to direct stiffness summation.

On the basis of the assembled operators in (5), we can now write the full set of discrete equations corresponding to finite element treatment of (3),

$$0 = \sum_j A_{ij} u_j + f_i, \tag{6}$$

where f_i is the discrete form of the nonhomogeneity in (3). It should be noted that the most difficult task in constructing (6) is typically not the generation of the elemental matrices, $\overline{A}_{\bar{i}\bar{j}}^k$ (which is relatively trivial for this particular equation), but rather the generation of the elemental connectivities as reflected in the $g_{\bar{i}}^k$ mapping.

We now turn to the time-dependent system described by (2). Using the spatial operators defined in (4)–(5) and an explicit time-marching scheme for the temporal discretization, the resulting evolution equations for the global nodal values will be of the form (e.g., for Euler forward),

$$u_i^{n+1} - u_i^n = \Delta t \left(\sum A_{ij} u_j^n + f_i^n \right), \tag{7}$$

where superscript n refers to time level, and Δt is the timestep. The use of explicit stepping will result in a severe stability restriction on Δt, which is why (7) does not constitute an efficient approach to the steady-state problem (6).

As regards the *solution* of (7) (up to this point we have considered only the *discretization*), it is clear from the form of (7) and the assembly procedure (5) that: a) updating of the dependent variable u at a given node

i can be performed independently of all other level $n + 1$ updates; and b) this updating requires access to only physically neighboring nodal values at level n. These observations suggest a massively parallel local-memory computer architecture for solution of (7), a realization that is now quite old.

It should be noted that (7) can correspond either to time-accurate solution of (2), or to solution of the steady problem (6) by Jacobi iteration [3]. The latter, however, results in quite slow convergence ($\mathcal{O}(M^2)$ iterations for a d-dimensional grid of M^d equally-spaced points), and more implicit techniques are therefore of interest. An example of an improvement for solution of (6) is the conjugate gradient iterative procedure [3], which entails evaluations of the general form of (7), but also inner products of the form

$$\alpha^{n+1} = \sum_i \tilde{u}_i^{n+1} \tilde{u}_i^{n+1}, \tag{8}$$

where $\tilde{u}_i^{n+1}$ is some representative intermediate result at iteration $n + 1$. This technique improves convergence (even without preconditioning, only $\mathcal{O}(M)$ iterations are required on an M^d grid), however, locality and concurrency are no longer as inherent. In general, there is a tradeoff between obvious concurrency and degree of implicitness; this is a reflection of the underlying mathematical fact that the Green's functions associated with (1) are, in fact, typically *not* local.

It is clear from this discussion that geometry enters into the finite-element solution of partial differential equations in two central ways: first, as a computational chore related to domain definition and construction of the g_i^k mapping; second, as the underlying basis that (potentially) allows for concurrency and locality in the solution algorithm. Although these problems of mesh generation and parallel solution described above may seem superficially unrelated, they are, in fact, intimately connected. In essense, mesh generation is related to the problem of connection topology, which is, in turn, a central issue in the parallel solution of partial differential equations. The proposed architecture aims to exploit this similarity.

III. Geometry-Defining Processors

Geometry-Defining Processors are microprocessors that are housed in *physical geometric packages,* that are aware of the parameters of these physical packages, and that are able to communicate this geometric information, as well as numerical data, to nearest neighbors. To simulate a physical system (that is, to solve a partial differential equation), GDPs are manually assembled in a "scale" model of the real-space domain D, as shown in Figure 3. The act of assembly automatically generates a symbolic

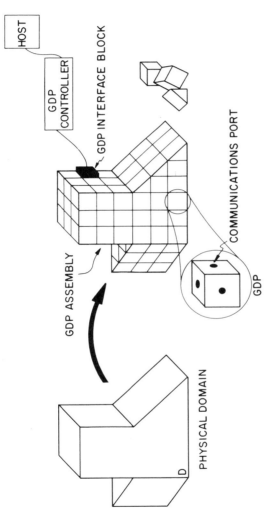

Figure 3. Geometry-Defining Processor assembly corresponding to the physical domain D. The GDP subsystem consists of the GDP assembly, a GDP interface block, and a GDP controller.

representation of the geometry (from which the mesh and equations directly derive), as well as creating a simple, "optimally-connected" dedicated parallel processor for the particular problem at hand. In a unified fashion, GDPs address the distinct, but related, issues of problem definition and problem solution.

The basic processor/communication structure of an individual GDP is shown schematically in Figure 4 for the simple case of a rectangular two-dimensional GDP. A communication port on each face of the GDP allows for two types of communication within the GDP assembly. First, each GDP is able to communicate through *local* buses that are reconfigurable in the sense that the lines emanating from different faces can be internally connected to route messages through the GDPs. These buses are termed local because in most applications they are used to connect only nearest neighbors; the reconfigurability does, however, allow for high-speed, parallel, non-nearest-neighbor communication, such as is used for vector-reduction operations. The second type of communication supported by the GDP faces is a *global* bus that all GDPs and the host computer can access. This bus is primarily used for communication between the host computer and one or more of the GDPs.

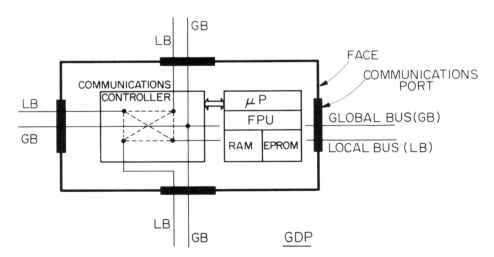

Figure 4. Schematic of a (rectangular, two-dimensional) Geometry-Defining Processor. A GDP consists of a package, communication ports on each face, a microprocessor (CPU), a floating-point unit (FPU), RAM and EPROM, a communications controller, a global bus (GB), and a reconfigurable local bus (LB).

Each GDP-resident microprocessor, in addition to controlling communications, performs local calculations related to mesh generation or equation solution using programs and parameters downloaded from the host computer via the global bus. The GDPs in an assembly can be synchronized by the global bus; however they otherwise operate independently, performing autonomous calculations on locally available data.

In assembled form, the GDPs can be thought of as an array of processor–switch units, with one global bus and a variable number of local buses. The local lines constitute a standard reconfigurable switching network, with f data paths incident to a particular processor–switch, where f is the number of faces of the "associated" GDP. The topology of a particular static GDP assembly (i.e., an arrangement for a *particular* geometry) can be interpreted in terms of several previously proposed parallel architectures, as will be discussed further in Section V.

Armed with the above brief description of GDPs and GDP-assembly architecture, we now turn to a discussion of applications of the devices to PDE solution. Some of the applications are relatively obvious (e.g., parallel solution algorithms), while some are less so (e.g., geometry input and mesh generation). The logical sequence in which to present these ideas is to start with geometry input and conclude with parallel computation, since this sequence is consistent not only with the order in which PDEs are actually solved, but also with the evolution of GDPs as regards internal complexity.

IV. Geometry Input and Mesh Generation

In this section we discuss the application of Geometry-Defining Processors to geometry input and mesh generation. Although our focus will be on partial differential equations, the examples in this section are representative of a general class of problems in which the computer must be interfaced to the physical, geometric world. In all of these applications, a set of GDPs is best thought of as an intelligent interactive peripheral attached to a conventional general-purpose host.

To input a geometry and generate a mesh using Geometry-Defining Processors, the GDPs are first manually assembled in the desired physical configuration, as illustrated in Figure 3. A GDP interface block is then connected to any (exposed) face of any GDP in the assembly, providing, via the global bus, communication between the assembly and the GDP controller. The GDP controller in turn communicates with the host computer. The various components of the system are illustrated in Figure 3.

On command from the host, the GDP controller then interrogates each GDP in turn for information of the form,

$$
\begin{aligned}
\text{GEOMTYP} &\quad (k) \\
\text{GDPNXTO} &\quad (k, f) \\
\text{FACNXTO} &\quad (k, f) \\
\text{ROTNXTO} &\quad (k, f)
\end{aligned}
\tag{9}
$$

where f refers to local face number (e.g., $f = 1, \ldots, 6$ for a cube) and k refers to GDP number. The array GEOMTYP contains the geometry type of GDP k (e.g., cube, triangular prism), from which the host can infer the relative position of all the local nodes using a database of geometry definitions. The array GDPNXTO contains the GDP number of the GDP next to face f of GDP k; the array FACNXTO contains the (local) number of the face adjacent to face f of GDP k; and the array ROTNXTO contains the relative rotation of these faces with respect to a fiducial orientation. This data is available and obtained automatically by virtue of the physical proximity (i.e., connection) of neighboring GDPs.

The data in the GDPNXTO, FACNXTO, and ROTNXTO arrays is readily translated into a local-to-global node transformation, g_i^k. Furthermore, as the GDPs are not only topologically, but also geometrically, representative of the physical domain, the positions of all the global nodes can also be inferred from the available information. This completes the mesh specification, the GDPs having provided all data necessary for subsequent finite element solution of partial differential equations on the geometry that they define. Examples of actual GDP mesh generation will be given in Section VI, in which details associated with hardware and communication will be described in greater depth.

As regards the generality of GDP mesh generators, GDPs have all the flexibility in three space dimensions that graphics tablets have in two dimensions, and in fact generate more information, since they discretize volumes (areas in two dimensions) rather than surfaces (lines in two dimensions). Practically speaking, it is certainly over-optimistic to conceive of three-dimensional GDPs of characteristic dimensions equal to the resolution of graphics tablets. However, we believe that reasonably small devices can be achieved, thanks to advances in VLSI and to the fact that the processing requirements for mesh generation are relatively minimal.

In terms of the ease of use of GDPs, the critical point is the simplicity with which geometries can be input using reconfigurable "real-space" elements. The GDPs allow for data input directly in physical space, with all symbolic, computational-space processing performed transparently to the user. Both the minimal learning curve associated with initial use of GDPs, and the minimal time required for subsequent particular realizations of GDP assemblies, should make the devices competitive with conventional software geometry-input techniques. Although it is clear that there are many geometry-input applications for which GDPs should not be considered (e.g., when boundaries are defined by nontrivial analytical expressions, as opposed to more "blocklike" structures), there are also many applications where GDPs should prove optimal.

Two particular applications in which we see a definite superiority for GDPs are as first-cut design workstations and as front ends for finite-element solvers used in university engineering and science education. In both cases, the construction of extremely user-friendly front ends (e.g., mesh generators) would allow numerical methods to be used for analysis of physical systems with sufficient ease so as not to change the emphasis from the physical phenomena of interest (i.e., solutions of PDEs) to the technical details of computation (i.e., the solution of PDEs). In such applications, ease of use and quick turnaround time are more critical than complete generality.

V. Parallel Solution of Partial Differential Equations

As described in Section II, the explicit solution of PDEs such as (2) results in discrete equation sets (7) which admit a high degree of concurrency and locality of communication. Although there are many general-purpose parallel implementations that do not explicitly exploit this "local" nature of continuum physics (e.g., pipeline, vector, and coarse-grain shared-memory parallel processors), there also exist massively parallel local-memory machines that have been constructed with precisely such applications in mind.

These "new" massively parallel architectures constitute great advances in computational speed for problems which conform to their respective connection schemes, or topologies. In particular, for problems defined on, or mappable to, regular two-dimensional domains, the lattice-structure processors appear to offer near-optimal architecture for solution of systems of the form given by (7). However, for many problems, the geometric complexity of the physical domain precludes effective mapping to a regular grid, resulting in greatly reduced computational efficiency due to processor latency and communication delays.

It is clear that for parallelism to have significant impact on a wide class of problems, the architecture must be sufficiently reconfigurable so as to reflect the underlying physics, topology, and geometry of the problem at hand (as well as to have sufficient communications flexibility to allow efficient "occasional" long-distance connections desirable for implicit algorithms). An ideal geometry for calculation from the point of view of optimal connectivity is certainly the actual physical space configuration of the domain of the partial differential equation of interest. To this end, we propose parallel solution of PDEs based on Geometry-Defining Processor assemblies.

A. GDP Solution of PDEs

GDP parallel solution of PDEs proceeds in a straight-forward fashion. First, the geometry and mesh are created following the procedure outlined in Section IV. However, now each GDP contains not only geometric descriptors, but also the values of the field variables at its local nodes, u_j^k, and the elemental equations, $\overline{A}_{ij}^k$, associated with the particular PDE of interest (e.g., (2)). The elemental equations, initial conditions, and nonhomogeneities in the problem are all downloaded to the GDPs from the host prior to simulation. In effect, each GDP represents (in fact, is) a finite element of the same shape. Note that in practice each GDP will no doubt represent a collection of elements, or a substructure [4] (see Section VII). However, for purposes of illustration we consider here a one-to-one GDP–finite-element correspondence.

Considering the explicit scheme (7), the solution u^n is advanced to the next time step, u^{n+1}, by first evaluating the right-hand side of (7) at an elemental (GDP) level by matrix multiplication,

$$\overline{q}_i^k = \overline{A}_{ij}^k u_j^{n,k} + \overline{f}_i^{n,k}. \tag{10a}$$

Direct stiffness summation, (5), then proceeds by summation of the $\overline{q}_i^k$ from neighboring GDPs,

$$q_{g_i^k} = {\sum_k}' \overline{q}_i^k, \tag{10b}$$

after which the global nodal values can be (locally) updated:

$$u_i^{n+1} = u_i^n + \Delta t\, q_i. \tag{11}$$

Note that in practice it is critical that the g_i^k data actually be represented as GDP-local pointers to adjoining elements and nodes in explicit recognition of the fact that the only contributions to the direct stiffness sum (10b) are from nearest neighbors.

It is clear from the above discussion that explicit solution of partial differential equations by GDPs automatically results in highly parallel, local calculations; the operation count (number of clock cycles) per time step on a d-dimensional assembly of K^d GDPs is $\mathcal{O}(1)$, that is, does not increase with K. Although the operation count per time step is "optimal," with K^d GDPs/finite elements the operation count to get to a steady state (i.e., to solve (6) by (10)–(11)) is of order $\mathcal{O}(K^2)$. The reconfigurable local buses can be used to reduce the operation count to reach steady-state by introducing more implicitness into the scheme.

For instance, solution of (6) by conjugate gradient iteration involves evaluations such as (10), but also inner products of the form given in (8). To perform the inner product (8) on the one-dimensional array of GDPs shown in Figure 5a, the local buses are dynamically reconfigured as indicated in Figure 5b. This architecture is similar to the partitioned linear array proposed in [5] for general vector-reduction operations. The resulting number of cycles required is $\mathcal{O}(\log K)$, an operation count which can be easily maintained in higher space dimensions by sweeping through each coordinate direction in succession. As the number of conjugate gradient iterations required to achieve convergence to a prescribed tolerance on a

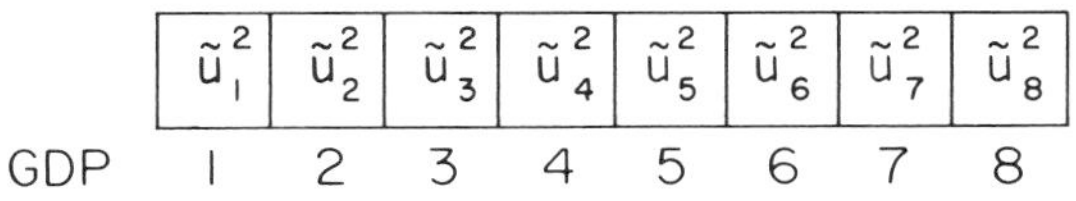

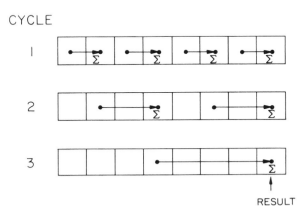

Figure 5a. One-dimensional array of GDPs to be used in the inner product summation (8).

Figure 5b. Use of the reconfigurable bus as a binary tree-like mapping to achieve an $\mathcal{O}(\log K)$ operation count for inner products. Here solid lines refer to the configuration of the local bus, with arrows indicating the direction of data flow.

mesh of K^d GDPs is $\mathcal{O}(K)$, the total number of cycles needed to solve (6) is $\mathcal{O}(K \log K)$, a substantial improvement over the Jacobi result. The same calculation would require at least $\mathcal{O}(K^d \log K)$ cycles if performed on a serial processor.

It is interesting to note that the parallel implementation of inner product summation described in Figure 5 does not correspond to embedding a binary tree into the GDP assembly topology, but rather to embedding one level of a binary tree at each cycle (a binary treelike mapping in which the same processor is used at multiple levels [6]). The former is really only superior to the latter in applications where input to the tree can be pipelined, a construction that cannot typically be exploited in solution of scalar (or low-order vector) partial differential equation systems.

From the operation count estimates above, it is clear that solution of PDEs by GDPs achieves the primary goal of parallel computation, namely an increase in computational speed and a decrease in computational cost through the use of many small processors to solve a single problem. Furthermore, it is expected that the reconfigurable geometric connection of the processors and the natural division of computation of the GDP scheme will lead to high parallel efficiency for a relatively large class of geometrically complex problems. The issue of computational efficiency for a GDP assembly is discussed further in Section VII.

B. Comparison of GDPs with Other Parallel Architectures

To put the GDP architecture in perspective, we now briefly compare it with other massively parallel machines that have been proposed. These machines all consist of K independent processors and associated local memories, with relatively few direct connections between the members of the assembly. Examples of this kind of architecture are ring and lattice structures with $\mathcal{O}(1)$ nearest-neighbor connections [7,8], generalized lattice constructions such as the hypercube [9], which has $\mathcal{O}(\log K)$ direct connections per processor, and reconfigurable switching networks [10-12]. A complete review of parallel architectures for PDEs can be found in [13].

We begin by discussing a lattice-based architecture — the Finite Element Machine [7] — that has much in common with the GDP concept as regards PDEs. The Finite Element Machine consists of a regular (fixed) square array of processors, nearest-neighbor links, a global broadcast bus, and an embedded binary tree connection. The design concept has each processor represent a finite element (or a substructure to minimize communication [14]), with the global bus to synchronize, the local bus to perform direct stiffness summation (10b), and the tree connection to facilitate inner product and norm calculations.

In practice, the principle limitation of the Finite Element Machine as a general-purpose PDE solver is the lack of reconfigurability. If the mesh graph cannot be represented on the available two-dimensional grid, or can only be embedded at the expense of unutilized processors or increased use of the global bus, significant processor latency and communication delays will result. Furthermore, even when relatively efficient mappings do exist, they may be computationally expensive to generate [15]. The GDP architecture, although similar to the Finite Element Machine for a particular, static GDP assembly, differs in the *reconfigurability of processors* that allows parallel efficiency to remain high even for general problems.

We discuss next the hypercube architecture [9], which is in fairly widespread use. The hypercube topology is designed to address a large class of parallel algorithms, and certainly not just the solution of partial differential equations. However, with regard to the solution of PDEs, the $\mathcal{O}(\log K)$ connections per processor ensure that many mesh topologies associated with PDEs can be embedded in the hypercube without loss of locality (i.e., with unit dilation). Furthermore, the extra available connections (i.e., as compared to $\mathcal{O}(1)$) allow for more implicit solution algorithms. For instance, the inner products (8) can be readily evaluated in $\mathcal{O}(\log K)$ using binary treelike mappings [6].

These positive features will no doubt lead to use of the hypercube architecture for parallel solution of PDEs. However, the fact that the number of connections grows relatively quickly as K increases will eventually imply increased (per processor) cost. Furthermore, the topology is not "optimal" in the sense that, although the number of available connections in a hypercube is greater than the number required for solution of lattice-based problems, a mapping problem still exists. It should be noted that the problem of increased communication delays due to non-nearest-neighbor interaction is being mitigated by more topology-transparent communication procedures, in which pipelining is used to reduce the time required to traverse intermediate nodes.

Lastly, we discuss GDPs in the context of reconfigurable switching networks, focussing on the CHiP [10], a parallel architecture that preserves locality by maintaining a high degree of reconfigurability. The CHiP solution to reconfigurability *and* efficient processor utilization is a dual system of processors and switches, a typical implementation of which would be a regular two-dimensional square array of processors and switches, with $\mathcal{O}(w^2)$ (w = corridor width) switches per processor. Processors are interconnected via the "underlying" switching system, with the switching system able to reconfigure according to globally broadcast commands.

Although perhaps not constructed with processor–finite-element correspondence in mind, the CHiP configuration is quite well suited for the task. General finite-element grids can be embedded in the array with high processor utilization due to the nonzero corridor width; furthermore, the (time-dependent) reconfiguring allows for embedding of more "implicit" structures, such as trees. The major issue as regards CHiP parallel solution of PDEs is the existence and construction of physical (often three-dimensional) grid-to-CHiP topology mappings.

The GDP topology can be thought of as a $w = 0$ three-dimensional CHiP layout in which reconfigurability is provided not through switches, but rather through changes in the geometry of the processor array. This eliminates the need for large corridor widths, and results in significantly less complexity at both the hardware and software level as compared to the CHiP architecture. This reduction in complexity will become increasingly important if large values of w are required, and thus a complete understanding of the tradeoffs between switch versus processor reconfigurability for PDEs must await more results on minimal embeddings and on algorithms for construction of such embeddings.

The clear advantage of three-dimensional GDPs for three-dimensional parallel computations is simplicity at both the hardware and software level. Used in conjunction with GDP mesh generation, optimal mappings (resulting in load balancing) are automatically created at the same time as the problem is defined. (Note that for parallel computation applications, efficiency only requires that the geometry of the assembly roughly correspond to that of the domain, and thus rigidity of GDP shape is not necessarily a crucial concern.) Furthermore, the size (e.g., number of processors) of the system is not set by decisions at the time of manufacture, but rather is determined by the requirements of a particular solution. This intrinsic modularity leads to optimality as regards sharing of resources, in that system expansion and subdivision is dynamic and unlimited.

VI. Prototype Implementation of Mesh-Generation GDPs

In order to investigate and demonstrate the viability and practicality of Geometry-Defining Processors at a very primitive level, we have developed prototype hardware and software to perform simple three-dimensional geometry input. These prototypes represent a tangible proof-of-concept of several important aspects of the GDP scheme: the GDPs are three-dimensional; the GDPs are aware of their geometry; the GDPs communicate with each other and the host processor; and the GDPs can be conveniently reconfigured. The simplicity of the prototype host software demonstrates the ease with which the GDP-generated data (9) can be processed to generate geometric information such as nodal positions. We now present some specific software and hardware details of the prototype GDPs, and demonstrate their use in inputting simple geometries.

A. *Configuration and Geometry Deconvolution*

Realizations of the GDP concept can take on many possible forms. The choice of the particular GDPs described here was influenced by considerations arising from their proposed use for finite-element mesh generation. These requirements suggest implementing GDPs as a set of volumetric elements that are capable of filling three-dimensional space, and that interface (connect) to one another through faces of identical shape and size. The shapes of the prototype GDPs are the cube and wedge elements shown in Figure 2.

The data base required to define a three-dimensional solid made up of nodes, edges, and faces is similar to, but more extensive than, that required to specify a nodal topology (i.e., a graph). The parameters used to specify an individual GDP geometry are identified in Figure 6 along with their particular values for the cube and wedge elements. The set of x, y, z-coordinates for the nodes fixes the relative geometry of the element but gives little topological information directly. In particular, the specification of faces and edges is carried out through an additional ordered list of nodes for each face. The first node in the list is a fiducial node, and subsequent nodes are those encountered as the perimeter of the face is traversed in a positive direction viewed from the outside of the GDP. An edge is defined by two adjacent nodes in a list.

The specification of the structure of an assembly of GDPs has already been given as the data set (9). That this set is sufficient to construct a GDP-defined volume can best be seen by examining the process of assembling a structure. The addition of GDP k' to an existing assembly consists of first specifying the geometry of the GDP to be added, GEOMTYP (k'). Then, a connection of one of its faces, f', is made to an exposed face, FACNXTO (k', f'), of a GDP, GDPNXTO (k', f'), already in the assembly. Finally, because GDP faces often have some degree of rotational symmetry, it is necessary to specify the relative rotational orientation of the two faces, ROTNXTO (k', f'). The set of numbers $\{k', f', \text{ROTNXTO } (k', f'), \text{GDPNXTO } (k', f'), \text{FACNXTO } (k', f')\}$ represents a *connection* between GDP faces. For example, the connection between the cubical and wedge elements shown in the detail of Figure 2 is given (when viewed from the cube) by $\{9, 2, 1, 12, 1\}$ or (when viewed from the wedge) $\{12, 1, 1, 9, 2\}$.

It is clear that the number of connections *necessary* to specify a K-element GDP configuration is K-1; however, the number of *all* (nonempty)

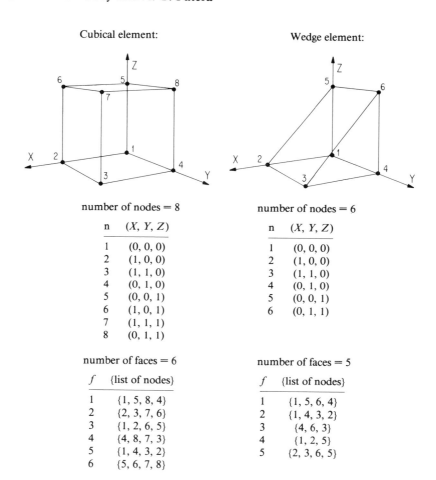

Figure 6. Parameter database used to specify three-dimensional cubical and wedge elements. Elements are defined by the number of nodes, the relative position of nodes, the number of faces, and an ordered node list for each face.

connections in an assembly will generally be of order $K\bar{f}$, where $\bar{f}$ is the average number of faces per GDP. Consequently, although a (properly chosen) set of K-1 connections can specify the assembly geometry, many of the connections will be present only implicitly. For efficient geometry-processing algorithms, the complete GDP-derived data set (9), in which all connections are explicit, is preferable.

With the framework outlined above, the data set (9) obtained from the

Assigning absolute coordinate values to the local nodes

Start with no GDPs having absolute positions assigned
  For all GDPs k
    XYZKNOWN(k) = false

Locate the assembly in space by positioning GDP k'
  Specify XYZ values for three nodes of GDP k'
  Calculate the rest of the nodal coordinates for GDP k'
  XYZKNOWN(k') = true

Locate the remaining GDPs by transferring coordinates
  For all connections
    IF there is a connection between GDP j' and GDP m':
      IF XYZKNOWN(j') is true and XYZKNOWN(m') is false:
        Use NODEMATCH(connection) to identify coincident nodes
        Transfer known XYZ(j') values to three nodes of GDP m'
        Calculate the rest of the nodal coordinates for GDP m'
        XYZKNOWN(m') = true
    IF any XYZKNOWN(k) is false: repeat

Figure 7. Algorithm used by the GDP host system to process the GDP-derived data to obtain absolute coordinates of all nodes.

GDP assembly can be processed to obtain two important results of mesh generation: the coordinates of all nodes in absolute problem-space, and a g_i^k mapping or equivalent data structure. For example, Figure 7 shows a simple host–resident algorithm for deducing absolute coordinate values of the nodes of the GDP assembly from the GDP-derived data (9). This algorithm makes use of the simple function NODEMATCH, which takes as its argument a facial connection, and returns a list of those local nodes of the connected GDPs which are coincident due to that connection. For instance, NODEMATCH operating on the connection shown in the detail of Figure 2 yields the pairs {2, 1}, {3, 4}, {7, 6}, and {6, 5}, where the first number in each pair is the local node in GDP 9, and the second number is the coincident local node in GDP 12. This algorithm represents a first attempt to make use of GDP-derived data, and it can no doubt be improved upon. In particular, one can consider designing *GDP-resident* algorithms to perform these same tasks.

B. Hardware Considerations and Design

Analogous to the generic GDP of Figure 4, the hardware of the prototype GDPs, shown in Figure 8, can be divided into two sections: the CPU and memory section, and the communications section. The microprocessor used in the prototypes is an NEC μPD70108, which is an enhanced CMOS

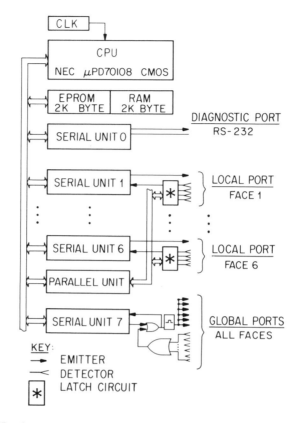

Figure 8. Hardware schematic of the prototype Geometry-Defining Processors. The face layout and latch circuitry are presented in Figs. 9a and 9b, respectively.

version of an Intel 8088. Nominal amounts of EPROM and RAM are used to store a small monitor program and the (host-downloaded) GDP program for geometry-input operation. A standard RS-232 serial port allows for diagnostic communication with the GDP processor; however, it is not used when the GDP is a member of a GDP assembly.

A GDP is capable of local communication through each of its faces via a serial unit and associated optical data ports. The choice of optical (rather than electrical) communication is prompted by the desire to have rotationally independent, easily reconfigurable connections. The layout of the electro-optics on each face of the GDP, shown in Figure 9a, allows mating GDPs to have matching emitters and detectors independent of their facial

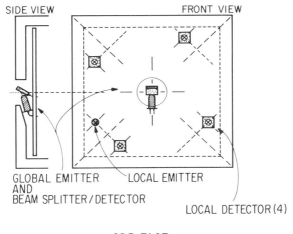

FRONT VIEW

GLOBAL EMITTER   LOCAL EMITTER
AND
BEAM SPLITTER / DETECTOR

LOCAL DETECTOR (4)

GDP FACE

Figure 9a. Layout of a typical GDP face showing the emitters and detectors used for local and global communication.

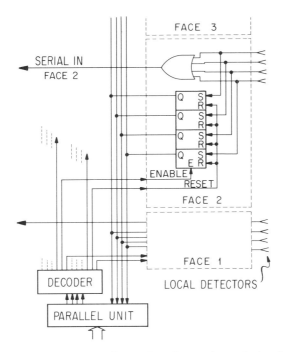

Figure 9b. Schematic of the logic used to determine relative facial rotation from incoming local signals.

orientation. In addition, the particular local detector on which data arrives indicates the relative rotations of the connected faces of the communicating GDPs. This is accomplished in hardware through the resetable latches and parallel unit shown in Figure 9b. Thus, the inter-GDP communication allows data to be passed between GDPs while simultaneously determining the rotational orientation of communicating GDP faces.

Global communication between the GDPs and the host computer is provided through another serial unit and an electro-optic system centered on each face. The emitter and detector axes are made optically coincident by a beam splitter; this beam splitter is, in fact, the casing of the detector, as shown in Figure 9a. Using a fixed-pulse-length data format, global signals received at any face are immediately rebroadcast on all faces of the GDP. Thus, the global communication propagates throughout the GDP assembly, ensuring near-simultaneous reception by all the member GDPs.

Figure 10. Prototype wedge-shaped (left) and cubical (right) Geometry-Defining Processors. The face communications hardware can be seen through the transparent GDP casings.

C. Examples of GDP Geometry Input

The GDP approach to geometry input and parallelism is novel, and it is therefore useful to show the GDPs in operation. The prototype cubical and wedge-shaped GDPs are shown in Figure 10. Note that, due to the use of off-the-shelf components, not all GDP hardware is contained within these prototypes, and not all faces of each GDP are active.

An example of the creation of a symbolic representation of the physical GDP domain is given in Figure 11a, where the results of interrogation of the GDPs are displayed on the host terminal to one side of the generating GDP assembly. The geometry here is that of the domain of Figure 1, albeit on a coarse-grained scale. For the purpose of illustration, we consider two further examples of GDP "mesh generation" in Figures 11b and 11c; these photographs were taken moments apart, demonstrating the flexibility and simplicity of reconfigurable, physical-space processors.

We believe that this first reduction to practice [16] of the GDP concept demonstrates the attractiveness of manually reconfigurable physical-space processors. We now discuss the design of next-generation computational GDPs.

VII. Performance Estimates for Computational GDPs

The implementation of the prototype mesh-generating GDPs in Section VI demonstrates that the hardware and algorithms necessary for GDP geometry definition are well within the capabilities of current technology. We now discuss the design and expected performance of an assembly of *fully computational* Geometry-Defining Processors. Of interest is determining the requirements on individual GDPs such that special-purpose GDP assemblies are competitive with current general-purpose supercomputers for solution of partial differential equations.

For purposes of illustration we consider solution of the steady-state heat equation (3) in a three-dimensional domain such as that shown in Figure 1. The equations are solved by conjugate gradient iteration, which at each iteration level is composed of the following three steps:

> Calculation of the $\bar{q}_i^k$ in (10a). This step requires approximately 50 floating-point operations per point for a trilinear element with 3^3 nearest nodal neighbors.   (12a)

> Direct stiffness summation of the $\bar{q}_i^k$ in (10b). This step is dominated by communication, with negligible computational effort as compared to the previous step (12a).   (12b)

(a)

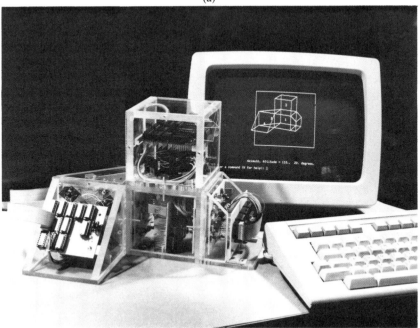

(b)

(c)

Figure 11. Demonstration of the prototype mesh generation GDPs. Figure 11a corresponds to a coarse-grained discretization of the geometry of Fig. 1. Figures 11b and 11c are photographs taken moments apart illustrating two examples of mesh generation, and demonstrating the flexibility and simplicity of reconfigurable, physical-space processors.

> Inner product summation in (8). This step requires approximately two floating-point operations per point (again negligible compared to (12a)), and a vector-reduction step, (12c) implemented in the GDP architecture using the embedded treelike mappings described in Figure 5 and Section V.A.

We assume that (12) is implemented on a GDP assembly of K^3 GDPs, with each GDP containing N^3 trilinear elements (and hence N^3 finite-element nodes). The total number of points in each coordinate direction is imposed by the accuracy desired in the numerical solution, and is specified as $M = KN$. To arrive at an expression for the work (i.e., computational time) required to effect (12) on a GDP assembly requires a last, critical piece of information: the relation between the time to calculate a floating-point result, the time to communicate a word (or words) through the local bus, and the time to reconfigure the local bus network for purposes of vector reduction.

We make the ostensibly specious but actually justifiable assumption that all of these times are of the same order, and are bounded by τ, which is some multiple of the basic CPU clock cycle. This assumption is justified by the following considerations: the GDP local bus network is a switching network and will have none of the startup problems associated with message routing and pipeline configurations; the GDPs are each running global-bus-synchronized special-purpose codes exchanging data on dedicated channels, thus avoiding the queueing, scheduling and allocation overhead associated with general-purpose parallel processors. Essentially, the limiting speed of the GDP is assumed to be set by the CPU instruction rate and memory bandwidth and *not* by floating-point or communications subsystem speeds.

With the assumptions stated above it can be shown that the *wall-clock time* required per iteration (12) per degree-of-freedom (recall there are $M^3 = K^3 N^3$ finite element nodes) is given by

$$W(K, N) = \frac{50\tau N^3 + 3\tau N^2 + 3 \cdot 3\tau \log_2 K}{K^3 N^3}, \tag{13}$$

where the three terms in the numerator come from the three steps of (12) respectively. The leading 3 in the second and third terms arises from performing the communications sequentially in each of the three dimensions; the 3τ in the third term is an estimate of the time required to reconfigure, add, and communicate data in the vector reduction operation. Ignoring the second term with respect to the first term and keeping whole number results, (13) becomes

$$W(K, N) = \frac{50\tau}{K^3} \left(1 + \frac{\log_2 K}{5N^3} \right), \tag{14}$$

where the term in brackets is the inverse of the usual parallel efficiency.

Minimization of (14) with respect to N for fixed $M = KN$ yields an optimal $N < 1$, implying that for the GDP architecture substructuring *increases* the solution time W; this result is due to the assumption of rapid communication and the dominance of the K^{-3} factor in (13). If we require $N^3 \gg \frac{1}{5} \log_2 K$, which can be easily satisfied by a small substructure of $N = 3$, the parallel efficiency of the GDP assembly is near optimal and (14) can be approximated as

$$W(K, N) = \frac{50\tau}{K^3}, \tag{15}$$

which will be used in all future calculations. (Although the actual numbers in these estimates are clearly very approximate, we maintain the pretense of precision to ensure that the final order-of-magnitude arguments are correct).

The wall-clock time $W(K, N)$ does not serve as an adequate figure of merit in that it reflects computation speed but not cost. Rather than simply increase computation speed, a more well-posed problem is:

> Find computing solutions that *minimize cost* for a *fixed computation time.*   (16)

To this end, we introduce the parameter MPIRS, which is *millions of point-iterations/resource-second,* where "resource" is used to denote some common measure of cost such as dollars or yen. Denoting by C_{GDP} the cost of an individual GDP, and defining $MFLOPS_{GDP} = 10^{-6}/\tau$, it follows from (15) that $MPIRS_{GDP}$ is given by $MFLOPS_{GDP}/50C_{GDP}$. The parameter $MPIRS_{GDP}$ is independent of the number of GDPs in the assembly due to near unity parallel efficiency and the fact that the cost of a GDP assembly scales linearly with the number of members in the assembly.

If we now consider the MPIRS of a current supercomputer, the CRAY X-MP, we find for (12) that $MPIRS_{CRAY}$ is given by $MFLOPS_{CRAY}/50C_{CRAY}$, where $MFLOPS_{CRAY}$ is the floating-point rate of the CRAY, and C_{CRAY} is the unit cost of a CRAY. (Note that even with the best non-parallelizable preconditioner, the number of iterations required on a CRAY for solution of (3) would be reduced by no more than a factor of five for general geometries.) As GDP cost and performance are linear in the number of GDPs, it can be shown that the optimization (16) is equivalent to requiring that $MPIRS_{GDP} < MPIRS_{CRAY}$, or

$$C_{GDP} < \frac{MFLOPS_{GDP}}{MFLOPS_{CRAY}} \cdot C_{CRAY}. \qquad (17)$$

Taking very roughly $MFLOPS_{CRAY} = 50$ MFLOPS, $C_{CRAY} = \$5 \cdot 10^6$, and assuming that $MFLOPS_{GDP} = 0.1$ MFLOPS, we find that $C_{GDP} < \$1 \cdot 10^4$. The limit of $\$1 \cdot 10^4$ is estimated to be one to two orders of magnitude larger than actual GDPs will cost using current device and packaging technology.

It is important to note that the requirement (17) is not equivalent to (16) unless an architecture's cost and performance scale linearly, *and* there is no limit to expansion of the system size. For instance, a minicomputer may well achieve the same MPIRS as a CRAY X-MP, but the time for a calculation will be fixed at a much longer time on the former as compared to the latter. The facts that the GDP architecture's cost and performance scale, and that the system is expandable, are due to the simplicity and optimality of nearest-neighbor connections for solution of partial differential equations.

These comparisons are graphically presented in Figure 12, where the time-per-point-iteration for solution of (12) is plotted versus machine cost for several machines. For the GDP system a set of points corresponding to different values of K^3 are plotted, demonstrating the flexibility of the GDP system. The value of $MPIRS_{GDP}$ for solution of (12) is 2 point-iterations-per-dollar-second, and corresponds to a $1 \cdot 10^3$ GDP operating at 0.1

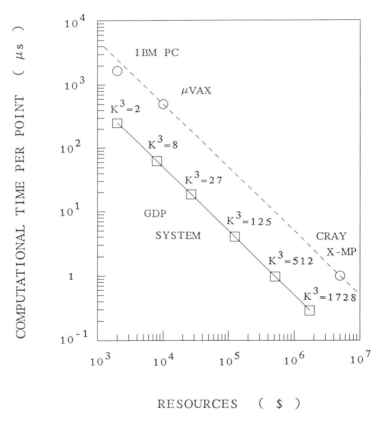

Figure 12. A plot of the locations of several existing machines and the proposed GDP system in time-resource space when applied to solution of (12). Because a GDP system is expandable it can occupy a *range* of locations in this space, parametrized by the number of GDPs in the assembly, K^3. For the problem (12), the time-per-point-per-iteration in microseconds is 50/MFLOPS.

MFLOPS, with a communication rate of 10Mbit/second, and a memory size of order 1 Mbyte to allow up to $N = 50$ substructuring. These values are all within current technologies.

The above arguments indicate that GDP architectures offer the possibility of fast and efficient parallel solution of partial differential equations. When this capability is combined with the geometric properties of GDPs, it is clear that Geometry-Defining Processor assemblies have significant potential as integrated special-purpose partial differential equation formulators and solvers. The question remains as to whether this potential is technologically realizable, and if so, whether the resulting technology is sufficiently general to be of engineering and scientific interest.

Acknowledgements

We gratefully acknowledge the support of the Massachusetts Institute of Technology.

References

1. Patera, A. T. (1984). "A Spectral Element Method for Fluid Dynamics; Laminar Flow in a Channel Expansion," *J. Comput. Phys.* **54**, 468–488.
2. Strang, G., and Fix, G. J. (1973). *An Analysis of the Finite Element Method.* Prentice-Hall, Englewood Cliffs, New Jersey.
3. Golub, G. H., and van Loan, C. F. (1983). *Matrix Computations.* Johns Hopkins University Press, Baltimore, Maryland.
4. Przemieniecki, J. S. (1963). "Matrix Structural Analysis of Substructures," *AIAA J.* **1** (1), 138–147.
5. Lin, H. X., and Sips, H. J. (1986). "A Parallel Vector Reduction Architecture," in *Proc. 1986 Int. Conf. on Parallel Processing,* pp. 503–510.
6. Saad, Y., and Schultz, M. H. (1985). "Topological Properties of Hypercubes," Research Report YALEU/DCS/RR-389, Yale University, New Haven.
7. Jordan, H. F. (1978). "A Special Purpose Architecture for Finite Element Analysis," in *Proc. 1978 Int. Conf. on Parallel Processing,* pp. 263–266.
8. Hoshino, T., Shirakawa, T., Kamimura, T., Kageyama, T., Takenouchi, K., Abe, H., Sekiguchi, S., Oyanagi, Y., and Kawai, T. (1983). "Highly Parallel Processor Array 'PAX' for Wide Scientific Applications," in *Proc. 1983 Int. Conf. on Parallel Processing,* pp. 95–105.
9. Seitz, C. L. (1985). "The Cosmic Cube," *Comm. ACM.* **28** (1), 22–33.
10. Snyder, L. (1982). "Introduction to the Configurable, Highly Parallel Computer," *Computer* **15**(1), 47–56.
11. Crowther, W., Goodhue, J., Starr, E., Thomas, R., Milliken, W., and Blackadar, T. (1985). "Performance Measurements on a 128-Node Butterfly Parallel Processor," in *Proc. 1985 Int. Conf. on Parallel Processing,* pp. 531–540.
12. Handler, W., Maehle, E., Wirl, K. (1985). "DIRMU Multiprocessor Configurations," in *Proc. 1985 Int. Conf. on Parallel Processing,* pp. 652–656.

13. Ortega, J. M., and Voigt, R. G. (1985). *Solution of Partial Differential Equations on Vector and Parallel Computers.* SIAM, Philadelphia, Pennsylvania.
14. Adams, L., and Voigt, R. G. (1984). "Design, Development, and Use of the Finite Element Machine," in *Large Scale Scientific Computation* (S. Parter, ed.),pp. 301–321. Academic Press, Orlando, Florida.
15. Bokhari, S. H. (1979). "On the Mapping Problem," in *Proc. 1979 Int. Conf. on Parallel Processing,* pp. 239–248.
16. Patera, A. T., and Dewey, D. "Geometry-Defining Processors." Patent application filed.

4   A Navier – Stokes Computer

DANIEL M. NOSENCHUCK,
WILLIAM S. FLANNERY, and
M. EHTESHAM HAYDER

Princeton University
Princeton, NJ

I. Introduction

A. Background

Fluid mechanics governs a myriad of physical phenomena broadly ranging from the hydrodynamics of microorganisms through the flow of interstellar jets. Included in this range are the hydrodynamics of boats and ships, and aerodynamics of air- and land-based vehicles. Although some of these flows are well understood, such as low-speed simple laminar flows, difficulty often arises when the flows become complex. Such is the case for turbulence, transonic and supersonic flows, flows near nonsimple boundaries, and chemically reacting flows. For example, very little is known about the external aerodynamics and heating of the proposed aerospace plane as well as the internal engine flow. The general control of flows, such as reducing wing turbulence to decrease drag on commercial transport aircraft, remains one of the fundamental unsolved areas in fluid mechanics.

As in most other areas of physics, three fundamental approaches may be used in the study of fluid flows. They are 1) analysis, 2) experimentation, and 3) numerical simulation. As discussed in the next section, the mathematical complexity of the governing equations renders unlikely the possibility of finding general analytical solutions. Moreover, the very difficulties that often lead one to perform physical experiments, in themselves limit the range of valid experimentation. Nonsteadiness and complexity of geometric boundary conditions (such as those encountered in rotorcraft and turbomachines) and turbulence are typical situations that do not efficiently yield to the experimental approach. Thus, effectively, one often faces the use of numerical simulation as a last practical resort to study a crucial flow. To understand the challenges inherent in this technique, one must consider the fundamental governing Navier–Stokes equations, along with numerical techniques that may be employed in a numerical solution.

1. Navier–Stokes Equations The governing equations of fluid flow are generally considered to be the conservative field equations of mass, momentum, and energy, together with appropriate state equations. Historically, these collective equations have come to be known as the Navier–Stokes equations (NSE), although formally only the combined mass and momentum conservation equations are so described. In this chapter, the NSE will refer to *all* of the equations of motion, including conservation of energy. The Navier–Stokes equations are given in Equations 1–3:

$$\frac{\partial \rho}{\partial t} + \nabla \cdot (\rho \mathbf{u}) = 0, \tag{1}$$

$$\rho \frac{D\mathbf{u}}{Dt} = \rho \mathbf{g} - \nabla p + \frac{\partial}{\partial x_j}\left[\mu\left\{\frac{\partial u_i}{\partial x_j} + \frac{\partial u_j}{\partial x_i}\right\}\right], \tag{2}$$

$$\frac{Dh}{Dt} = \frac{Dp}{Dt} + k\,\nabla^2 T + \Phi, \tag{3}$$

where Φ is a nonlinear function of velocity gradients. As can be seen in Equation 2, conservation of vector momentum introduces significant nonlinearities. The generally variable thermodynamic transport coefficients provide strong coupling between energy and the mass/momentum equations through variations in temperature. Both of these occurrences provide severe overall difficulties in seeking analytical solutions to problems with arbitrary initial and boundary conditions.

2. Computational Approaches One of the most forbidding tasks one faces is the selection of the appropriate fundamental equations coupled with an adequate numerical solution scheme. Although the governing equations of fluid motion are generally taken to be the Navier–Stokes equations, these equations form a set of coupled, highly nonlinear partial-differential equations that describe a very wide range of continuum flows. Fortunately, as discussed below, these equations can often be simplified by eliminating terms that are extraneous to the flow at hand. Once a subset of the Navier–Stokes equations are selected, a computational method must be selected from the myriad of available numerical techniques. These methods can be broken down into two broad classes: those that deal with the spatial discretization of the domain, and those that solve the equations on the resulting grid. The former classes include techniques to create grid structures with uniform, nonuniform, embedded, and multigrid meshes. Methods that deal with the solution of equations include finite-difference, finite-element, and spectral techniques. Other approaches are sometimes based on combinations and enhancements to these three methods. Due to constraints in the available computing resources, there have been no universal approaches developed for general flow simulation. The remainder of this section discusses several considerations that are often made when attempting to model fluid flows.

a. Simplifying Physical Approximations.   Based on flow geometry, Reynolds number, Mach number, fluid properties, and other parameters, it is often possible to simplify the equations of motion. For example, in the limiting case of zero viscosity, constant density flow with no vorticity (i.e. $\nabla \times \mathbf{u} = 0$), the governing equations reduce to the Laplace equation for stream function ψ and velocity potential ϕ. Although this equation yields to the implementation of a wide range of numerical techniques, the range of applicability to real flows are quite limited. Most flows-of-interest involve viscous and/or compressibility effects.

In the absence of viscosity and body force, the momentum equation reduces to the Euler equation:

$$\rho \frac{D\mathbf{u}}{Dt} = -\nabla p. \tag{4}$$

The essential nonlinearities in the equations of motion are seen to emerge with viscosity not being present. The Euler equation governs flows that are primarily inertial, often compressible, where viscous-related phenomena such as boundary-layer effects are negligible and flow separation does not occur. Transonic and supersonic flows over aircraft are representative of such flows. At this stage of approximation, supercomputer flow simulation is generally performed to yield insight into mean velocity and pressure fields (Jameson, 1987). With the additional consideration of viscosity, the "full" Navier–Stokes equations are reached. A fundamental impact of this is the introduction of the "no-slip" boundary condition at all solid surfaces. This results in a shear region that gives rise to viscous drag and promotes flow instabilities. As the Reynolds number increases, the flows become increasingly inertial. Consequently, violent instabilities form which ultimately lead to turbulence.

Time-averaging the NSE provides solutions of various mean flow parameters such as average velocity distributions. This technique, known as Reynolds-averaging, results in the emergence of statistical parameters in the equations that are not known a priori. In the case of a predominantly two-dimensional mean flow, such as that which occurs over a wing section, the NSE reduces to

$$\rho \frac{D\mathbf{u}}{Dt} = \rho \mathbf{g} - \nabla p + \frac{\partial}{\partial y}\left[\mu \frac{\partial u}{\partial y} - \overline{\rho u'v'}\right]. \tag{5}$$

The terms in the equation are fundamentally the same as those found in the laminar-flow equations, with the exception of the term $-\overline{\rho u'v'}$. To provide closure to Equation 5, this so-called turbulence correlation term must be modeled. The turbulent models that are invoked often give reasonably accurate results for conditions close to those used in calibrating the model. However, for flows with differing boundary conditions, the models often fail to capture the essential physics.

Based on this experience, it has become desirable to seek solutions to the "full" NSE without resorting to modeling. The NSE may be solved using direct application of standard numerical techniques such as finite-element or spectral methods. Recently, renormalization group (RNG) theory has been applied to the Navier–Stokes equations in an effort to obtain high-Reynolds-number solutions to flows involving complex geometries. Although the method is powerful in that it uses no adjustable constants, a large number of computations are still required to tackle complex, nonsteady flows.

Finally, a novel approach to the problem of flow simulations involves the use of cellular automata. In this approach, the flow field is discretized into a finite collection of cells. Each cell is provided with a simple set of rules that govern interactions with adjacent cells. At the present time the cellular automata approach is limited to two-dimensional simple flows, and even then the physical significance of the results are somewhat unclear (e.g. ambiguous flow Reynolds numbers).

b. Brief Overview of Numerical Methods. A fluid flow governed by the Navier–Stokes equations occurs in a region called a field. Thus, the Navier–Stokes equations are often referred to as the field equations of motion. As such, they may be rendered in discrete form for application to the global discretized domain of the field. The independent variables are generally those which describe space and time. Velocity, temperature, pressure, density, and other fluid properties are the dependent variables.

The Navier–Stokes equations, as most partial-differential equations, may be solved using a variety of techniques. The selection of an appropriate numerical solution scheme is dependent on the specific problem. A list of applicable numerical methods includes

- finite-difference methods
- finite-element methods
- spectral methods

The first two offer advantages for particularly complex, arbitrary boundary conditions, although they are finite-order accurate. The latter, although constrained to relatively simple (often periodic) boundary conditions, potentially offers infinite-order accuracy. This is due to the selection of a series solution to the governing equation truncated at a point appropriate to the extent of the global computational domain. In general, a solution need only contain a finite amount of wavenumbers to be meaningful and instructive. Thus, if a Fourier series were employed in the spectral method, the number of terms included would directly scale with the desired resolution in the field.

Finite-difference techniques were among the first to become popular, primarily due to their conceptual simplicity. Derivatives are cast as algebraic difference operators, and the dependent variables are then calculated in discrete form. This involves the solution of large, banded matrices. Although explicit techniques are occasionally implemented, they typically suffer from stability limitations. To overcome this difficulty, implicit schemes are often invoked. Such approaches typically rely on iterative methods to solve the linear systems of equations. Finite-difference schemes are readily adaptable to geometries with regular, linear boundaries. Difficulty is often encountered when an attempt is made to implement the technique in irregular spaces.

Problems with arbitrary, complex boundary conditions, such as those found in studying heat transfer in the neighborhood of high-power circuit elements, are often best attacked through the implementation of a finite-element method. Based on arbitrary meshes, the technique is well-suited for problems with irregular boundaries. A minor drawback of this method is that the discrete variables are not uniformly stored or accessed in the computer. This provides a challenge to the machine architecture that may result in decreased performance. At the present time, however, this approach generates a wide-ranging potential for complex flow simulations. One such example is the efficient three-dimensional simulations of flow around a complete aircraft. Jameson's FLO-code series, based on a finite-element scheme applied to the Euler equation, has been extensively applied to this class of problems.

Implicit numerical schemes often rely on repeated iteration to achieve a solution of specified precision. Typically, the majority of time spent in a calculation is related to the rate at which the solution converges. Since most methods rely a great deal on various matrix solution methods, one is tempted to invoke efficient techniques. One such approach involves the use of recursion to invert matrices. The general form of the operation is

$$x_{i+1} = A_i x_i + B_i.$$ (6)

Since the x-array is dependent on its previous values, they must be made available to the computational section of the computer as soon as they are generated. This operation is difficult to perform at high speed in most computers, as discussed below.

B. Available Computing Resources

To date, virtually all flow simulations have been carried out on commercial, "general-purpose" computers. The overall success of a numerical approach is often intimately tied to the design of the machine on which the algorithm is coded. This is especially the case when the global domain of simulation is large, which usually prompts the programmer to select fast, large-capacity machines. These machines have differing designs, with varying strengths and weaknesses that must be considered when extensive simulations are performed. In this section, a brief overview of applicable computer architectures will be discussed. These machines generally fall into categories that may be classified according to Flynn's taxonomy:

- SISD—Single Instruction, Single Data-path architecture
- SIMD—Single Instruction, Multiple Data-path architecture
- MISD—Multiple Instruction, Single Data-path architecture
- MIMD—Multiple Instruction, Multiple Data-path architecture

The SISD machine, also known as the von Neumann architecture, represents the ubiquitous class of computers referred to as micro-, mini-, and mainframe computers. The VAX is a typical example of a midrange computer in this class. Since the fundamental aspect of the architecture is that instructions and data are individually fetched and operated upon, SISD machines are very flexible. The maximum performance of this class of machines is related to the bandwidth of the single data and/or instruction paths. To realize increased performance, multiple data-fetch capability was added into several computers in the early 1970s. The ILLIAC IV is representative of the SIMD machine where one instruction commands multiple data operands to be processed. This type of machine works well in the area of regular array processing where the same operation is performed on all parts of the array. The array is partitioned and individual segments are loaded into different data-path units. The computation then proceeds in lockstep among the individual elements. Such units comprise parallel elements of the overall machine. Thus, the SIMD computer may be called the first parallel machine.

1. General-purpose computers In the class of general-purpose computers, one can point to mini/mainframe SISD units that are typified by machines such as Digital Equipment Corporation's VAX, or to MISD machines that often perform multiple pipelined operations repetitively on single long data streams called vectors. The Cray Research Cray-series has become a symbol of such machines. Even though one may argue that vector machines are geared towards numerically intensive operations, the architectures of many vector-oriented computers often include SISD scalar units that generate a general problem-solving environment.

2. Special-purpose computers When a given class of problems requiring greater computational capabilities than available from general machines, it is sometimes justified to create a computer with high-performance hardware supplied in those areas needed to address the given task, and with all nonessential units removed. This creates the situation where the program-handling state-machine portion of the computer is vastly simplified, or removed, with "hard wires" taking the place of certain flexible or programmable elements in the machine. Digital signal-processors formed one of the earliest classes of special-purpose computers. Recently, parallel computers have begun to make inroads in areas related to numerically intensive scientific computing. Although many of these machines were designed with an eye towards general applications, to date most have proven to be effective in particular applications. This can be in part attributed to the requirement that many nodes are interconnected with a specific internode topology. This is coupled with the node characteristics. For example, a node may be considered to be a microprocessor with local memory, it may include a vector element, or it may be as simple as a several-bit boolean processing unit with a minimal number of registers and memory. Such machines have proven to be effective on problems ranging from cellular-automata modeling of physical systems to image-processing.

The remainder of this chapter is devoted to one such parallel computer, called the Navier–Stokes Computer (NSC). The original motivation for the NSC was based on the need for a very fast, high-capacity machine that was geared toward invoking a somewhat wide range of numerical techniques aimed at solving various forms of the Navier–Stokes equations.

C. Navier-Stokes Computer

Based on the discussion in Section I.A. it is clear that a multitude of physical approaches and mathematical models exist to tackle various problems in fluid flow. Over the past several decades, numerical approaches, algorithms, and computer codes have advanced in performance at rates that often outstrip analogous increases in hardware capability. A hardwired "solver" would primarily suffer from not being capable of adapting to emerging codes, in addition to not being cost-effective when applied to widely varied flow fields. Thus, it is evident that in order to create a useful device with a finite lifetime before obsolescence, the device must be general-purpose. In fact, such a machine must be far more flexible in efficiency and scope of application than existing general-purpose supercomputers.

In this chapter, FORTRAN will be used as the example programming environment, and examples of NSC utilization will frequently draw upon concepts taken from FORTRAN conventions.

II. Architectural Overview of NSC

The underlying theme of the Navier–Stokes Computer is the use of multiple scales of reconfigurable parallelism. This approach was taken because it was felt that most physical systems inherently possess multiple phenomenological scales that behave in fundamentally different ways. For example, in the case of fluid flow, multiple scales occur in the flow around wings where phenomena such as turbulence, separation, shock-wave formation and potential flow all combine and interact in a single field. It appeared that it was not sufficient to create a number of multiple nodes and exploit a simple MIMD environment where one portion of nodes were assigned to one task, with others programmed to implement codes to deal with differing flow features. This was because the individual phenomena were often quite complicated, and would benefit from a more powerful treatment within a node than, for example, a single microprocessor and floating-point unit could provide. However, the need for global interconnects was persistent in that the various flow zones often covered a domain that extended beyond the capacity of a single node, with strong interactions (requiring computational coupling) among the different zones. This suggested that a powerful node, with internal parallelism, would be capable of dealing with locally complex phenomena, while a number of interconnected nodes operating concurrently would be capable of simulating a globally complex, heterogeneous flow field.

The majority of the overall effort has been placed in the design of the nodes. The nodes are interconnected using somewhat standard topologies and techniques, as described below. The individual node was designed to be a very powerful entity, with memory and processing power roughly equivalent to present-day Class VI supercomputers.

It was noted early in the conceptual planning phases of the NSC that vector-oriented processes often dominated the computations. Therefore, the floating-point/logical pipelined functional unit was chosen to be the key ALU building block. It was further observed that highly chained operations frequently occurred within the innermost FORTRAN DO-loops. This necessitated the inclusion of multiple processing elements that were arranged in a reconfigurable network to provide for the creation of arbitrary processing pipelines. Finally, to account for the somewhat stochastic nature of certain algorithms, and the need to handle scalar operations on a demand basis, the overall architecture of the node was designed to be *dynamically reconfigurable* within one clock period. This flexibility has proven to be invaluable in handling a number of unrelated computational schemes.

The overall layout of a multinode NSC is given in Figure 1. The nodes are individually linked with local interconnects to provide appropriate data and instruction passing between nodes. A front-end is connected to the individual nodes via a bus as well as discrete serial and parallel interconnects. The number of nodes in the present NSC ranges from 1 to 128, with between four and eight common in the early systems. A node may run in a

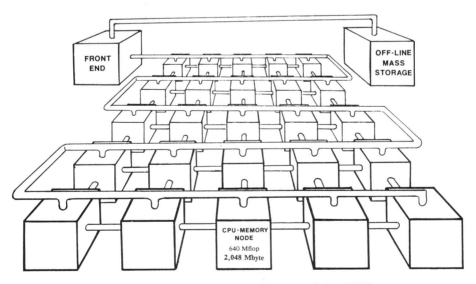

Figure 1. Overall block diagram of the NSC.

complete stand-alone mode operated by the local console. However, to afford the user with high-level interactive capability, a front-end is generally utilized for program editing, data storage, and off-line data processing.

The architecture of a generic node is given in Figure 2. A node achieves a high efficiency by configuring a large number (up to 32) of individual processing units into one or more pipelines to provide multistage processing on an input operand stream from memory with a minimum of inter-

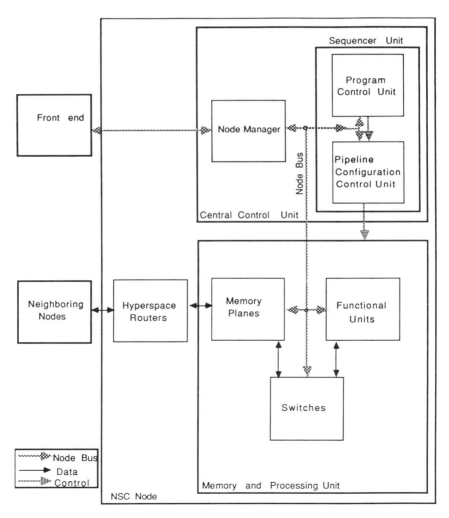

Figure 2. Block diagram of a NSC node.

mediate storage. Given the large number of arithmetic and logical operations that can be performed on the data, several lines of FORTRAN can typically be compacted into a single ALU pipeline configuration. Since the pipelines are formed with a crossbar switching network, continuously changing code structures can be accommodated by reconfiguring the processor interconnects. In the NSC this function can be implemented in a single clock period as a result of an unconditional or conditional event. This provides the capability to nest conditional, recursive, and difficult-to-vectorize statements within inner FORTRAN DO-loops.

To support multistage processing, a number of independent operands have to be simultaneously read from memory. Many of these operands have a typical vector data type, and are conveniently stored *within* a single memory unit called a plane. Other data types such as scalars and mixed-type variable-length records are often stored *across* individual planes, in a fashion similar to conventional banking. The memory plane also serves as the internode communications port. A portion of each memory plane's local address space is multiply mapped into a two-port internode message/data cache that serves as the gateway/buffer between the global nodes.

Internode communications occur over standard network topologies. Initially, a hypercube interconnect scheme was invoked. However, as switching technology improved, and dense, high-speed switching chips became available, the internode connections were upgraded to a full-crossbar switch. This provided a fully nonblocking route between all nodes, which became nearest-neighbors. The routing algorithm was also vastly simplified. Since the initial configuration supported nodes that ranged in numbers up to 128 nodes, the crossbar switch proved very practical and easy to implement.

III. NSC Hardware Organization

The NSC nodes fall into three hardware classes: the micronode, mininode, and fullnode. The micronode was the proof-of-concept unit used to validate several key NSC concepts such as one-cycle dynamic reconfigurability. The mininode and fullnode are operational "production" NSC nodes. Both share an identical architecture with nearly identical hardware attributes, the main difference being the number of functional units in the ALU and the number and size of the memory planes. The mininode will be discussed in detail, and hardware extensions in the fullnode will be noted where appropriate. The speed and capacity of the micro, mini, and fullnodes are

Micronode: 60 Mflop (32-bit); 1 Mbyte

Mininode: 200 Mflop (32-bit); 16–64 Mbyte

Fullnode: 640 Mflop (32/64-bit); 256–2,048 Gbyte

A. Single Node

The mininode is comprised of five units:

1. Node manager
2. Memory (with internode router)
3. Switch
4. Arithmetic logic unit
5. Node sequencer

In addition to these units, the fullnode has some additional hardware to provide vector shift/delay operations. The node manager provides high-level supervisory capability, effects front-end communications, and interacts with the node sequencer to start, monitor, and stop high-speed pipeline processing. The memory is distributed between the node manager and the main memory planes. Since address-flow is directly associated with the memory hardware, the internode communications unit is directly located in the memory unit in the mininode. Internode data routing is handled by an external unit, closely coupled with memory, in the fullnode. The arithmetic logic unit (ALU) provides floating-point, integer and logical, and special-function and local register storage capabilities. ALU inputs and outputs are routed to memory through a cross-bar switching network. High-speed memory, ALU and switch operations are directly controlled by the node sequencer. The node manager does not interact with processing unless a high-level request is sent from the sequencer. This occurs when a major section of processing is done, or when a major fault is encountered that cannot be locally rectified (by the node sequencer). In the following sections, the individual units will be described more fully.

1. Node Manager   The node manager primarily acts as an autonomous local controller, subservient only to the front-end host. Its primary task is to supply managerial support to the local memory and ALU. The node manager supervises and provides a parallel interface for host data transfer. Two serial lines to the front-end serve as a command interface. High-level interrupts issued by the host are bused to all the nodes. The node manager uses, at present, an Intel 80286 microprocessor as the local controller. The 80286 is run in nonprotected mode, and has a local 256 kbyte RAM/ROM program control store. The node manager has the usual complement of numerical coprocessor, interrupt and DMA controllers, along with a special-purpose unit that formats integer and floating-point data prior to host transfer for immediate use by the front-end. Communication with the sequencer, memory planes, switch, and ALU occur over the synchronous nodebus, generated and used primarily by the node manager. It must be stressed that although the node manager is a complete stand-alone micro-computer in its own right, because of its severely limited speed and capacity it does not become involved in specific numerical operations. Both the mininode and fullnode have identical node managers.

2. Node Sequencer   In a fashion similar to the global management tasks for which the node manager is responsible, the node sequencer controls the detailed operations of the memory planes, switch, and ALU. The sequencer is the primary state generator for directing the control flow of the high-speed node elements, in that it generates the addresses that ultimately point to the configuration tables of the node. These tables are collectively referred to as *nanocode* (or ncode). The ncode is nested one level below the *microcode* (or μcode). Overall state operation is regulated by the μcode. The relationship of μcode to ncode, and their implementation and use, will be more fully discussed in Section IV.

The relation of the node sequencer to both the node manager and the high-speed computational elements (memory, switch, and ALU) is shown in Figure 3, which illustrates the intranode control flow and indicates the processing of interrupts. A very simplified block diagram of the node sequencer is given in Figure 4. The sequencer unit itself is somewhat traditional in that it selects the next μcode address based on various conditional and unconditional directives in the μcode. The address sources may be supplied by the node manager (MAP), interrupt vectors (VECT) or from the branch field of the μcode. In addition, addresses may be generated by a sequential program counter, popped off an internal stack, or indirectly accessed using a loop counter to provide appropriate loop control. Microcode is used to supply

1. The instruction for the address sequencer
2. Programming instructions for the direct memory access (DMA) address generators
3. Interrupt initialization and mask instructions
4. Multiple concurrent pipeline timing control instructions
5. Node manager interrupts
6. Pointer field table (nanocode) addresses
7. Nodebus addresses for main memory/microcode memory data and instruction transfers

Thus, the node sequencer is used to point to the ncode which configures the memory, switch, and ALU, to generate linear vector addresses available for immediate use or translation, to respond to interrupts from the ALU or to generate its own interrupts to node manager, and in general to monitor and remap its own microcode as required.

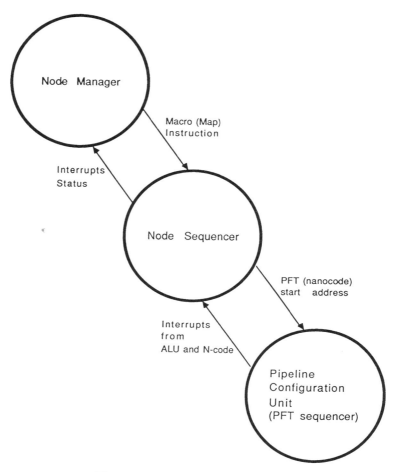

Figure 3. Intranode control flow.

The ncode and associated control hardware are distibuted among the memory, switch, and ALU units. The node sequencer generates a pointer-field-table (PFT) address in a microcode field that maps onto the distributed nanocode. Low-level flags primarily generated by the ALU, such as sign and zero flags, are processed by the PFT sequencer. This unit is tasked with pointing to the next ncode address, analogous to the sequencer directing μcode selection. Up to two-level nested conditional operations are handled by the PFT sequencer at full speed (within one clock). This permits a reconfiguration of the switch, ALU, and memory, without slowing the computational rate. Conditionals with more than two levels of

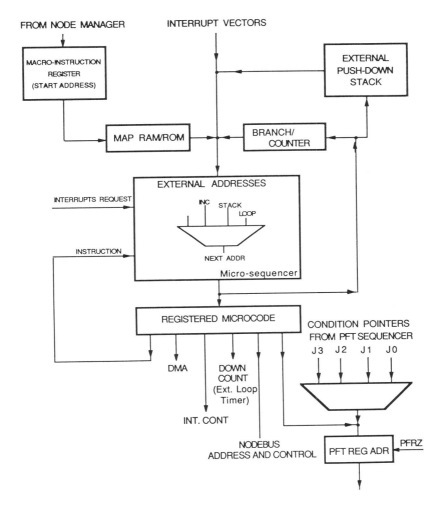

Figure 4. Node sequencer block diagram.

nesting are governed by the node sequencer, with process wait states inserted as appropriate.

3. Memory and Internode Router The nodes have between four and 16 independent memory units called planes. These memory planes provide primary storage for ALU operands and results. Each plane has a bidirectional port to the nodebus, and a split vector bus for independent read/write operations. In general, at a given time several of the memory planes are sourcing operands to the ALU, while others are used to receive the results. Memory is used to store a variety of data types, ranging from zero-dimensional arrays (scalars), and relational strings, through multidimensional arrays (vectors). For scientific computing, vectors occupy the vast majority of the available memory, and are individually stored within and/or across memory planes. When a local computation requires access to multiple array data elements, a stride across two or more memory planes is often selected. A common case arises when the arguments of a Laplacian or similar operator are fetched in parallel from multiple memory planes. However, in scientific computation, often only single vector elements are required, such as the nonhomogeneous terms of a differential equation. An example where a single plane is used to store one vector, and stride is invoked to simultaneously retrieve a second vector from memory, is the Poisson equation:

$$\nabla^2 \psi = -\omega.$$

This equation is among those solved for two-dimensional viscous flows. (In this case, ψ is the stream function, and ω the vorticity.) Note that both ψ and ω are two-dimensional arrays. If this equation were to be put into finite-difference form, the ψ-array is multiply subscripted (five immediate references) in the inner DO-loop, while the vorticity has but a single reference.

The overall layout of a memory plane is given in Figure 5. To provide the flexible storage required by differing algorithmic needs, each memory plane has a local address generation unit as shown in the figure. Three modes of addressing are supported by this unit. They are

1. Linear addressing
2. Translated (scatter/gather) addressing
3. Computed addressing

All of these modes make use of an offset- and stride-generation unit. The first and second modes completely generate the on-board address given a linear source count. Computed addressing uses an ALU-generated address that is routed through the switch to the memory plane. This latter mode provides immediate "on-the-fly" indirect vector/scalar addressing.

Each memory plane has a local nanocode store. This control store is used to provide read/write configuration, select the address mode and port, and provide offset and stride values. Secondary control functions include translate memory control and hyperspace cache management.

Internode data and message communications occur directly between memory planes. This is facilitated through a hyperspace routing switch. Each memory plane has a portion of its address space mapped into an

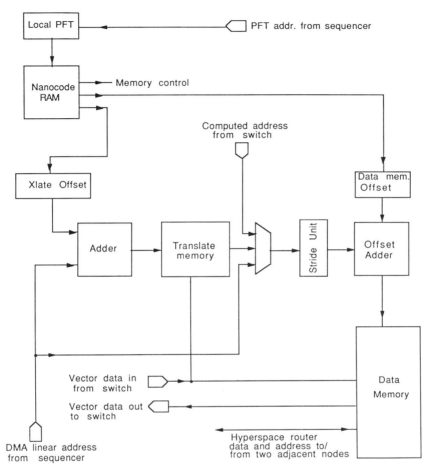

Figure 5. Block diagram of a node memory plane.

extended hyperspace address whose least significant portion is contiguous with the local memory plane, with the most significant portion encoded with the memory plane number and the local node address, thus forming a unique hyperspace address. The hyperspace cache is used to receive data from neighboring nodes, and provide local access by placing the cache adjacent to the main memory physical address space. This enables the use of translate memory to logically map internode data randomly within the local node's address space. In an analogous fashion, when data is written to local memory within the physical hyperspace transfer region, a copy is sent to the appropriate neighboring nodes' hyperspace cache. The address of a word has the following format:

|Node|Plane|Base address|

4. Arithmetic Logic Unit   All logical and numerical processing that is related to the primary application task is performed by the arithmetic logic unit (ALU). This unit is occasionally used to pre- and post-format host–node data transfer. The ALU provides the capability to create multifunction pipelines to meet the needs of computationally intensive algorithms. When required, the ALU may be structured as multiple independent pipes, each similar or distinct in its configuration from the others. Moreover, the overall pipeline topology may be dynamically altered in response to code flow or local conditionals within one clock period.

The ALU is organized as a collection of discreet building blocks, each called an arithmetic-logic-structure (ALS). The ALS has three configurations: the singlet, doublet, and triplet. These names refer to the number of floating-point/register-file units in the ALS. Additionally, each ALS has one integer/logic unit. Figure 6 shows the interconnects of the three ALSs. As illustrated, the singlet has one level of internal pipelining, while the doublet and triplet each have two levels. Since most numerical and logical processing requires multistage computations for a given set of operands, the ALS structure minimizes the required number of interconnects between processing units, without sacrificing any significant amount of generality. The singlet is the most general of the three ALS units, having two operand inputs and one result output. The processing units of a singlet include floating-point and integer-logic units, a 32-word four-port register file, and a special-function unit. Functions such as min/max, negate, and absolute value are performed on the results at the ALS output stage. Each of the other two ALSs have a final pipeline stage identical in processing attributes to the singlet. As indicated in the figure, the doublet and triplet have additional floating-point and integer-logic processing units that feed the final processing unit.

The register files have several primary functions. They are to

1.   Synchronize the pipeline
2.   Store scalars
3.   Delay vectors to create a secondary operand vector

5. Switch Networks   Fundamentally, the switching networks within a node provide for complete general interconnects between the memory planes and ALS units. Although a single network is sufficient to provide all the requisite data routing in a node, hardware and construction considera-

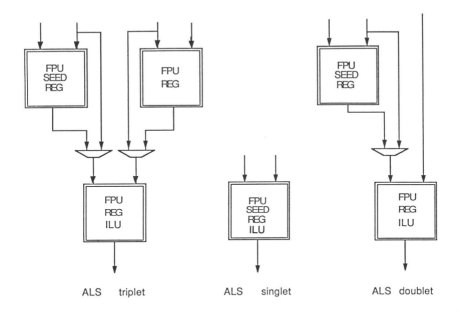

ALS   triplet   ALS   singlet   ALS   doublet

FPU : Floating Point Unit
REG : Register file
SEED : Look-up table
ILU : Integer/Logic Unit

Figure 6. ALS configurations.

tions necessitated the use of two switching networks called MASNET (Memory/ALU Switching Network) and FLONET (Functional/Logical-unit Organizational Network). MASNET routes operands from multiple memory plane outputs to the ALU inputs, while the FLONET is used to interconnect the ALS units to form the computational pipeline. Both of these units are crossbar switches that independently route 32-bit (with byte parity) operands with a one-clock delay through the switches. Both switches are reconfigurable within a single clock period.

B. Multinode Interconnects

The nodes were initially interconnected using a hypercube interconnection scheme, with standard data routing practices. Recently, the internode communications channels were replaced with a general-purpose high-performance crossbar switch that essentially establishes all nodes as nearest neighbors. This affords the use of very simple routing algorithms, non-blocking message and data routing and broadcast, along with a predictable one-clock delay between global nodes. The data, once received by a node, enters an internode buffer (also called a hyperspace cache — a term that survived from the earlier internode communications network) where it is tagged with bits indicating that the data is new, and is available to the local memory plane on demand as controlled by the node sequencer. Data sent to other nodes passes directly through the internode crossbar switch. Since multiple data elements may arrive simultaneously at a given node, the internode buffer has appropriate hardware to effect priority resolution and arbitration to assure orderly flow of operands and results within the multinode NSC.

IV. NSC Software

Navier–Stokes Computer software is classified in two categories: low-level drivers, and the various support programs provided to facilitate user operation. The drivers are written in machine language, which permits direct NSC control. This involves pipeline setup, memory setup and manipulation, and switch configuration, in addition to a variety of other basic tasks. Ultimately, user programs are translated into NSC machine language. In the case of the NSC, user programs are placed into two categories. The first comprises those programs that execute and control computations in the pipeline, while the second is made up of user-generated support programs that are executed on the node manager. NSC machine code comprises two separate instruction sets. The node manager is based primarily on an Intel 80286 microprocessor, and hence uses the 80286 and 80287 instruction sets as the machine language. The computational, memory, switching, and internode communications units are controlled by NSC machine language. This language is a multileveled machine language with a wide horizontal format.

Support software largely runs on the node manager board, excluding the firmware for the address sequencer and the front-end support programs. Included are an operating system, debuggers, compilers, and peripheral support programs. Additionally, libraries of subroutines, such as scientific subroutines, are provided to aid in the development of application programs. The remainder of this section discusses the overall structure of the NSC software including the operating systems, subroutine libraries, and applications programming. No discussion is made of the machine language of the 80286 and 80287, since it is not a characteristic unique to the NSC, and information on it is readily available.

A. Internal Structure of the NSC Software

The complexity inherent in a parallel architecture, with a large degree of flexibility and reconfigurability, such as that of the NSC, led to the implementation of a multileveled machine language. This permits ready pipeline multitasking, which is essential to maintain high, efficient throughputs. To simplify, both conceptually and in practice, the programming of the NSC, a hierarchical language structure composed of two levels was developed. At the lowest level, the NSC is a state machine where a large number of bits compose an instruction. This is used to define the hardware configuration at each clock cycle. These instructions are stored in configuration tables collectively referred to as nanocode. To facilitate programming and enhance the sustained throughput, the nanocode itself is nested. The microcode (μcode) resides at the highest level of directly executable code within a node, which establishes coherent control flow. At this level the NSC may be viewed as a microprogrammed machine. Unified sequences of microcode execute operations that govern flow of the executing program. Micro-instructions are comprised of series of bits used to define all aspects of the machine as well as set up and determine potential next states. Typically a number of micro-instructions executed sequentially is required to perform operations. Together these two code levels provide for efficient NSC utilization based on its powerful reconfiguration capabilities.

1. Nanocode   The nanocode is a collection of configuration states that are stored in tables nested one level deep. This code is used to directly configure the current state of the node. The lowest level is a number of independent state tables, whose entries are referred to as nanocode instructions. Nanocode instruction access is governed by a table of addresses pointing to one of the nanocode instructions nested one level above the state tables. This table is called the Pointer Field Table (PFT). Thus an entry in the configuration table is merely a pointer plus a nanocode instruction.

a. State Tables and Nanocode Instructions.   To enhance the utility of the NSC, multiple state tables are employed rather than a single table with an entry that defines the configuration of the entire machine. The efficiency of numerous independent tables will become more apparent in the following sections. These tables have logical and natural divisions defined by the various fundamental structures in the NSC architecture that are controlled by the nanocode. These include ALS units, switching elements, and memory planes. Each nanocode instruction table physically resides on the same circuit board as the fundamental NSC element it configures, reducing interboard busing.

Nanocode instructions define the hardware configuration of its substructure at each clock cycle. The bits of this instruction are latched directly to the hardware components they configure. Structurally, the nanocode instructions are words of varying bit size. For example, 64 bits control mininode memory and 192 bits control the mininode ALS. The n-bits of the nanocode instruction can be divided into groups of bits, called fields, corresponding to the particular component of the NSC substructure they define. These fields also vary in size, from one bit to several bytes. In the case of the ALS, parameters such as arithmetic operation of the floating point units, special functions, and internal data paths are defined. For the memory planes, addressing modes, read/write mode, and address calculation operands and operators are determined by the state table entry. It is by changing the nanocode instruction that the NSC can be reconfigured dynamically, from one clock cycle to the next.

2. Intermediate Level: Pointer Field Table   The Pointer Field Table is a table of address pointers to each of the nanocode groupings: the ALSs, memory planes, switches, and the various elements in the central control unit (CCU) such as the logical flag controller (LFC). These tables are physically located on the board whose nanocode instruction address they define (i.e. the board containing the NSC substructure being configured). In addition to nanocode addresses, there are a number of special PFT entries. These include pointers back to itself, as well as some special control bits for sequencing conditionally or unconditionally PFT entries. Also, a special control bit, called a chain bit, is associated with each pointer. Since PFT entries point to all the nanocode instructions, and thus set the state of all the control bits, each entry in the PFT completely defines a pipeline configuration.

The predominant reasons for a nested structure in the nanocode are to enhance performance and simplify programming. The most important simplification in programming is conceptual, since the number of bits that need be considered at one time are minimized and related to one NSC pipelined functional block. There are also significant savings in program storage because individual configurations of NSC substructure are only stored once.

In addition to the somewhat modest gains in the programming of the NSC, performance is greatly enhanced by the nested nanocode structure in three ways: reducing pipeline latency times, allowing multitasking, and facilitating vectorization of logical operations. Since the PFT contains pointers back to itself, the sequencing of addresses to the PFT is self-sustaining. This allows the address sequencer to perform other tasks concurrent with pipeline execution. Such tasks include computing values for loop indices, DMA counts or start addresses, and fetching data from unused memory, thus reducing the setup time for the next pipeline. Another aspect of the NSC is the capability to multitask the ALU. This creates multiple pipelines to increase processor utilization. For example, while a pipeline of vector length 100 is running, a number of pipelines with smaller vectors (e.g., length 10) can be run. These tasks execute independently. The chain bit in the pointer field permits currently executing nanocode instructions to be chained to the next pipeline configuration. This protects the configuration of the currently executing pipeline. Only unused portions of the pipeline are reconfigured. Finally, the PFT facilitates the vectorization of logical operations (nested IF-THEN-ELSE structures) by providing a number of pointers back to itself that can be accessed with no penalty in computational speed. Depending on the evaluation of Boolean expressions by the LFC, entries in the PFT can be sequenced at high speeds without using the address sequencer.

3. Control Level: Microcode   The highest level of machine language is the primary control flow mechanism or state generator for program execution on the NSC. Although the hardware on a mininode and fullnode differ slightly, the control mechanism is the same. Once program execution is initiated by the node manager, after it loads a program, data, etc., the address sequencer acts as an autonomous controller of program execution and runs independently until either board makes a request to the other via an interrupt. The address sequencer on the mini- and fullnode have an instruction set of 16 and 64 instructions respectively, but there are additional bits in the micro-instruction for performing operations other than address fetches. Similar to the manner in which the nanocode instruction is partitioned into fields, the bits of the micro-instruction can be divided into fields corresponding to the devices they program. The micro-word consists of fields that perform the following operations:

1. Provide an instruction for the address sequencer
2. External address sources for the address sequencer
3. Interrupt definition and masking
4. Node manager interrupts
5. DMA programming
6. Loop controls
7. Multitasking control
8. Node bus addresses for main/μcode memory data and instruction transfers
9. Provide initial PFT address

Since all the bits to perform the above operations are stored as one contiguous control word, a greater degree of parallelism is generated for the NSC since several devices can be programmed simultaneously. This minimizes the clock cycles required to reprogram the program control structure.

Operations that are performed by the microcode may be placed in four categories: address sequencing, control flow device programming, memory fetching via the node buses, and PFT initialization. The first two items provide the means for the address sequencer to generate its next address, first by giving the sequencer an instruction, and then by providing a number of external addresses such as the branch and map addresses. In the second category are fields to program the various control devices such as the DMAs and interrupt controllers. A number of fields are provided to allow the address sequencer to do its own memory fetches, minimizing the need to use the node manager for memory operations.

The last field above the address sequencer acts as the primary state generator for the NSC by initiating the address of the PFT. A convenient way of interpreting this operation is as a subroutine call, similar to the call instruction in FORTRAN. Parameters are passed to the subroutine by the definitions provided by the sequencing of micro-instructions. For example, data is passed by setting the starting DMA address and word count, thus passing an array or vector to the block of code in the PFT. In addition to passing data, configurations can be passed to the subroutine, by changing any number of the pointers in a block of entries in the PFT. Blocks of code in the PFT are executed repeatedly simply by initializing execution to that block through this field in the micro-instruction. This is completely analogous to the concept of a subroutine in other programming languages.

4. Summary of Low-Level Software   The machine language is dual-leveled language consisting of a control level called the microcode and a configuration level known as the nanocode. In addition, the nanocode employs a nested structure of pointers and state tables. This particular arrangement of the internal structure enhances performance and simplifies programming. It is not proper, in the case of the NSC machine language, to talk of an instruction set because the structure allows effectively an infinite number of permutations of pointers, nanocode instructions, and fields. Instead the NSC can be thought of as an infinite state machine in which a small subset of these states are sequenced in a manner defined by the control level of the machine language.

To further clarify the internal structure of software on the NSC, the sequence of operations required for program execution is described below. First, the front-end is used to load all initial data and the program to the node or nodes involved in the computation. The front-end then requests the node manager to commence program execution. The node manager sets the initial address to the address sequencer, and then, via an interrupt, initiates program execution. The address sequencer executes a series of micro-instructions to set up the control flow of the first pipeline. A block of code is then called via the PFT, configuring the entire machine. While this pipeline is executing, the address sequencer may perform other operations to set up the next pipeline. After pipeline termination, an interrupt is sent to the address sequencer, which can set up the next pipeline and initiate another execution. If the program is finished, an interrupt to the node manager board is generated. The node manager then informs the front-end of the program status, thus completing program execution.

B. Support Software

Support software provides system management and aids in program development. System management is handled by the operating system. In the case of the NSC there are two operating systems to consider, one resident on the node, and one resident on the font-end. In addition a number of development tools are provided. Among these are assemblers, compilers, debuggers, libraries, and a simulator.

1. Operating Systems

a. Node Operating System: NSC Executive. The basic support program provided on the node is a local operating system called the NSC Executive Program. This program provides all the facilities needed in order to run the node. Among the functions it performs are front-end communications, data management, interfacing with a local terminal, and monitoring local program execution. Through the local user interface the node can be operated in a stand-alone mode, independent of the front-end. From a local console terminal a user can examine or fill memory, check or set various I/O ports, issue requests to the front-end, and execute and monitor an application program. The Executive is written primarily in C language, with a number of hardware directives written in 80286 assembly language, and is part of the firmware on the node manager.

b. Front-End Operating System. The front-end performs three major functions in the NSC: arbitrating multiple node execution, program development, and data storage and management. File management is provided by the operating system resident on the front-end. At present, two front-end units support the NSC. They are a Concurrent Computer Corporation

3250 running a version of UNIX, and a Digital Equipment VAX 8200 running VMS. Program control is effected with a special operating system known as the NSC Node Monitor.

The NSC operating system is the NSC Node Monitor program, which has ultimate control over the nodes. Among the tasks performed by the Node Monitor are downloading data and programs to the nodes, retrieving data from the nodes, issuing directives for program execution on the nodes, monitoring the program execution, replying to node manager directives, and processing user requests.

2. Program Development Tools In addition to the operating systems, a number of support programs are being developed to facilitate the applications programming. These include assemblers, compilers, debuggers, scientific subroutine libraries, and a simulator.

To write low-level code, two assemblers are being developed. The first is a hand assembler that provides the means to enter microcode line by line. A second assembler takes advantage of the visual nature of creating computational graphs for creating the pipelines. This is a graphical assembler intended to run on a graphics work station such as a Silicon Graphics IRIS 4D. A FORTRAN compiler is under development for high-level language application programs.

Debuggers are being implemented on both the front-end and the node. For programs that use multiple nodes, a debugger resident on the front-end is under development. At the node level a debugger is used to permit insertion of breakpoints, single stepping, and examination of the primary registers used in pipeline execution. A second program for debugging use is an assembler/disassembler that allows examination of micro- and nano-code by giving the configuration represented and allowing it to be modified.

A library of scientific subroutines is being developed. These not only reduce program development time but also make the most efficient use of the hardware. For example, routines for matrix multiplication, random number generation, and FFTs reside in this library.

A library of microprograms is provided on the node to simplify operation of the address sequencer. Among the functions performed by these routines are programming the DMA, memory transfers via the node bus, and programming the interrupt controller, as well as the other control-flow devices. This library allows a user to program the address sequencer without detailed knowledge of its operation. This is particularly useful at the early stages of program development so that the majority of effort can be placed in creating efficient pipelines. Once the configuration tables are defined, the user then writes specific microprograms to improve the efficiency at the control level.

3. Simulator The hardware of any computing machine can be simulated using a suitable software package that mimics the attributes of the target system. Such a code is called a simulator, and typically runs on a general-purpose computer. To aid the architectural developments of the NSC and to support code development and testing, an NSC fullnode simulator was written (Hayder, 1988). This permitted many subtle, alternate architectural changes to be rapidly tested and evaluated, which proved very useful in that not all of the hardware in the final version of the NSC was designed when the simulator came on-line. In a simulator, the functionality of different hardware blocks is replaced by suitable software subroutines. The state of the machine at each clock cycle is computed, and information about different resources and the overhead associated with computation often indicates ways to improve the computational efficiency either by hardware or by software changes. Thus, vast improvements to the robustness of the architecture and the mapping of algorithms to the machine are added with simulator tools.

The Navier–Stokes Computer node simulator has been developed and is written in FORTRAN77. There is a one-to-one correspondence between different blocks of hardware and software modules.

C. Applications

Nosenchuck et al. (1986) presented viscous flow simulation results on the NSC mininode. For the model problem a sustained computational speed of 179 MFLOPS was achieved. It was also found that the internode communications had little (< 2%) overhead, and performance scaled almost linearly with the number of nodes. Note that there are minor differences between the mininode architecture presented in their paper with the current configuration illustrated by Hayder (1988).

Estimates of a Navier–Stokes algorithm on the fullnode were given by Nosenchuck et al. (1987). This algorithm solves time-dependent incompressible flow problems. Solution techniques involve relaxation schemes with multigrid acceleration. Their projected timings are given in Table 1.

Hayder (1988) simulated several fluid dynamics algorithms on the NSC fullnode simulator. Some of those simulations are briefly discussed in the following.

1. Two-Dimensional Laplace Equation The first model problem in the discussion is a two-dimensional Laplace equation with boundary condi-

Table 1. Projected Performance of Algorithms on the
NSC (Nosenchuck et al. (1987))

Methods	Sustained operation rate MFLOP/NODE
Point Jacobi	519
Red – Black SOR	259
Multigrid	403

tions shown in Figure 7. For simplicity, only the Dirichlet-type boundary
condition is used. This model problem can be solved using many different
numerical techniques. Here, the focus is on mapping an explicit and an
implicit iterative algorithm onto the NSC. These algorithms are known as
the point Jacobi iteration and point Gauss – Seidel iteration schemes. Alternative programming approaches are discussed to illustrate the flexibility
that the NSC provides in permitting many different, efficient approaches
to solve a given problem.

At any point of computation with the fixed boundary conditions, only
the interior points are required to be updated. One way of performing this
is to use a translate table (i.e. address the operands indirectly) and make a
single sweep over the two-dimensional array. Computed results corresponding to the boundary points are then discarded, and only the interior
points are updated. When a translate table is used to access memory
planes, there is a one-clock delay for prefetching the initial address. After

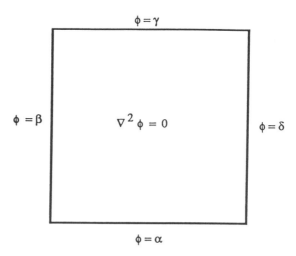

Figure 7. Two-dimensional Laplace equation domain.

that, both translate table and memory planes are accessed in pipeline fashion.

The point Jacobi iteration for a two-dimensional Laplace equation is given by Equation 7:

$$\Phi_{i,j}^{k+1} = \tfrac{1}{4}(\Phi_{i-1,j}^k + \Phi_{i+1,j}^k + \Phi_{i,j-1}^k + \Phi_{i,j+1}^k), \tag{7}$$

where k is the level of iteration. Because of its explicit nature, this algorithm is easily vectorizable. An algorithm mapping to an NSC node is given in Figure 8. The four input operands are different elements of a vector output from a single memory plane with offsets. A shift/delay unit

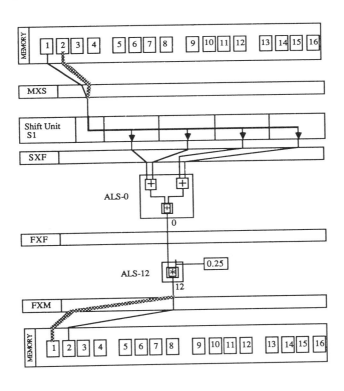

Figure 8. Mapping of the Laplace equation to the NSC architecture.

(SDU) is used to generate the four operands from the data stream. Three addition operations are done in the ALS-0 triplet, and the multiplication operation is performed in the ALS-12 singlet. In Figure 8 the box around 0.25 indicates that the constant 0.25 is stored in the register file in ALS-12. One of the inputs (constant 0.25) to ALS-12 comes from this register file location, and the other input comes from the FLONET switch. The variable Φ is stored in memory planes 1 and 2. Storage in memory planes 1 and 2 is used for operand and result vectors, which alternate between sweeps. In a particular sweep, data are brought from memory plane 1 and the output vector is stored in memory plane 2. In the following sweep, memory plane 2 sources the input data stream as the output vector of the previous iteration and memory plane 1 receives new results.

Applied to the Laplace equation, the Gauss–Seidel method results in the same finite-difference formulation as in the Jacobi method. The only difference is that the computation immediately uses any points that have been updated. Because of its implicit nature, this approach converges faster than the Jacobi method. The Gauss–Seidel algorithm is given by Equation 8 and a pipeline configuration for computation on the NSC is shown in Figure 9.

$$\Phi_{i,j}^{k+1} = \tfrac{1}{4}(\Phi_{i-1,j}^{k+1} + \Phi_{i+1,j}^{k} + \Phi_{i,j-1}^{k+1} + \Phi_{i,j+1}^{k}). \tag{8}$$

Two input operands (RHS of Equation 8) at any sweep $k + 1$ are from the previous k sweep, and the other two operands are from the sweep $k + 1$. Since computation at any point depends on results at some grid points from the same sweep, this generates a problem for vectorization. When a sweep is made in the I direction, all operands for the computations of $\Phi_{i+1,j}^{k+1}$ and $\Phi_{i,j}^{k+1}$ are not available at consecutive clock cycles. This is due to $\Phi_{i,j}^{k+1}$ being computed and made available as an operand before the computation of $\Phi_{i+1,j}^{k+1}$ can begin. For computation of a Gauss–Seidel iteration with the pipeline configuration shown in Figure 9, this process takes six clock cycles. Clocks associated with pipeline DMA can be slowed down by a given factor. In the present simulation, the pipeline DMA clock associated with memory planes 1 and 2 is slowed by a factor of six. This arrangement permits sweeps to occur for a point Gauss–Seidel iteration in a pipeline fashion. However, the throughput is six times slower than in Jacobi iterations.

Both boundary values of Φ and interior updated points are needed at the input of SDU-1. Note that the input of SDU-1 is connected to outputs of memory plane 3 and ALS-12. Memory plane 3 stores the initial array of $\Phi_{i,j}$. At any particular clock cycle, both ALS-12 and memory plane 3 deliver Φ from the same (i,j) location to the input of the switch leading to SDU-1. When (i,j) corresponds to some interior point in the field, ALS-12

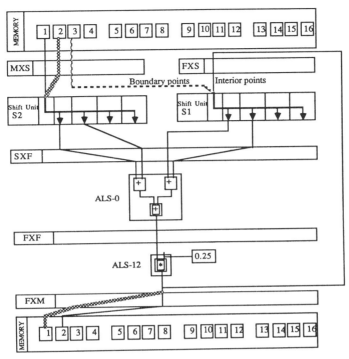

Figure 9. Pipeline configuration for point Gauss–Seidel iteration.

output is routed to the input of SDU-1. On the other hand, when (i,j) corresponds to a boundary point, output of memory plane 3 is routed to the input of the SDU-1.

Implicit schemes usually have faster convergence rates than explicit approaches. Explicit schemes are easy to vectorize, while implicit schemes generally impede vectorization. If neighboring points are not decoupled, one may still be able to vectorize the algorithm on the NSC, if the pipelining technique shown in this section is applicable.

Simulation results for point Jacobi iterations on the fullnode are shown in Figure 10. The average computational speed for this algorithm exceeds its 50% value for a 10×10 grid size. Note that only four out of 32 floating point units and one out of two SDUs are used in these computations. The computational domain can be divided into two subdomains. One pipeline composed of a SDU and four floating point units may be employed to compute Φ in each subdomain. This arrangement doubles the computational speed. This technique is used for the simulation of the model problem 2 and is discussed in the following section.

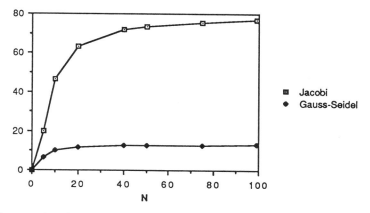

Figure 10. Simulation results of the Laplace equation on the NSC.

Simulation results for Gauss–Seidel iterations are also shown in Figure 10. The reconfigurable pipeline mode is used to deliver switch between boundary and interior computed point deliveries to SDU-1. Since this is done in pipeline mode, there is no overhead associated with these reconfigurations. However, since clocks associated with memory planes 1 and 2 are slowed down by a factor of six, the computational speed with the Gauss–Seidel scheme is about one sixth of the point Jacobi scheme.

2. Thermal Boundary Layer Temperature profile in a fluid flow can be calculated solving the energy equation. A two-dimensional model problem is shown in Figure 11. The temperature distribution in this flow is solved using Equation 9

$$\frac{\partial}{\partial t} T + u_j \frac{\partial}{\partial x_j} T = \alpha \frac{\partial}{\partial x_j} \frac{\partial}{\partial x_j} T. \tag{9}$$

This equation is written in finite-difference form as

$$
\begin{aligned}
T_{i,j}^{k+1} = {} & ax_{i,j}(T_{i-1,j}^{k} - T_{i,j}^{k}) + ay_{i,j}(T_{i,j-1}^{k} - T_{i,j}^{k}) + T_{i-1,j}^{k} \\
& + bx_{i,j}(T_{i+1,j}^{k} - 2T_{i,j}^{k} + T_{i-1,j}^{k}) + by_{i,j}(T_{i,j+1}^{k} - 2T_{i,j}^{k} + T_{i,j-1}^{k}).
\end{aligned} \tag{10}
$$

An efficient mapping of this problem is shown in Figure 12a–c. In this mapping, the computational domain is split into two sections. Duplicate copies of output and the coefficient matrices are stored in memory planes. This arrangement gives 100% utilization of the memory planes, floating point, and shift/delay units. Pipeline 1 updates the grid points in domain 1 and similarly pipeline 2 updates the grid points in domain 2. In sweep 1, pipeline 1 receives temperature data from planes 5 and 7 and writes

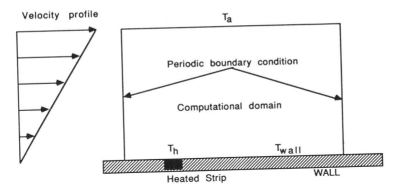

Figure 11. Model problem 2.

outputs to planes 6 and 16. It should be noted that planes 5, 6, 15 and 16 contain the temperature data of domain 1 and planes 7, 8, 13 and 14 contain the similar data of domain 2. Therefore, pipeline 1 has access to temperature data of the whole flow field from the previous time-step. This is also true for pipeline 2. Interconnections of the memory planes to the pipelines are interchanged to assure the accessibility of the temperature data over the two different domains.

Simulation results are shown in Figure 13. Computed isotherms of this model problem are given in Figure 14. The given mapping uses all floating point units, SDUs, and memory planes, and exceeds 50% of the peak computational speed for a 20x10 grid. For a 100x100 grid, there is a SDU fill overhead equal to 4% of the total computational time, and the average computational speed reaches about 95% of the peak computational speed.

3. Three-Dimensional Flow Calculation Aerodynamic flows have many important practical applications. Various mathematical models have been developed to gain insight into these flows. These models invoke many simplifying assumptions, and many fail to make accurate quantitative predictions of complex flows. With the advent of high-speed computers, direct numerical solutions of more complete mathematical models are becoming feasible. As bigger and faster computers are designed, simulations of more complete mathematical models of aerodynamic flows are becoming feasible. These simulations could provide reliable predictions and tools for the designers. At present, a few flow codes are routinely used as design tools for aerodynamic designs. In this section, one such complex and state-of-the-art flow code is discussed. This code is known as FLO57 and solves steady-state three-dimensional transonic flow problems over an

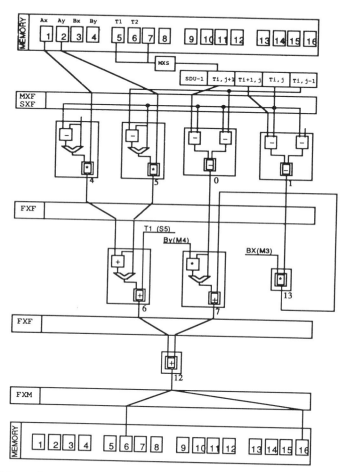

Figure 12a. Pipeline configuration in mappings 2 and 3 of model problem 2.

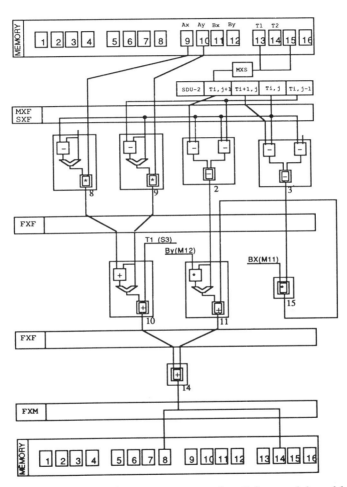

Figure 12b. Pipeline configuration in mapping 3 for model problem 2.

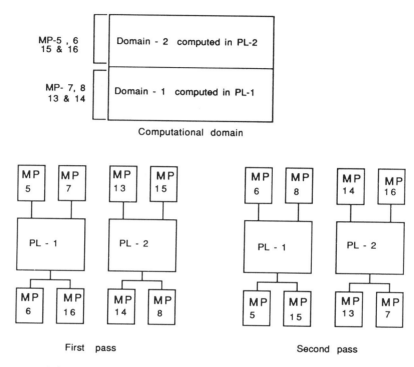

Figure 12c. Memory plane assignments in mapping 3.

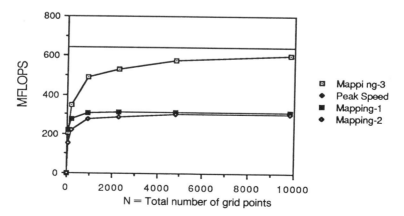

Figure 13. Simulation of thermal boundary layer on the NSC.

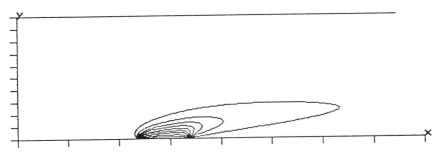

Figure 14. Isotherms in model problem 2.

airplane wing. A. Jameson has developed this code, which is used widely by many aircraft companies for their research and development of airplanes (Jameson, 1987). The algorithm used in this code is an extension of the algorithm developed by Jameson et al. (1981). The three-dimensional Euler equations are the governing equations used for this flow simulation. This code uses the finite-volume technique for spatial discretization and the Runge Kutta method for time-stepping.

Simulation results for one subroutine of FLO57 are shown in Figure 15. On the average 30% of the functional units remain filled for the computations in FLO57. Therefore, the average computational speed would exceed 200 MFLOPS when more than 100 points are used in the I-direction in the computation.

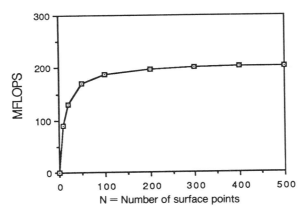

Figure 15. Simulation of subroutine EFLUX on the NSC.

References

1. Jameson, A., Schmidt, W. and Turkel, E. (1981), "Numerical solution of the Euler equations by finite volume methods using Runge-Kutta time stepping schemes," AIAA paper 81-1259.
2. Jameson, A. (1987), "Successes and challenges in computational aerodynamics," AIAA paper 87-1184-CP.
3. Hayder, M. E. (1988), "The Navier–Stokes Computer," Ph. D. Thesis, Mechanical and Aerospace Engineering Department, Princeton University, NJ.
4. Nosenchuck, D. M., Littman, M. G. and Flannery, W. (1986), "Two-dimensional non-steady viscous flow simulation on the Navier–Stokes Computer mini-node," *Journal of Scientific Computation* 1: 53–73.
5. Nosenchuck, D. M., Krist, S. E. and Zang, T. A. (1987), "On multigrid methods for the Navier–Stokes Computer," presented at the 3rd Copper Mountain Conference on Multigrid Methods, Copper Mountain, Colorado.

5 Parallel Processing with the Loosely Coupled Array of Processors System

E. CLEMENTI AND D. LOGAN

IBM Corporation
Data Systems Division
Kingston, New York

I. Introduction

The concept of supercomputing, while relative at best, is complicated by consideration of vast areas of problems that require solution. One area that has traditionally been associated with the need of supercomputing, and in which our primary interest lies, is that of scientific and engineering problems. Success in these applications has invariably given impetus to the development of more elaborate calculations. Thus there has always been constant pressure to expand the limits of currently available computer resources. However, the extent to which traditional sequential processors can be pushed into higher realms of computational power is limited by pragmatic or fundamental constraints. Of general importance is the constant need of developing more efficient algorithms and languages. Of a more fundamental nature are limitations that deal with density of packing integrated circuits, heat dissipation and finally the speed of light. Such considerations have lead to alternative strategies in attacking the problem.

One of the first and most successful approaches has been the development of vector-oriented processors such as IBM 3838, the CRAY series computers or the CDC CYBER 205. However, the useful application of this technique has to a large extent been limited to applications that are inherently vectorizable. While such applications are significant in number, they do not include many areas of scientific computing. An alternative approach has been the development of parallel structures, i.e. systems of many independent processors that may be concurrently applied to the solution of a single problem. It is now generally conceded that both approaches are complementary. Tomorrow's supercomputer probably will have the properties of massive parallelism incorporating processors that retain the highest possible performance in vector and scalar computation; certainly a high degree of parallelism and vector features will be typical in future architectures.

With this comment on the necessary attributes of supercomputing it is logical that one of the first concerns should be that of the parallel structure. In this work we shall expand on some of our previous review papers, particularly [1e]. The idea of parallel computers is certainly not new. It has already been the subject of numerous research projects and a very vast literature. For a representative subset see [1] and references therein. Even a system intended specifically for computational chemistry has been talked about [2]. Our interest in such systems has been spurred by the need of extending calculations in theoretical chemistry and biophysics, with which our laboratory has been traditionally involved, well beyond what is obtainable on current systems.

As a first step in this direction we have defined our objectives as follows: to develop a kernel architecture that 1) is at minimum the equivalent of a CRAY 1S or CYBER 205, 2) is easily extended well beyond this limit, 3) has much more flexibility and versatility, 4) permits the quick migration of large scientific applications to parallel execution, and 5) doesn't cost too much.

Many of the characteristics of our parallel strategy follow from these priorities. These characteristics are 1) not thousands, nor hundreds of processing units (PUs) are considered, but very few, less than 20; 2) each PU is a *well-developed engine* which executes asynchronously or even independently as a stand-alone from the others; 3) the system softwares needed to execute application programs are as much as possible those commonly available for sequential programming; 4) to start with we constrain ourselves to FORTRAN, since this is the most widely used scientific application language; 5) we restrict ourselves to the minimum level of programming variations relative to the old sequential codes; 6) because of the applications we are interested in, 64-bit hardware precision is required;

and 7) if a larger number of PUs is advisable, then a *hierarchical* system will be considered from the very beginning.

With respect to point 1), we wish to implement a *pragmatic approach* which is in no way critical of more ambitious attempts that are likely to become standard and available for general application programming, but only in the next decade. Concerning point 2), we use an IBM host or hosts (for example, IBM-4341, IBM-4381 or IBM-308X) with several FPS-164 or FPS-264 attached *array processors* (AP). Since the latter could in principle be either standard scalar CPUs (Central Processing Units) or APs, in the following we shall refer either to "slave CPUs" or to "attached APs" as equivalent approaches to obtain parallelism. Concerning point 3), we note that we have implemented our architecture in two physical systems, referred to as LCAP-1 and LCAP-2. They differ in two important respects in the identity of the IBM host and the operating systems employed. The systems softwares that are needed for parallel programming, as opposed to sequential programming, are those concerned with communication of commands and files. These issues, which are operating system imperatives, will thus be explored from two approaches. Concerning point 4), one would eventually like to have a compiler and/or an optimizer which would include the above communication facilities. As a first step we have developed precompilers that permit the insertion of directives that may be interpreted as extensions to the FORTRAN language. These directives, described in a later section, incorporate basic functions such as "fork" and "join" needed in expressing parallelism. Concerning point 7), we note that we have explored ways to connect LCAP-1 with LCAP-2 in a hierarchical manner.

Additional description of our initial hardware configuration is provided in Section II below. In Section IV we present the strategies we have developed to modify our applications programs for effective parallel execution on our system. In order to more precisely understand how these strategies are implemented, we describe the operating system communication considerations in Section III. Section V studies performance of our initial system in practical applications. Finally, in Section VI, we discuss performance enhancements that were made to this initial system along with a short survey of additional applications.

II. Initial Configuration for LCAP

As mentioned previously there are at present two parallel processing systems working in our laboratory. Both share the same fundamental architecture of a distributed system with a front-end CPU and attached PUs (or

APs) with initially no emphasis on the ability to achieve direct slave-to-slave communication. For this reason we termed our architecture a *loosely coupled* array of processors (LCAP). The first of these systems, called LCAP-1, was originally hosted either by an IBM 4341 or 4381 and attached to 10 FPS-164 processors. The second and more powerful system, called LCAP-2, originally employed as host a dyadic IBM 3081 and as slaves six FPS-264s processors; it was later expanded to include 10 of these processors. In spite of these differences, the two systems were, and continue to be, very similar (aside from operating system considerations, which will be discussed in the following section). Thus for the purpose of brevity we confine ourself here to description of the LCAP-1 system as it was operating in the second half of 1984. We recall that the systems are experimental and have evolved continuously in hardware and software applications.

This system was structured such that seven FPS-164s were connected to an IBM 4381 host and the remaining three were attached to an IBM 3314 switching unit so they could be switched between the IBM 4341 host or the IBM 4381 host. The FPS-164 processors were attached to the IBM hosts through IBM 3 Mbytes/sec. channels available on these hosts. A third IBM 4341, connected to a graphics station, completed the host processor pool. The graphics station included an Evans and Sutherland and an IBM 5080 graphics terminals and a large set of graphics packages for such diverse uses as cad/cam applications or molecular modelling. The three IBM systems were interconnected, channel to channel, via an IBM 3088 connector. A schematic diagram of the configuration appears in Figure 1a.

One attractive feature of the above system was that a variable number of APs could be attached to either the 4381 or the 4341; the former configuration was used primarily for production jobs while the latter served for debugging and experimentation. When we ran a given job on two or more APs (parallel mode) we attempted to ensure that the amount of data flowing from one AP to another AP, via the host processor, was kept to a minimum. Indeed, jobs requiring transfers of long files from AP to AP

Figure 1. a: The initial structure of the LCAP-1 system. See Section II for a detailed discussion.

b: Performance comparison between an FPS-164 with and without the inclusion of one MAX board in executing a matrix multiply. The use of fast table memory is not automatically invoked by the compiler and must be explicitly declared.

c: VM operating system considerations in creating a master/slave system with IBM hosts and FPS attached processors. Communication is achieved through the VMCF system utility.

a.

Loosely Coupled Array of Processors (LCAP-1)

Scientific/Engineering Computations, Dept. 48B, IBM–Kingston, DSD

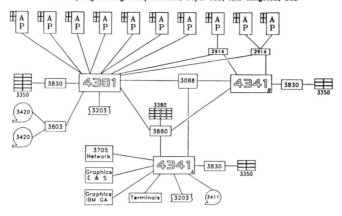

b.

Matrix Multiplication

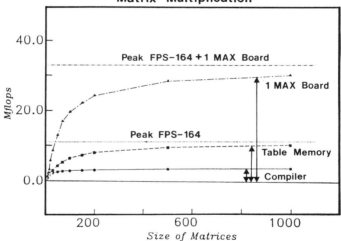

c.

System Considerations Under VM/SP

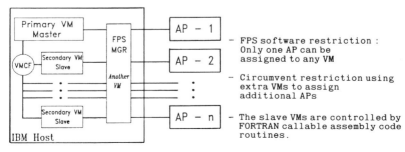

– FPS software restriction :
  Only one AP can be
  assigned to any VM

– Circumvent restriction using
  extra VMs to assign
  additional APs

– The slave VMs are controlled by
  FORTRAN callable assembly code
  routines.

were not optimal on this configuration because of channel transfer rate limitations. To offset this condition, the system was later expanded to include both a fast common bus as well as a number of shared memories that permitted direct AP-to-AP communication. These extensions will be discussed in Section VI since they constitute a departure from LCAP and a step towards TCAP (*tightly* coupled array of processors). Aside from these modifications the following describes the essential features of LCAP-1 and LCAP-2 as they exist today.

Each AP contains an independent PU and its own memory and disk drives for either temporary or permanent data sets (the latter is a rather seldom occurrence). The CPU on the FPS-164 runs at 5.5 million instructions per second (MIPS), and several concurrent operations (up to 10) can take place on each instruction cycle. In particular, one 64-bit floating-point addition and one 64-bit floating-point multiplication can be initiated each cycle, so that peak performance is about 11 million floating-point operation per second (11 Mflops). Of course, one must make the distinction between peak performance (a characteristic of the machine hardware) and sustained performance (depending on the application and the code which implements it as well as the hardware).

Communication between the host computer and the attached FPS-164 is handled by hardware and software that is provided and supported by Floating Point Systems as a standard feature. An optimizing FORTRAN compiler and supporting utilities (including disk I/O) are also standard products for the FPS-164. The compiler produces reasonably compact pipelined machine code that takes advantage of the unique multiple independent functional units of the FPS architecture. An extensive library of subroutines is also provided. Many of the latter have been enhanced in terms of execution speed as well as error detection through efforts within our laboratory [3].

Each of our FPS-164s has at least eight Mbytes of real random access memory. The memory on the IBM 4341 model M2 and model P2 are 8 Mbytes and 16 Mbytes, respectively. The IBM 4381/3 has 32 Mbytes. Thus, taken as a whole, there was 136 Mbytes real storage available in our system.

Each AP also has four 135 Mbyte disks, for a total of 5.4 Gigabytes. In addition there are banks of IBM 3350 and IBM 3380 disks accessible to the host computers, totalling about 25 Gigabytes of disk storage. Tape drives, printers, and communication networks interface and complete our configuration.

To complete the description of LCAP-1, we should note briefly that Floating Point Systems supplies the FPS-164 MAX; the latter is a special-purpose board that can be added to the FPS-164 to augment performance, particularly on vector operations. Each MAX board contains two additional adders and two additional multipliers, and so adds 22 Mflops to peak attainable performance. Up to 15 boards can be placed in a single FPS-164, converting it to a machine with a peak performance of 341 Mflops.

A library of mathematical routines will be available for use of the MAX boards. When properly used, they may permit a gain in performance that is impressive. This is illustrated in Figure 1b for the operation of a matrix-by-matrix multiplication. It compares the processing speed as a function of matrix size on one AP to that with the addition of one vector board. It is seen that for large matrix sizes the processing speed increases by approximately 22 Mflops, i.e. the rated peak performance of the supplemental vector board.

At present each of our APs has been equipped with two MAX boards. This has upgraded our peak performance from 110 to 550 Mflops. Ultimately our system could grow to 3410 Mflops peak capability, but (recalling the distinction between peak performance and realized performance) it is clearly desirable first to explore the gains that one can realistically obtain with only a few 164MAX boards per AP. Consequently we have settled at 550 Mflops. The rated peak performance of the FPS-264 is 38 Mflops so that the peak performance of the LCAP-2 system is 380 Mflops.

It should be noted that such upgrades have no effect on the parallel programming strategy to be discussed later. The strategy is equally effective for APs of any architecture or computational speed. In principle, we could substitute 10 vector-oriented supercomputers for our 10 FPS-164s. However, given the notable differences in cost between these options, the latter one is unrealistically high.

III. System Considerations

Our system is a multiple instruction stream/multiple data stream (MIMD) system [4], in the form of a distributed network of nodes. The distributed nature of the system allows appropriate utilization of the parallelism of the code; i.e. the "degree of parallelism" [1b] of the software is matched by the hardware. An important advantage of high-level parallelism, as in high-level programming languages, is portability. A high-level parallel code may be executed on any system with a rudimentary communication protocol. In addition, improvements at the instruction level can be independently pursued without disturbing the setup of the parallel algorithm.

As previously mentioned, we have implemented our basic architecture in two physically different systems. They differ in one important aspect in the operating systems that the host employs. This directly dictates the mode by which each system achieves host-to-slave communication. In the following we describe this issue for both systems. It will be seen that, aside from some details of implementation, the overall communication structures are logically equivalent. Thus parallel programs written for either system may with ease migrate to the other.

The LCAP-1 system, hosted by either an IBM 4341 or 4381, runs under the IBM Virtual Machines/System Product (VM/SP) operating system [5]. For the APs, we use the software provided for hosts running under this system by Floating Point Systems. We have not found it necessary to modify either set of software in order to run our applications in parallel.

VM/SP is a time-sharing system in which jobs run on virtual machines (VM) created by the system; these VMs simulate real computing systems. The standard software provided by Floating Point Systems to use the FPS-164s embodies the restriction that only one AP can be attached to a VM. Of course, for a task running in parallel, more than one AP is required. Our solution to this is to introduce extra "slave" VMs to handle the extra APs we need. To make this work, one must have a way to communicate between different VMs; this is provided by the Virtual Machine Communication Facility (VMCF), which is a standard feature of VM/SP [5].

In general, then, a parallel task will consist of several FORTRAN programs, each running on a separate VM in the host system, and each controlling a particular AP on which additional FORTRAN code runs. On one of the VMs, the "master", is the part of the original FORTRAN code intended to be run on the host, combined with utility subroutines that handle communication with the "slave" VMs and with the AP attached to the "master" VM. The logical structure of this system is illustrated in Figure 1c. The programs running on the "slave" VMs are much shorter, since the "slave" VMs are nothing more than transfer points for communication between the "master" program and the APs attached to the "slaves." In essence, the "slave" VM programs consist of code to handle communication with the "master" and utility subroutines to communicate with the AP attached to the "slave." Since each VM is attached only to a single AP, the standard utilities provided by FPS [6a] for communication between host and AP can be used without modification.

It remains to describe the utilities that handle communication between "master" and "slave" VMs. As mentioned, the vehicle for communication between VMs is provided as part of the VM/SP system, namely VMCF, thus reducing the dependency on system programming. Since use of VMCF requires calls to the system from assembler code, it is desirable to package this code in utility subroutines that can be invoked from normal FORTRAN code. Development of this set of utilities, which we call VMFACS (Virtual Machine FORTRAN-Accessible Communications Subroutines), was one of the first steps in implementing our parallel system.

The VMFACS utilities packages are experimental, as is our entire parallel system. They may be expected to change as our system undergoes further development. One possibility is to replace or supplement the use of VMCF by Inter-User Communications Vehicle (IUCV), another feature of VM/SP [7]. Ultimately, one might expect to eliminate the need for these communication packages by replacing the standard FPS utilities with utilities that would allow many APs to be attached and controlled by a single VM. Our tests indicate that VMCF communications are no great burden on the system. They amount to a small fraction (about 1/10) of the time required for channel transmission between host and AP.

The LCAP-2 system initially used as host a dyadic IBM 3081 that ran under the IBM Multiple Virtual Systems (MVS) operating system [7]. In contrast to the VM operating system it has traditionally been employed in a batch-oriented processing environment. Another distinction between the two architectures is that the LCAP-2 system uses FPS-264 attached processors. These processors roughly outperform their earlier-164 counterparts by a factor of three to four [6b].

Aside from these differences, much the same issues must be addressed in both systems. The important concern of host/slave communication was bridged in the former case through the creation of a set of virtual machines and the use of the VMCF system utility. For LCAP-2 we require the equivalent of this intermediate set of slave machines or processes that will connect uniquely to the set of attached processors. This requirement is effected within the MVS operating system through the creation of subtasks which serve in an analogous fashion. Communication between the subtasks and the attached processors is functionally identical thereafter. However, there are several important distinctions between the two environments in carrying out communication between the master and the slave processes. In the VM system the code being executed in each virtual machine may be considered as a subroutine that is invoked by a call in the master. Here argument and common-block transmission of data is accomplished by use of the VMCF utility and subsequent copy-memory-to-memory instructions. In the MVS environment, system software permits the overlap of virtual memories of master and slave subtasks such that they may share common memory. The operation of data transfer in this case reduces to negligible system interaction followed by simple address translation and single memory reference instructions. The cost of communication along this path is thus significantly reduced in the MVS system. Later on we shall comment on the bulk shared memory system we have added to

LCAPs; this addition brings about new features that reduce some of the above-explained differences between VM and MVS.

The remaining differences in executing parallel code in the two environments are concerned with subtask or VM initiation and synchronization. The latter, while operationally different on the two systems, is roughly equivalent in terms of efficiency and execution overhead. Moreover, existing software in either case requires little or no modification to achieve the desired result. Of major importance is that, aside from the considerations above, programs written for either system have been found to be easily adapted to the counterpart system. In other words, the strategies employed in parallelizing a code are largely invariant with respect to the host operating system. In the following section we discuss these strategies.

IV. Parallel Programming Strategy and Considerations

We begin with the observation that large-scale, typically CPU-bound, calculations almost invariably involve loops, either explicitly or in an equivalent sense, that are traversed many times. Most of the CPU time is consumed in such loops, so that if we adapt the tasks contained in these loops to parallel execution, we shall find that we actually have most of the code (as measured by execution time) running in parallel.

This is easy enough to accomplish. Let us suppose that our sequential FORTRAN code has an explicit or a logically inferred DO loop of the form

```
DO 500 I = 1, N

   .   .   .   .   .   .

   .   .   .   .   .   .   ,
```

with some computational kernel inside the loop (up to statement 500). Then, if we suppose that NCPU is the number of APs available for parallel execution, we can keep the same computational kernel and modify the loop to read

```
DO 500 I = ICPU, N, NCPU

   .   .   .   .   .   .

   .   .   .   .   .   .
```

This portion of the program, with the computational kernel and modified loop, is dispatched to each of the NCPU APs. Each AP must of course have a different value for the index ICPU, with $1 \leq \text{ICPU} \leq \text{NCPU}$.

This fundamental scheme has been applied to all the applications pro-grams we have migrated to parallel execution, and has been effective in every case. Thus, after migration, typical program flow would consist of an initial sequential part handling initial input, setup, etc., followed by a parallel part running simultaneously on several APs. At the end of this portion, the results from the parallel execution must be gathered up and processed by another sequential portion. This may be a prelude to another period of parallel execution, or, ultimately, to development of final results and the end of the run.

There is an obvious limit on this scheme: the computational kernel for a particular value of I in the loop example above must not depend on results computed in earlier passes through the loop with a different value of I. Our experience so far indicates that this is not a severe restriction; indeed, we find many codes tend to fall naturally into such a form. There are some "exceptions," of course, and, to start with, we have simply left the ones we have encountered in the sequential part of the code.

The procedure above constitutes a classical fork-and-join process whereby a master forks off a number of subtasks to an equal number of slaves and upon their completion joins the results. Accordingly, our exten-sions to the FORTRAN language for parallel programming have centered around this concept. These language extensions have taken the form of precompiler directives which the programmer inserts in the original body of code. The fork directive takes the general form of EXECUTE ON ALL/SLAVE: SUBROUTINE (arguments). It effectively initiates the exe-cution of the subroutine named either on all the attached processors or on a particular slave. Accordingly, the partitioning of the DO loop described above necessitates the loop being restructured as a callable subroutine. Data to be passed to the routine (such as the loop index of the previous example) may be passed either as arguments of the routine or through common blocks. The join directive takes the general form of WAIT FOR ALL/SLAVE. It effects a synchronization point within the master's se-quential code for task completion either on all the attached processors or optionally on a particular slave. This directive is usually followed by one or several directives which specify the data to be returned as well as their subsequent treatment or merging conditions.

The precompiler, through which the modified code is processed, then generates the transfer or communication programs that will run on the slave VMs. This is effected through the translation of the above directives into the desired sequence of primitive communication routines alluded to in Section III. Its output is a pair of FORTRAN programs each of which is compiled and executed on the host and slave VMs accordingly. The mod-ules that run on the attached processors, which contain the parallel sub-tasks, are compiled and downloaded in a separate phase.

Before discussing our performance studies on a variety of applications, it is worthwhile to consider some underlying principles that will determine their success. These observations, while pertinent to the LCAP system, are quite general and address the larger body of parallel processing systems now built or under investigation.

The analysis of the performance of a parallel processing system is a very complex undertaking. It may be approached at a variety of levels. First, one may examine the system-wide performance in a very general context. Analytic or quasianalytic methods may be employed without detailed specification of the actual problems that will be run on the machine; here one is concerned with the manner in which resources are scheduled in a general time-shared multiple user operating environment. Two approaches, not necessarily mutually exclusive, are usually employed in this regard. The first utilizes queueing models with explicit representation of Markov chains with the goal of determining steady-state performance of such system features as memory bandwidth, process average waiting times in specific queues, etc. Several important inputs in this scheme are the assumed distributions of arrival times and processing times at queues for various resources. For computational ease these are usually taken to be memoryless distributions, i.e. Markovian decaying exponential functions. In this method then the modelling of a parallel system is similar but more complex than that of a sequential time-shared system. For further details on this approach see [8] and [9] and references therein.

At the same level of examination, one may wish to avoid the arduous mathematics of the analytic method discussed above by using simulation techniques. These invariably use Monte Carlo methods in sampling the time behavior of the system in terms of the input distributions that govern the work load and component performance. The disadvantage of this approach is that the amount of sampling required to model complex systems may require unobtainable amounts of computer time. For a discussion of the principles involved in this process see [9, 10]. It is often desirable that some combination of both the analytic and simulation techniques be employed, perhaps embodied in a queueing language [11].

The two methods discussed above are useful for gaining some estimate of the *general* performance of a time-shared parallel processing system. The later developed versions of LCAP were indeed of this nature and we have performed analysis of the latter type, i.e. discrete event simulation, in developing a parallel job scheduler and in optimizing the parameters under which it runs. Initially however, the LCAP systems were effectively single user partitioned systems and the usual queueing analysis tools were inappropriate in predicting performance. This afforded a much simpler perspective of performance in terms of examining the parallel structure of single programs. Focussing exclusively on a parallel processing system running a single program, one may model the resulting performance in several crude but useful means. In one simple scheme we imagine that the system may be effectively partitioned into three computational subsystems: a sequential processor, a vector or SIMD (single instruction stream/ multiple data stream) facility and lastly an asynchronous set of parallel processing units. Then following Bucher [12], we may express the total execution time for the job with the following proportional approximation as

$$T \propto \frac{F_{seq}}{S_{seq}} + \frac{F_{syn}}{S_{syn}} + \frac{F_{par}}{S_{par}} = \frac{1}{S_{eff}} \tag{1}$$

where F is the fraction of the code that is respectively sequential, vector and parallel and S is the corresponding system speed in performing each of these computations. S_{eff} is the effective speed with which the system may process the particular application. This expression equivalently restates Amdahl's law that the slowest execution speed will dominate the effective processing power unless the corresponding fraction F is very small. Because these fractions vary widely from application to application, it is then of paramount importance in designing supercomputers that all three capabilities be maximized to the extent possible.

The most complicated parameter in the above expression, and the one of present interest, is the effective execution rate of parallel computation, S_{par}. Following Axelrod [13], one may gain some insight into the behavior of this rate by expressing it in the following simple approximation:

$$S_{par} = P \times R(A) \times f(P,A) \tag{2}$$

where P is the number of independent parallel (assumed identical) processors and $R(A)$ is the execution rate of performing the calculation on application A with a single unit. The last term, $f(P,A)$, is the degradation factor or efficiency of distributing the solution of A among P processors. As expected, it is a function of the interprocessor communication required and the structure and performance of the interconnection scheme of the parallel processing system.

Several observations may be made concerning the efficiency factor $f(P,A)$. The first is that it is a function of how uniformly A may be partitioned among the P processors. Ideally one would want each processor to perform an identical amount of work such that no processor remains idle waiting for the last processor to complete its assignment. In the example cited earlier, this would imply an exact division of the DO loop equally among all NCPU processors with the further requirement that the amount of execution within each iteration be identical. Under this condition the system is load balanced and $f(P,A)$ is maximized.

Another important criterion in determining efficiency concerns the required synchronization after each processor has completed its task. This synchronization is algorithm-dependent and will be influenced by the interconnection scheme that the system employs for interprocessor communication. An example is a strictly master/slave system wherein the master is used to perform a global synchronization following the completion of all the slaves tasks. For simplicity we consider the case of a totally load-balanced calculation with each slave initiating execution simultaneously. Again following Axelrod we may express the total execution time of the parallel job as

$$T = \frac{W}{P} + T(p) + P \times T(c),\tag{3}$$

where W is the total amount of work to be done and P is the total number of parallel units. $T(p)$ is the amount of communication code that each slave must execute (again in parallel) to communicate to the master. The master in turn requires the execution of $T(c)$ units of time to process each message from each slave. Included in this parameter is the performance of the actual hardware employed in the transmission of data (an IBM channel in the initial LCAP case). Then the speedup factor (of using our parallel system compared to a single processor) may be written as

$$\frac{T(1)}{T} = \frac{P}{(1 + (T(p)/W) \times P + (T(c)/W) \times P^2)},\tag{4}$$

from which one may identify the efficiency factor as

$$f = \frac{1}{(1 + (T(p)/W) \times P + (T(c)/W) \times P^2)}.\tag{5}$$

Several important and rather general properties of parallel processing may be appreciated from this very simple model. The first is that there exists a maximum speedup factor that is for the application under study a function of the number of processors employed. The addition of one more processor after this point will result in subsequent slowdown. This maximum is a function of the value of $W/T(c)$ and thus may be increased either through decreasing $T(c)$ or increasing W. In the former case this could correspond to increasing the transmission speed while the latter would correspond to solving a larger scale problem, i.e. increasing granularity.

These effects, although arrived at through very simple models, will be seen to be reflected in the applications that we now consider.

V. Initial Applications and Performance

Several points should be stressed prior to discussion of the applications areas considered. The first is that while the architecture of the system is experimental and evolving, we intend, as suggested above, to address problems of significant computational merit. Thus we are interested in measuring performance of problems as a whole rather than that of isolated 'loops' or kernels. In this regard we shall explicitly consider real rates and turn-around times and not focus exclusively on the sometimes ill-applied speedup measurements. The latter, while often impressive, may be misleading when total elapsed times are considered. Another area that was felt to be important was that many of the applications could be developed elsewhere and adapted to the LCAP system by researchers other than LCAP personnel. The ongoing visitors' program has met with this goal. It has been invaluable in assessing the ease of use of the system and the related areas of precompiler design and language extensions necessary for sequential-to-parallel code conversion.

An additional concern, and one that we hope to explore here, is how universally the concept of parallel processing may be applied to scientific and engineering problems. Many of the examples cited here deal with applications in chemistry and physics. Their goal is typically to describe the behavior of a system of n constituents or particles. The exact description of what behavior is to be examined, the interrelational forces that pertain and the system itself vary from application to application. However, one unifying principle that is useful in adapting the computations to parallel implementation is the following [14]. In general, given a system of n particles, either classical or quantized, the computation of the interactions between the i-th particle and the remaining n-1 particles is independent from the computation of the interactions of the j-th particle with its remaining n-1 particles; this computational independence leads to parallelism in simulations in physical sciences.

In other applications similar unifying principles are sought. Some are simple, such as in many image-processing applications, where parallel computation may often result from a straightforward domain decomposition of the image into nonoverlapping subimages. The concurrent application of local neighborhood operators on each subdomain effectively achieves the desired result. In other problems, this decomposition may be applied to a list of tasks whose independence allows a similar partitioning of work among processors. However in other areas, such as those dealing with many structural engineering problems where one is often concerned with the solution of large systems of linear equations, the technique may be more elusive. It may involve parallel algorithm development in either modifying existing solvers (e.g. SOR, conjugate gradient methods) or perhaps creating entirely new ones. These techniques in turn must often be designed within the constraints imposed by the architecture of the parallel system, i.e. the connectivity imposed by processor interconnection networks, bus, cache and memory limitations, etc.

In general the importance of algorithm development, parallel or otherwise, cannot be overstressed. Often "supercomputing" rates of computation may be achieved not by massive parallelism but alternatively by clever restructuring of sequential algorithms. Such was the case, for example, in the implementation of the discrete Fourier transform by the fast Fourier transform (fft) technique. The aim in parallel processing is to map the best possible sequential algorithm onto the architecture in question. The main goal will remain the maximization of the ratio of independent parallel computation to the sum of remaining sequential calculation and communication.

We consider first three applications that were investigated as part of the theoretical chemistry program of our laboratory. The first is a quantum chemistry code employed in the *ab initio* determination of molecular wave functions and the resultant expectation properties such as energies, dipole moments, etc. The next two are, respectively, a Metropolis Monte Carlo program and a Molecular Dynamics program. Both are employed in the determination of equilibrium properties of large ensembles of particles (in our case liquids and solutions). In addition, the latter program may lead to predictions of time-dependent properties such as diffusion constants, speeds of acoustic waves, etc.

Thereafter we consider four applications that were ported to our system through the visitors' program. The first is a seismic data analysis code developed at the IBM research center at Palo Alto, California [15]. It is used to determine geologic structures below earth surfaces from seismic data recorded on the surface. The second in this category is a program developed at McMaster University in Ontario, Canada, to investigate from fundamental principles the properties of atoms in molecules [16]. Next we consider two nuclear reaction data analysis codes written at CERN, Switzerland to analyze high-energy physics data obtained in accelerator experiments [17]. Finally, we consider a simple linear algebra algorithm (matrix multiply) whose parallel performance on the LCAP system was investigated by the Triangle Universities Computation Center (TUCC) in North Carolina [18].

All applications will be briefly described (detailed discussions are referenced elsewhere) in terms of their purpose and the differing demands placed upon the system. Thereafter we present the performance of these applications in their parallel implementation on the earlier LCAP-1 system prior to incorporation of the vector boards described in Section II. We are presently developing software to properly use the MAX boards, which we expect to yield significant gains in performance in applications that have a strong vector character.

Benchmark efforts on the LCAP-2 system indicate a gain in performance of roughly a factor of between three and four over the LCAP-1 system with the same number of processors. This is consistent with the ratio of the processing speeds of the base-attached processor in each system, i.e. the FPS-264 to FPS-164, and the large parallel grain size of the problems examined. However, the area spanned by these problems is deemed representative of a broad class of calculations that are currently of major importance in scientific and engineering computing.

The first three programs, developed within our laboratory, are concerned with determining from first principles fundamental properties of matter. This is approached from a molecular viewpoint at two levels of detail, microscopic and macroscopic. The first is represented by our quantum mechanics code, which attempts to describe the properties of a single molecule. It executes a self-consistent field calculation within the Hartree-Fock approximation to predict the ground state electronic configuration of the system and the basic properties that this infers. For purposes of analysis it may be logically divided into two parts. The first calculates the values of all electron-electron interactions within the framework of representing the electronic system in terms of a set of basis functions (each function is related to an atomic orbital to some degree of approximation). Each such interaction requires the calculation of a six-dimensional integral between the electronic density of electron i and the electronic density of electron j at the distance $r(i,j)$ for any position of i and j; we call this portion of the code the "integrals program." The latter stage of the calculation proceeds from an initial guess of the electronic structure and, using the data of the integrals program, iteratively improves on the structure until convergence is achieved. This portion is generally called the "SCF program." Typically one needs about 20–30 functions to describe the electrons on an atom on the first row of the atomic table. The number of integrals is about N^4, where N is the sum of the number of functions on each atom in the molecule.

The *integrals program* repeatedly evaluates algebraic expressions with various sets of parameters. Evaluation of any one integral is fast, but any complete run will include huge numbers of these integrals. The computed integrals are stored on disk files which can be larger than a Gigabyte in size. Computation of any integral is independent of any other integral, which make it easy to run the integrals program in parallel; one simply decides how the set of integrals is to be divided among the available APs. Once the run is set up, there is no communication between the tasks running on the different APs, and even disk I/O takes place entirely on the AP (parallel I/O). The time a particular task runs without interruption on the AP is the elapsed time for the entire run (a unique feature of this application), and this is typically on the order of hours. The only obstacle to ideal parallelism is that we have not found a way to divide the set of integrals in the run that can guarantee perfectly even distribution among the APs; however, one can expect that the larger the value of N relative to NCPU, the better the synchronization.

The *SCF program* iteratively improves on an initial guess for molecular electronic structure until convergence is achieved. Each iteration can be divided into several steps, of which the most time-consuming by far is combining results from the last iteration with the integrals file generated by the integrals program to develop the current iteration. This step is the only one running in parallel at present. It involves heavy disk I/O (which again takes place in parallel) and also very substantial CPU time. The time for this step running in parallel is typically a fraction of an hour, and requires transmission of several hundred Kilobytes of data between host and AP. A more detailed description of both the integrals program and the SCF program can be found in a previous report [19].

The remaining two classes of programs attempt to determine macroscopic or thermodynamic properties of large ensembles of molecules. In particular our *Metropolis-Monte Carlo programs* predict such properties of liquids or solutions by tracking the random motion of one molecule at a time. The main task in this process is the evaluation of the potential energy of the bulk each time a molecule is moved. It is this task that may run in parallel provided that the potential energy expression is complex enough to guarantee a large parallel grain size. All other tasks are so fast that they cannot benefit from parallel execution. There are several versions of our Monte Carlo code, depending on how elaborate (and hence realistic) an energy expression is being used. Thus the time a task runs in an AP without interruption varies from a fraction of a second up to several seconds. Data transmission between host and AP may be on the order of 100 bytes per task. For more detail concerning our Monte Carlo programs, the reader is referred to our previous report [20].

The second of these classes of programs is represented by our *molecular dynamics* codes that simulate the kinetic motion of molecules in bulk liquid or solution over a period of time. Dividing this time into many smaller timesteps requires at each stage the evaluation of many intermolecular energies and forces. These may be calculated in parallel in the same sense as with the Monte Carlo codes. This is the bulk of the computation. Again, there are several versions of our molecular dynamics codes, depending on the energy expression being used. Typical time for a task run in an AP without interruption is a fraction of a minute, and this involves data transmission between host and AP of as much as a few megabytes. We again refer the reader elsewhere [21] for additional details of these programs.

We have timed specific application runs for all four of these programs running sequentially (one AP), and running in parallel on three APs, six APs, and 10 APs as well as on a CRAY 1S and CRAY XMP. The applications code for the CRAY was developed under constraints analogous to the constraints for our parallel applications codes, that is, the minimum modifications required to run properly under that system. Efforts to modify the code to better exploit the vector architecture of the CRAY would certainly have resulted in faster timings for that machine, but, conversely, we could gain on our parallel system by adapting our code to the architecture of the FPS-164. We believe our results are useful as they stand even though they cannot be regarded as anything like a definitive comparison between the two systems.

Our timings can be found in Table 1a. We find that for the integral, Monte Carlo and molecular dynamics programs, the execution time on our system with six APs almost equals the CRAY 1S. For the SCF program, results are not as good. We can attribute this to the sequential part of the SCF code, which grows in significance as more APs are used for the parallel part. We have started improvement of the SCF code, expecting that this will bring its performance into line with the other applications. This is shown in Table 1b where we repeat and extend the data in comparing performance with a CRAY-XMP with one processor. For comparison we show the performance of LCAP-2 versus the CRAY-XMP in Table 1c

Table 1a. Computational Chemistry Applications Comparisons.*

Comparison of execution times for LCAP-1 with different numbers of APs versus the time needed on the CRAY 1S (application codes not optimized for either system), in minutes. Measurements for up to three APs were performed with an IBM 4341 host, except for the molecular dynamics runs; all runs with more APs took place with an IBM 4381 host.

ELAPSED TIME FOR LCAP-1 (Minutes)					
JOB	1 AP	3 APs	6 APs	CRAY-1s	10 APs†
Integrals (27 atoms)	71.7	24.0	12.3	10.6	7.8
SCF (27 atoms)	46.7	21.0	17.5	8.6	12.0
Integrals (42 atoms)	203.4	68.9	38.3	32.3	21.1
SCF (42 atoms)	108.5	44.9	34.1	19.6	22.0
Integrals (87 atoms)	2163	730	380	309	247
Monte Carlo	162.1	57.8	32.0	28.4	18.1
Molecular Dynamics	87.1	38.3	23.1	20.1	—

* Application codes have not been optimized.

† Applications using 10 APs were run with an IBM-4381 host. Cases with fewer number of APs were run with an IBM-4341 host.

Table 1b. Computational Chemistry Applications Comparisons
   Comparison between the LCAP-1 system on selected applications in Table 1a
   versus the CRAY XMP with one processor. Lower repeated entries are several
   applications with code modifications (see text).

ELAPSED TIME FOR LCAP-1 (Minutes)					
JOB	1 AP	3 APs	6 APs	10 APs	CRAY-XMP
Integrals (27 atoms)	71.7	24.0	12.3	7.8	7.6
SCF (27 atoms)	46.7	21.0	17.5	12.0	6.8
Integrals (42 atoms)	203.4	68.9	38.3	21.2	23.2
SCF (42 atoms)	108.5	44.9	34.1	22.0	20.4
Monte Carlo	162.1	57.8	32.0	22.0	20.4
Molecular Dynamics	87.1	38.3	23.3	—	19.8
SCF (27 Atoms)	25.2	9.4	5.9	4.9	3.6
SCF (42 atoms)	73.0	26.0	14.3	10.6	8.7
Molecular Dynamics	99.6	34.6	19.3	13.7	17.0
Seismic	33.8	11.8	6.6	4.3	5.6

Table 1c. Computational Chemistry Applications Comparisons
   Comparison between the LCAP-2 system on selected applications in Table 1a
   versus the CRAY XMP with one processor. Lower repeated entries are several
   applications with code modifications (see text).

ELAPSED TIME FOR LCAP-2 (Minutes)					
JOB	1 AP	3 APs	6 APs	10 APs	CRAY-XMP
Integrals (27 atoms)	19.1	6.5	3.3	2.3	7.6
SCF (27 atoms)	13.6	5.5	4.2	2.7	6.8
Integrals (42 atoms)	55.0	18.7	9.3	6.1	23.2
SCF (42 atoms)	30.0	11.1	7.0	5.3	13.5
Monte Carlo	60.0	20.9	11.4	7.7	20.4
Molecular Dynamics	29.6	10.6	5.9	4.2	17.0
SCF (27 Atoms)	10.6	5.2	3.7	3.4	3.6
SCF (42 atoms)	24.1	9.1	5.6	4.7	8.7

where it is seen that three APs have aproximately the same performance. In all cases, we see some degradation from full parallelism. For example considering LCAP-1, for the integrals run with 42 atoms (see Table 1a) we would expect the three-AP result to be $\frac{1}{3}$ the execution time with one AP or 67.8 minutes. The actual execution time for three APs is 68.9 minutes, so we have a little over a minute of "overhead time" in this case. Additional overhead shows up as one progresses from three to six APs, and from six to ten APs. The causes of this overhead, and the strategies that can be used to minimize it, have already been discussed in Section IV.

To illustrate more comprehensively the degradation to parallelism as a function of the number of APs employed and the problem size, the representative case of the integrals program is chosen. In Figure 2 are shown the elapsed times as bar graphs for three problems of successively larger size. They are the solutions for a system with respectively 27, 42, and 87 atoms. Also indicated are the percent parallelizations for each solution as a function of the number of APs used. We define this metric as

$$\% = \text{total-job-time}_{(1AP)} \times \frac{100}{(n \times \text{total-job-time}_{(nAPs)})}. \qquad (6)$$

This measure expresses the gain in execution time when going from one AP to n APs in units of what is theoretically reachable. It is identical to the efficiency factor, $f(P,A)$, expressed as a percent, as employed in Equation (2) in the previous section. The corresponding speedup factor may be calculated simply as the number of APs multiplied by this percent.

It is evident from this figure that, for a given size problem, the performance decreases as the parallel portion of the job is distributed more thinly over increasing numbers of processors. This is a consequence of emphasizing, in a relative manner, the portion of the problem that must be performed serially, the increased number of data transfers required and synchronization overhead that must be paid. As is also evident, increasing the problem size readjusts the parallel grain size upwards and reimproves overall performance in this case. This result will always obtain when parallel computation grows at a much larger rate than the competing sequential execution and data transmission. We should note that small problems probably do not need supercomputer systems; thus the trend is exactly in the correct direction.

We now consider four applications that were ported to our laboratory through the visitors' program. They are representative of much larger class of such codes that have been successfully adapted to the LCAP system. Much of the following information is extracted from reports (not published as yet) made by the pertinent visitors on their perceptions of the physics of their applications, the degree of inherent parallelism therein, and the relative ease of use of the LCAP system [15, 16, 17, 18].

The first case considered is a program developed at McMaster University in Ontario, Canada. The code, PROAIMS, is used in the theoretical analysis of atoms in molecules [16]. Within such a structure an atom may be uniquely defined by the topologic properties of the charge density. Thus atomic boundaries are implied by solving for surfaces through which the flux of the first derivative of the charge density is zero. The estimated properties are then computed by integrating the appropriate quantum mechanical operators over the volume of the atom in question.

As suggested, this calculation may be considered in two distinct phases

a.

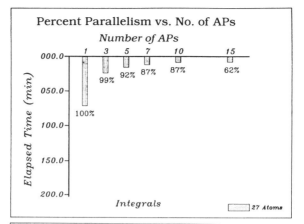

b.

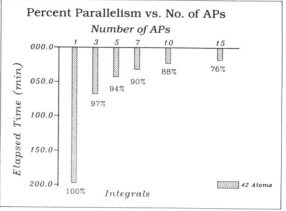

c.

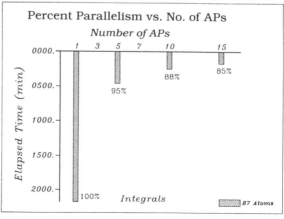

—the first is the determination of the volume's surface and the second the actual integration. Considering the first part, the root of calculation lies in tracing a large set of paths of the charge density over various surfaces. Each such path may be considered computationally independently. Thus the algorithm seems to be well suited for parallel processing. However the procedure is complicated by the requirement that no two paths be further apart than some preassigned distance from one another. Should this requirement be violated it is necessary to dynamically insert one or more additional paths. Thus in order to distribute the work load as efficiently as possibly over the slave APs, or stated equivalently to perform load balancing, it was determined that a parcel policy be adopted. In this method the master processor keeps an internal list of all the paths that must be traced and successively allocates to each slave a small portion of these. Upon completion the slave processors asynchronously receive their next allocations. Thus the dynamic expansion of the list that occurs as computation proceeds may be distributed evenly among processors.

The second part of the program involves the actual volume integrations. In the sequential version of the program they are carried out over regularly spaced rays starting from the atomic nucleus and extending to the surface. This portion of the program seems to be well suited to parallel execution as well. Further since there are no "on-the-fly" adjustments as there were in the first part, implementation is easily accomplished by giving to each AP the task of performing the integrations over fixed and equal segments of space.

With the program modified in this manner, calculations were performed to estimate properties of C atoms in the molecular structure of $C_3H_7PC_3$. The total elapsed times ranged from 44 minutes with one AP to six minutes with eight APs. The overall performance is indicated in Figure 3a, illustrating both the speedup factor and the percent parallelization as a function of the number of APs employed. Here is seen the usual degradation of performance as the parallel grain size decreases. This is largely attributed to the first part of the program, where 100% parallelization is never attained due to the host/slave communication required to dynamically load-balance the system.

In the following two examples we consider applications that require the

---

Figure 2. a: Degradation to parallel performance on increasing the number of slave processors cooperating on the solution of the integrals problem for a molecule of 27 atoms.
b: As in a, but for a molecule of 42 atoms.
c: As in a, but for a molecule of 87 atoms.

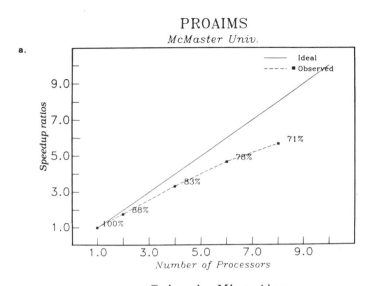

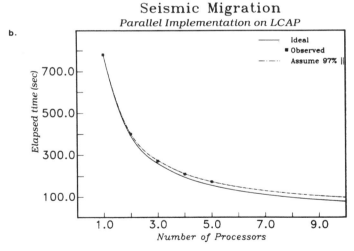

Figure 3. a: Performance of the parallel version of the program PROAIMS (property of atoms in molecules) on the LCAP-1 system.
b: Performance of the parallel version of the PSPI seismic data analysis program on LCAP-1. With 10 processors the percent parallelization is 75%.

analysis of large amounts of experimental data in two entirely different fields. The respective storage requirements of the raw data represents a related problem that is of paramount importance in both areas. This latter problem will not be explicitly dealt with here. Rather we will focus our concern on the treatment of this data by parallel processing.

First we consider an important application in determining subsurface geologic structures through the analysis of seismic data. In a typical seismic study, a pressure wave generated by a source (an explosion generally) is dispersed by reflective surfaces inside the earth and then measured by detectors placed on the surface. The problem to be solved is to derive the geometries of the reflective structures from the pressure/time measurements collected over a specified grid of detectors.

The essence of the calculation, considering for simplicity only one surface dimension, is the solution of the scalar wave equation:

$$\frac{\partial^2 p}{\partial^2 z} = \left(\frac{1}{v^2}\right) * \frac{\partial^2 p}{\partial^2 t} - \frac{\partial^2 p}{\partial^2 x}, \tag{7}$$

where x is the surface coordinate, z is the depth coordinate, t is time, v the velocity of the pressure wave in a particular medium, and p is the pressure. It is the latter variable's values that we wish to map out over the subsurface domain from the boundary data recorded. Discontinuities over this domain will reveal the structures sought.

The problem posed in this manner is not amenable to parallel computation. However, if the equation and the boundary values are transformed from the time/position domain to the frequency/wave number representation (by a standard double Fourier transform), then the equation reduces to a large set of independent equations, one for each frequency component. These may be solved in parallel to map out partial pressures as a function of depth. Finally, discontinuities in total pressure may be deduced when all the partial pressures are summed. To retrieve the original coordinates of pressure/time, the inverse Fourier transforms are applied (in parallel) prior to the summation. This procedure in essence is the method called Phase Shift Plus Interpolation proposed by Gazdag and Squazzero [15].

The problem was decomposed as described above and run on the LCAP system. The sequential part of the calculation that remained in the master consisted of a time normalization on the measured data followed by the initial two-dimensional Fourier transform. The master then issued to each slave a subset of the total number of frequencies and the task of performing the pressure tracking (called migration) for each frequency. On completing these tasks, each slave performed the back transformation and reported its data to the master. Here the summation was done and output as a mapping of the subterranean structure. [15]

A test case was run for a problem size of 256 by 256 (number of detector points, number of times samples) and for a depth of 256 units of the same magnitude. The elapsed times using different numbers of APs as slaves are shown in Table 2. The first column reports these values for the original code while the second indicates those times when more efficient math library routines were introduced (e.g. pipelined ffts). In both cases the percent parallelizations are given in parentheses. Figure 3b illustrates the elapsed times versus number of slaves and compares this with the ideal minimum. The fit to the data points corresponds to an implied result that the parallelizable portion of the original code constituted 97%. Successive degradation on increasing the number of processors results from the increased relative significance of the sequential 3%. Initial measurements indicate that most of this degradation is due to the host-to-slave I/O, namely the transfer of the 256-by-256 binary matrices. While the speedup is impressive, we judge that increased performance will be obtained by extending the method to two-dimensional geometries of detectors and three-dimensional volumes where the parallel computation becomes ever more dominant.

In the second of our data analysis applications, we examine the field of experimental medium or high-energy physics. To aid us in studying this area for application to parallel processing, a joint study was done with a number of researchers who perform experiments at the accelerator complex at CERN, Switzerland. High-energy physics (HEP) computing involves processing large quantities of real data gathered by complex and imperfect devices. It is also necessary to make Monte Carlo simulations of the data, under various assumptions about the underlying physics. HEP detectors are necessarily asymmetric and time-dependent devices, and extraction of the maximum information from such apparatus requires large computer programs with very many conditional branches. Typically

Table 2. Timings for the PSPI LCAP-1
parallel code (in seconds).
Seismic data analysis code performance
on the LCAP-1 system. First column employs user math routines while the second employs the FPS math library.

	Original Code	Math-Library
1 AP	2300	782
2 AP	1038 (97.8%)	402 (97.3%)
3 AP	—	274 (95.1%)
4 AP	—	212 (92.2%)
5 AP	—	175 (89.4%)

one FORTRAN statement in three is an 'IF.' Thus a large fraction of HEP code cannot be pipelined, and even where pipelining is possible its recognition by the compiler is impeded.

However, the applicability of the parallel processing concept to high-energy physics computing is obvious. Since data come in independent units of one event, and a few thousand of them can be processed independently with any granularity, the problem is inherently parallelizable without great effort. Moreover as far as the simulation task is concerned, parallel execution can even be implemented on the track level, since showers caused by different primary particles are independent until digitization occurs.

The strategy thus employed in adapting these programs for parallel processing was the parcel policy employed in the previous example of determining properties of atoms in molecules. A slave processor, in executing either a simulation code or in analyzing experimental data, would be given a fixed number of events to process from a large pool of such events. Upon completing the analysis of this parcel, the host would dynamically assign to it a new parcel. Load balancing was achieved by the asynchronous execution of the slave processors.

Two typical programs were run to determine the effectiveness of this strategy. The first, a code named GHEISHA, was a Monte Carlo code to simulate detector response to hadron showers formed in nuclear collisions. The second was a typical data analysis routine. Left to the programmer's discretion was the specification of how many events constituted one parcel. The codes were run with various sizes to investigate the effect of increasing the parallel grain size. It was found that with any more than 10 events per parcel very good performance was obtained. Typical results for the first program with 100 events per parcel are shown in Figure 4, which illustrates as a function of the number of slaves used the elapsed times (a), the percent parallelisms (b), and the fractional load on the host (c). With 10 APs it is seen that 90% parallelization is obtained while 10% of the execution is involved in data transfers initiated by the host. Similar behavior is observed for the second program as shown in Table 3. It is to be noted that improvement in these results is simply achieved by increasing the parcel size because a major portion of the data transmission time (the I/O latency) is constant and independent of the number of data items transferred. In summary it is felt that applications of this type are ideally suited to parallel processing and that this conclusion holds for a substantial fraction of HEP codes in general.

These last three examples, ported to the LCAP system through the visitors' program, illustrate that a high degree of parallelism may be exploited in a variety of diverse applications. To reinforce this conclusion we briefly mention several additional among many such codes that achieve similar

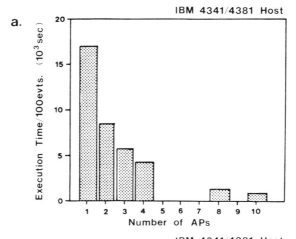

a.

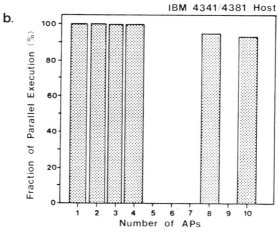

b.

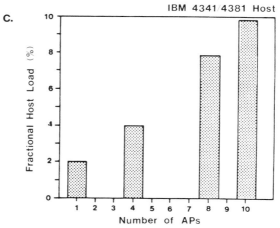

c.

Table 3. Performance of LCAP-1 for the parallel GEANT task.
Performance of the high-energy physics data analysis program on the LCAP-1 system.

Host	# of APs	# of Events	Time Per Event (sec)	Fraction of Parallel Ex. (%)	Host Load (%)
4341	1	100	51.0	(100)	<0.5
4341	2	100	25.6	99	<1.0
4341	3	200	17.5	97	<1.0

results. Illustrated in Figure 5 are the performance graphs of four such programs. One of these, the program ASTAP, is an IBM Installed User Program (IUP; program number 5796-PBH) used in circuit analysis and simulation. Another is a program employed at Tampere in Finland to study the dynamics of crystal growth in fabricating wafers such as silicon semiconductors [22]. A third was originally written at Cornell University to obtain the equilibrium structure of such macromolecules as proteins; presently it is jointly used to investigate the structure of interferon [23]. And lastly is illustrated an application from the University of Florida used to predict the mass of the fundamental particle of the neutrino [24]. These examples are representative of a much larger body of programs that have been successfully adapted for parallelism on the LCAP system.

To complete this brief survey of applications on the initial LCAP system we now consider the area of parallel algorithm development. As a very simple example, the algorithm considered here is a parallel version of matrix-by-matrix multiplication. The performance was measured on the LCAP system by the Triangle Universities Computation Center (TUCC) situated in North Carolina as part of their benchmarking program on supercomputers. It was selected because it is easy to write, the results can be easily and automatically verified, and further the number of floating-point operations required can be computed accurately. Thus the execution speed (in Mflops — millions of floating-point operations per second) may be measured without any problems resulting from different possible paths through a complex application program.

The manner chosen to implement the parallel matrix multiplication was straightforward; each processor was designated the task of calculating an

Figure 4. a: Execution times of the high-energy physics Monte Carlo code on LCAP-1 as a function of the number of APs employed.
b: Percent parallelizations for the applications in a.
c: Fractional load on the host for the applications in a.

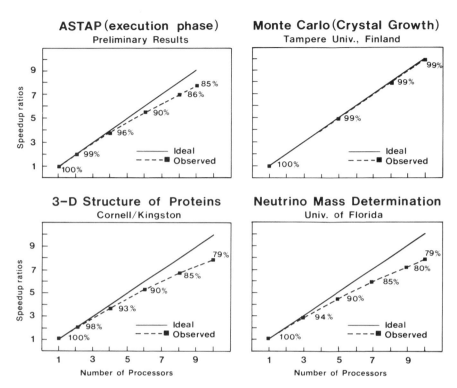

Figure 5. Performance of four additional programs run on the LCAP-1 system. They are: a program (ASTAP) used in the simulation and analysis of circuits; a Monte Carlo code to examine the dynamics of crystal growth; a program to determine the equilibrium structure of proteins; and a code used to predict the mass of the neutrino.

equal but different fraction of the final columns of the result matrix. In order that this be accomplished, each processor was required to receive prior to calculation the entire body of the first matrix and a corresponding fraction of columns of the second matrix. Each processor thereafter performed independent calculations in obtaining their portions of the final result matrix. Load balancing was achieved by segmenting the columns as evenly as possible among processors. The final step consisted of the complementary communication from slaves to host of partial results for final assembly.

An important aspect of this experiment was to model the entire process such that auxiliary information, such as effective communication speed, could be extracted from the time measurements. Therefore included in the calculation was an adjustable parameter that dictated the number of times the kernel computation was to be redundantly performed within each slave prior to reporting its results to the host. Typical results for a 300-by-300 problem size as a function of this repetition factor and the number of APs employed are shown in Figure 6. Figure 6a shows elapsed times for job completion while Figure 6b illustrates aggregate computational rates.

Evident from these measurements is the familiar pattern of performance enhancement as parallel computation grain size grows in comparison to communication. Near linear speedup is realized with a repetition factor of 300, i.e. the Mflops rate increases linearly with the number of APs used. However, because the problem is well structured in terms of operational sequence, it is possible to extract more basic information from these measurements. To do this it is necessary to build models that describe the overlap of communication and calculation that obtains in spawning off the subtasks to the slaves. One such model is shown in Figure 7a for the case where the calculational phase is greater than the data transfer phase per processor. Indicated in Figure 7b is the reverse case.

Based on such models and including the easily computed number of floating-point operations required per subtask and the amount of data transferred, it is possible to fit the measured completion times to functional forms that include as extractable parameters the base-processor execution rates and the effective data transfer capabilities.

For the 300-by-300 matrix case, it was found that the individual base processor (the AP) executed at an effective rate of 9.9 Mflops while receiving and sending data to the master at approximately 0.6 Mbytes/sec. The smooth curves in Figure 6 represent the least-square fits to the data within the context of the models and with these parameter values. For the 100-by-100 matrix case, the values were found by a similar least-square fit to be 9.3 Mflops and 0.9 Mbytes/sec. These processing speeds may be compared to the maximum achievable rate of 11 Mflops that is obtained if full pipelining is realized. These results are due in large part to employing the FPS math library dot-product routine required in calculating matrix elements. This routine, like the others in this library, is expressly written to achieve high performance.

The two parameter models are able to describe the major features of the measured data, yielding plausible values for both the processing speeds and the data transfer speeds. However, the slight variation in these values as a function of problem size indicates that more terms may be needed in the models. For example, to reconcile the variation in processor speeds it may be necessary to incorporate a term that describes the overhead in initiating and terminating dot-product pipelines as a function of vector length. The

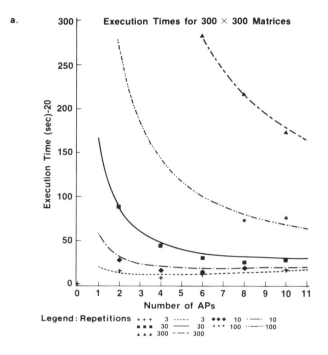

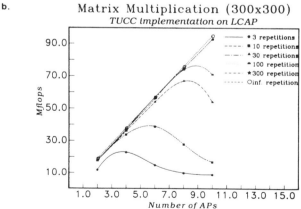

Figure 6. a: Execution times for performing a parallel matrix multiply on the LCAP-1 system. The repetition factor refers to the number of times the kernel calculation is redundantly performed prior to synchronization.
b: Sustained execution rated for the matrix multiplies of above.

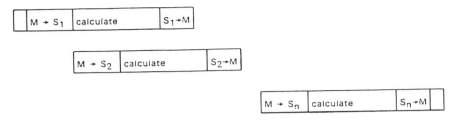

a. Overlap between calculation and data transfer for **long** calculation times;

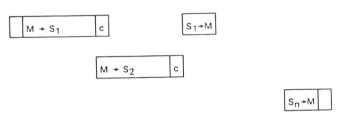

b. Overlap between calculation and data transfer for **short** calculation times.

Figure 7. Models employed in extracting performance data on the LCAP system for the matrix multiply algorithm (base processor execution rate and data transmission speed between host and slaves).

variation in transfer speeds may be attributable to the effects of such system factors as buffer sizes, saturation of I/O capacities or perhaps data-size-dependent algorithms for scheduling I/O. Additional and much more detailed measurements would be necessary to clear up these points.

In conclusion, this example as well as the previous ones demonstrate that it is possible to achieve a high degree of parallelism on the LCAP system provided that enough work per byte transferred can be done by the slaves and that the proper number of slaves is selected. In short, LCAP does work, it can be very cost effective, it requires intelligent users, and it can be used to solve significant problems that may be beyond the limits of sequential processing.

VI. Extended LCAP, Applications and Performance

From the previous section it would appear that many scientific programs naturally decompose into parallel structures and further that a loosely coupled approach to their solution is a method that works with high efficiency. However, left undiscussed were a large subset of applications that require a more tightly coupled approach to solution. By more tightly coupled we imply the ability of direct and rapid communication between slave processors without the need of message passing through a host intermediary.

Many examples of the latter type are found for example in the areas of hydro- or fluid dynamics. There the partial differential equations that describe the system are usually discretized by either finite difference or element approximations and coupled with boundary conditions; this may lead to the need of iteratively solving large sets of linear equations. Many algorithms, either direct or iterative, are available for the solution of such systems of equations. Moreover such solvers may often decompose into parallel structures [25]. However, it is usually the case that the ability to communicate intermediate data between the processors involved in the parallel computation presents a bottleneck when a master/slave topology is employed. This is particularly the case with the initial LCAP system, where one master serves a large number of slaves and the maximum communication rate between host and slave is approximately three Mbytes/sec.

To address problems of this nature the basic LCAP architecture was extended in two independent but complementary ways, both of which increase the speed of AP-to-AP communication. The first was to incorporate six shared memories, developed by Scientific Computing Associates (SCA), that are directly addressable by the APs. Five of these memories are each 32 Mbytes in capacity and support four-way multiplexing. They are connected to the 10 APs in a double ring topology. Each memory is capable of a peak transfer rate to an AP of 44 Mbytes/sec. on LCAP-1 and 38 Mbyte/sec. on LCAP-2. The sixth memory was 512 Mbytes in size and was multiplexed 12 ways. It thus represented a global shared memory for the 10 APs. The peak bandwidth of the latter is approximately 130 Mbytes/sec. A diagram of LCAP-1 and LCAP-2 with these inclusions is shown in Figure 8. As is also evident in this figure the structure of LCAP has evolved into a single host system (an dyadic IBM 3081 for LCAP-1 and a four-processor IBM 3084 for LCAP-2).

The second approach to improving interprocessor communication was the inclusion of a fast bus, built by FPS, that directly links all 10 APs. It is also represented in Figure 8. This bus supports broadcasting as well as direct communication between any two APs. It is 32 bits wide and has a peak 32 Mbytes/sec. transfer speed from node to node and 22 Mbytes/sec. rate AP to node. The software to use the shared memories was initially developed by SCA [26] and later extended by us to include functions such as synchronization, locks and memory management, all accessible through user-friendly precompiler directives. The software to employ the fast bus was developed by FPS [27].

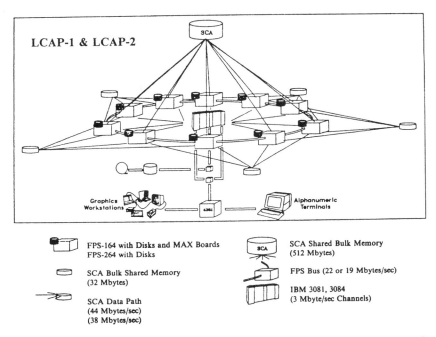

LCAP-1 & LCAP-2

	FPS-164 with Disks and MAX Boards FPS-264 with Disks		SCA Shared Bulk Memory (512 Mbytes)
	SCA Bulk Shared Memory (32 Mbytes)		FPS Bus (22 or 19 Mbytes/sec)
	SCA Data Path (44 Mbytes/sec) (38 Mbytes/sec)		IBM 3081, 3084 (3 Mbyte/sec Channels)

Figure 8. Expanded structure of the LCAP systems using shared memories and fast buses to achieve tight coupling between the APs.

The FPSBUS software is based on a message-passing scheme; the user has to specify from which processor to which processor data is to be sent and received. If the same data is to be sent from one processor to all the others then the broadcast mode can be used. On the other hand, the facilities provided by the precompiler for using the bulk memories offer a choice of two modes of communication: shared memory and message passing. In the shared mode, the data to be shared is stored in memory at locations known to all the processors, and it is passed between processors by specifying a write-of-data from one processor and a read-of-data by another. In the message-passing mode, messages, in the form of contiguous blocks of data, are passed between processors via a network of paths transparent to the user, who specifies in his code the "send" and the "receive" transactions along with the targeted processors.

Performance measurements have been made, using as processors either the FPS-164s or -264s, exploiting the three communication schemes described above for the three patterns of data transmission given in Figure 9. Pattern a has been called the STAR. In this configuration one processor (considered the master) sends data to the others (the slaves). Pattern b has been called the RING (RNG for short). In this case each processor sends

a.

b.

c.

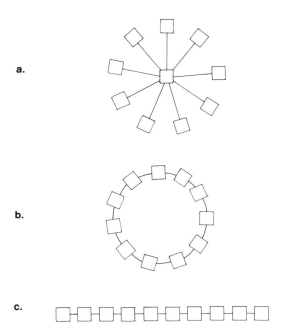

Figure 9. Three communication topologies studied for interprocessor transmission rates: STAR, RING, and LINE.

and receives data from its two neighboring processors. Pattern c has been called LINE (LN for short). This configuration can be achieved by cutting the RING configuration, so that the two end processors have only one neighbor.

The measurements varied numbers of processors, the configurations and data transmission sizes. In the top two insets of Figure 10 we report the results for the minimum number of processors used in each configuration (two for pattern a and three for b and c) for the FPS-164s and FPS-264s respectively. In the bottom two insets the curves are for the same cases but using eight processors. Plotted are the measured transmission rates per receiving processor in Mbytes/sec. (ordinate) against the logarithm (base 10) of the number of bytes transmitted (abscissa). Data sizes range from 8 bytes (one word) up to 800K bytes (100K words).

The notation for each curve in Figure 10 has to be interpreted as follows. First the configuration is specified, either RNG, LN, STAR or BROAD for broadcast. STAR is assumed to differ from broadcast in that different data is sent to each receiving processor. Next the device used for the communication is given, namely BUS means that the transaction occurs through the

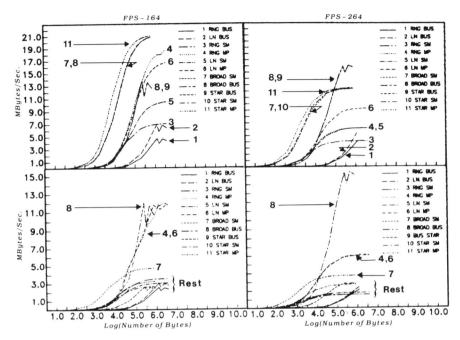

Figure 10. Transmission rates (Mbytes/sec.) per receiving processor as a function of communication topologies shown in Figure 9, and number of bytes transferred. Top left is for minimum number of processors using LCAP-1. Top right is for minimum number of processors on LCAP-2. Bottom left is for eight processors using LCAP-1. Bottom right is for eight processors using LCAP-2. For a detailed description of the legend see text.

FPS-BUS, SM is the short notation for the bulk memories in shared mode and MP for the bulk memories in message passing mode.

Two features are common to all curves illustrated in Figure 10, namely the notable initialization delay (latency) time (see how "slowly" the curves rise up) and the consistent degradation in going from two to eight nodes (compare top curves with bottom ones). Concerning the degradation one notes that the total bandwidth to a particular device, be that a shared memory or the bus, remains roughly the same (of the order of 22 Mbytes/ sec.), but that it is more or less divided evenly between the number of processors accessing it. Thus for eight processors the asymptotic rates per processor are of the order of 3 Mbytes/sec., i.e. at rates typical of the peak performance of the channels. For example, using the bulk memories in the STAR configuration in shared mode, 22 Mbytes may be transferred in 1 sec. if one FPS-164 processor is used but of the order of 3 Mbytes are transferred per processor in 1 sec., when eight processors are used. The corresponding numbers are approximately 13 and 2 Mbytes/sec. when the LCAP-2 FPS-264 processors are used (different implementations of the I/O ports for the FPS-164 and -264 are responsible for these differences in performance). The latencies are due in most part to software path and not hardware and thus there exists the possibility of improving small transfers significantly.

The implications of relative performances of these communication modes for a representative application were studied for a Metropolis Monte Carlo calculation. Here we study the dynamics of 512 water molecules confined in a periodic box and subject to two- and three-body potentials. Using such simple potentials (compared to, for example, four-body potentials) implies that the parallel grain size, i.e. how much work is distributed to each parallel processor, is relatively small when compared to the frequency and the amount of data communication needed between processors. Shown in Figure 11 are speedup curves for this application as a

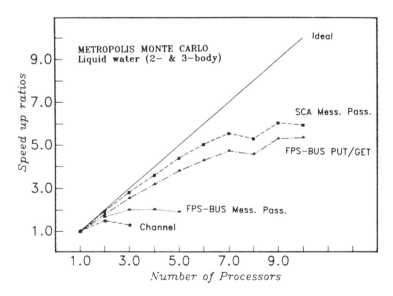

Figure 11. Performance curves for executing a Metropolis Monte Carlo code as a function of communication devices used. Problem is for simulation of liquid water using 512 molecules and employing two- and three-body potentials. FPS-BUS PUT/GET refers to use of FPS primitives; FPS-BUS Mess. Pass. refers to extended software.

function of the number of processors employed and the communication mode. It is seen that channel communication is wholly inadequate for such a problem size but that the bus or shared memories give reasonable performance (and that the bulk memories are optimal).

To make the preceding example more definitive we consider the performance of several applications which correspond to successive levels of decreasing parallel grain size. Parallel grain size is defined in a relative manner by comparing the amount of computation that can be distributed among cooperative processors to the amount of communication that is required between them.

The study and prediction of the motion of water-borne particles in bay areas subject to tidal forces is critically dependent upon the ability to solve for the tide-induced residual circulation [28]. We present here the solution of the tide-induced residual circulation in Buzzard's Bay and Vineyard Sound, Massachusetts. The problem is formulated by specifying the boundary conditions and applying a finite difference discretization of the two-dimensional shallow water equations. These in turn are obtained by depth-averaging the full three-dimensional equations which express the conservation of mass and momentum of a fluid in motion. Since the sought-for features, which include current direction and water elevation, are typically small scale, the number of grid cells needed to resolve the flow even in modest domains can be very high. In the model problem, a grid size of order 200-by-200 was chosen and is shown superimposed over the region in Figure 12a. The solutions obtained were found to be consistent with the observed means at several locations. The parallelization strategy for this computation was to partition the explicit updating of grid points, per time step, evenly among processors, i.e. domain decomposition. This calculation may be considered to be characterized by a large parallel grain size as there is order n^2 parallel computations to be completed for every synchronization that requires order n data exchanges between processors. The parallel performance, using LCAP-1 with shared memories and exploiting the LINE interprocessor communication topology required of this problem, is shown in Figure 12b. Previous experience with the same program, without using the shared memories, resulted in a "speed down," i.e. the computation time increased with the number of processors [29].

Next we consider a problem of smaller parallel grain size. The pseudospectral method is a relatively recent method for the solution of time-dependent partial differential equations. It is gaining in importance because of the very high accuracies achieved with this technique [30]. It works by using a dual representation of the variables in the physical grid domain and wave number domain, and performing a transformation between them at every timestep. High efficiencies in the transformations

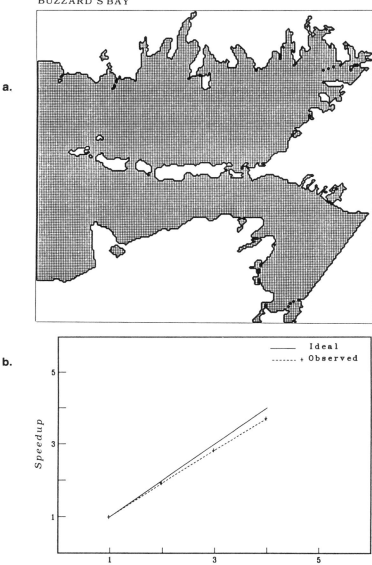

Figure 12. a: Buzzard's Bay, Massachusetts, with computational 200-by-200 grid superimposed for finite difference discretization of shallow water equations solution.

b: Performance of the shallow water simulation program with the LCAP-1 system using shared bulk memories for interprocessor communication.

between the two representations are achieved through the use of the fast Fourier transform. This constitutes the major computational component of the calculations. A 2-D program that employs this technique for the solution of a hyperbolic equation, that in turn can be used to describe pollution migration, was adapted to the LCAP-1 system. The model problem dealt with advection of an initial concentration of pollutants (shown in Figure 13a), in a region with a circular velocity distribution and is described in [31]. To make this program run in parallel required the development of a block two-dimensional parallel fast Fourier transform [32]. The observed efficiencies for various problem sizes, indicated in Figure 13b, were obtained using a shared bulk memory to effect the parallel block

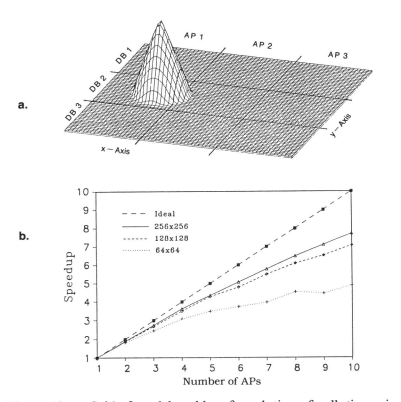

Figure 13. a: Grid of model problem for solution of pollution migration. Pollutant concentration indicated by cone. Domain decomposition for parallel processing for three processors indicated by dark lines.
b: Performance of model problem for various grid sizes as a function of number of processors employed on LCAP-1. Bulk shared memory used for interprocessor communication.

transpose operation required in a two dimensional transform. Again previous experience, for similar problem sizes but using channel communication to the host, showed an increase in running time with increasing processors. The parallel grain size of this calculation was of order $n^2\log(n)$ while synchronization and data exchanges required order n^2 operations. It is apparent from this figure that an efficient parallel implementation requires dealing with problems that are large if one wants to use many processors.

At a smallest level of parallel grain size we consider the parallel implementation of the multigrid algorithm. This method is one of the fastest techniques for the solution of systems of algebraic equations originating from the discretization of elliptic partial differential equations [33]. The domain of solution is covered by a scheme of nested grids, with the major computations being the smoothing of the solution, restriction of the residual and prolongation of the solution at various grid levels. Of these operations only the smoothing operation is an intrinsically sequential procedure. However, if a red-black ordering is employed for the grid points then both the smoothing operation is made more efficient and the operation can be implemented in parallel. Red-black ordering is a process of "coloring" alternate nodes in the grid; the smoothing is done alternately for the red nodes and then for the black nodes. The parallel efficiency of the overall process, on the LCAP-1, when used for the model problem of solving Poisson's equation on a square is shown in Figure 14 for a small problem size of 128-by-128. Again it is to be noted that running this algorithm without a shared memory (using the host channels for communication), would result in a slowdown rather than a speedup with increasing processors. The order of complexity of the parallel computation and that needed synchronization and data exchanges for each grid size n are similar to the explicit solver described above, i.e. n^2 and n respectively. However, because the problem as a whole proceeds through a series of smaller and coarser grids at each iteration, the parallel grain size is effectively much smaller for the multigrid algorithm when comparing equal size problems. This unfavorable balance is reflected in the relatively poor performance shown and, unlike the previous examples, cannot be as dramatically improved by addressing larger size problems.

The above examples, which emphasize the parallel implementation of explicit solver, fast Fourier transforms and the multigrid method respectively, illustrate the great importance of parallel algorithm work. This is particularly relevant to engineering applications where often the ability to parallelize a code is tantamount to being able to solve large linear systems or solve eigenvalue problems in parallel. Thus we have developed parallel linear system solvers for dense systems (LU and Cholesky factorization) as

PARALLEL RED-BLACK MULTIGRID

Poisson Equation

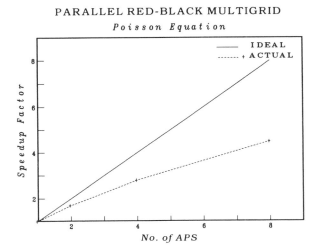

Figure 14. Performance curves for executing a parallel Multi-Grid algorithm for the solution of Poisson's equation on a square using LCAP-1 and bulk shared memory. Grid size is 128-by-128 and 7 lower nested levels.

well as techniques for sparse systems (such as Conjugate Gradients with different degrees of preconditioning). For eigenvalue solvers we have experimented successfully with parallel block Jacobi methods as well as traditional methods based on Householder reductions. To perform linear least square problems in parallel we have developed parallel versions of both QR factorization (using either block Givens rotations or Householder reductions) as well as block versions of Single Value Decompositions. Additionally we are beginning to explore the parallel potential of optimization algorithms such as linear programming's Simplex algorithm and that due to Karmarkar. Details of some of these efforts may be found in references [34, 35, 36].

In the previous examples we have considered nuclei, electrons, atoms and molecules, liquids and solutions, simple fluids, and applications in meteorology and oceanography. It seems proper to conclude with an application in celestial mechanics. Project Spaceguard is a numerical experiment, carried out by Drs. Milani and Carpino (University of Pisa), dedicated to understanding the long-term dynamics of planet-crossing asteroids. It is meant to extend and improve current theory based on analytic and semianalytic models [37] that attempt to predict asteroid–planet probabilities of collision. The calculations differ from traditional computations of hierarchical organized planetary trajectories [38] by recognizing the essential chaotic nature of the asteroids' orbits, i.e. they are associated with positive Lyapunov exponents. The experiment was thus a statistical measurement that involved integrating through classical mechanics the positions of all known, approximately 400, asteroids whose orbits intersect those of Earth, Venus and Mars in conjunction with the seven major planets of the solar system over a time span of 200,000 years.

The computation amounted to approximately 8.5 Teraflops and generated approximately 3 Gigabytes of output associated with nearly one half million close encounters. The statistical analysis of the output is in progress. These calculations were performed on the LCAP-2 system using 10 APs for approximately 40 hours and at a sustained rate of 95 Mflops. The parallelization efficiency corresponded to approximately 90% of linear speedup and was achieved by partitioning the calculation of the orbits of the asteroids and the planets evenly between the available processors. In particular one processor was responsible for the planets' orbits and all output to the host. The remaining processors divided up the asteroids and received data at a given number of time steps from the planet-tracking processor of the planets' positions. Communication between these processors was achieved through the shared memories. Computation was thus both parallel and pipelined. Futher details of this calculation may be found in [39].

Lastly we mention two further experiments in parallel processing with LCAP systems. The first was the construction of the LCAP-3 system to explore the potential of a hierarchic and heterogeneous parallel architecture. This was achieved by linking LCAP-1 and LCAP-2 to an IBM 3090, model 200, with two processors and vector attachments. The system as a whole has a peak processing rate of well over a Gigaflop/sec. and over a Gigabyte of real memory. The pyramid structure of this system is illustrated in Figure 15a. As is evident, the large global shared memories have been employed directly to couple the LCAP-1 and LCAP-2 clusters and connect the 3090 to its own subset of FPS processors. A sample SCF program was successfully run on the entire complex, but at the expense of a large effort in programming to effectively distribute load balancing over the clusters.

Figure 15. a: Diagram of LCAP-3 showing LCAP-1 and LCAP-2 clusters coupled to an IBM 3090 (model 200, vector). Additional coupling achieved by large bulk memories.
b: One proposed structure of LCAP/3090 showing four IBM 3090s (model 300 with three tightly coupled nodes each with vector features). Coupling between 3090s achieved with channels, shared memory and a fast bus. Also indicated is a large shared disk farm.

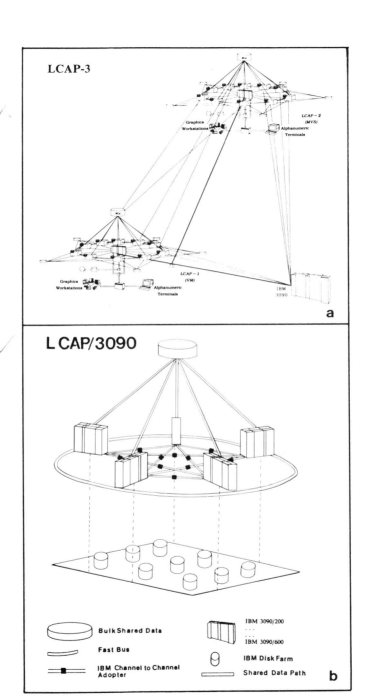

LCAP-3

Graphics
Workstations

LCAP – 2
(MVS)

Alphanumeric
Terminals

LCAP – 1
(VM)

Graphics
Workstations

Alphanumeric
Terminals

IBM
3090

a

L CAP/3090

Bulk Shared Data

Fast Bus

IBM Channel to Channel
Adapter

IBM 3090/200
· · ·
IBM 3090/600

IBM Disk Farm

Shared Data Path

b

Presently we are assembling one more supercomputer constructed of multiple clusters of processors, called LCAP-3090. In this system each cluster is an IBM-3090 system that can have up to 6 nodes (IBM-3090/ 600). We are considering up to five clusters. (In Figure 15b we have shown an LCAP-3090 built up by IBM-3090/300 clusters.) The advantages of LCAP-3090 over LCAP-3 are 1) one single vendor for all hardware and softwares, 2) very high hardware and system software reliability, 3) portability of application programs relative to LCAP-1 and LCAP-2, 4) peak performance up to 3 Giga-Flops, 5) growth opportunity starting from a single node and 6) vector hardware, system softwares and math library availability.

VII. Summary

The LCAP system seems to be well adapted to the efficient implementation of a large and diverse collection of scientific and engineering problems. Further, the extensions to the system discussed in the previous section would seem to make this parallel processing system a truly general-purpose machine. Future experiments will be needed to verify this conclusion.

A superficial examination of the methods employed in making parallel the applications discussed does not reveal a useful abstraction in describing parallel decomposition in general. Each problem or class of problems did find its own mode, for example the parcel policy of the high-energy physics problems or the transformation of the equations into a different domain as in the seismic application. Clearly, there is a need for an "in-depth" analyzer for general methods for migrating codes from sequential to parallel. We should however recall that *new* supercomputing tasks can now be written directly for our parallel systems, and with time the need of conversion might be less pressing.

The most fundamental conclusion that we wish to emphasize in closing is the following. It is essential in achieving supercomputing performance in the domain of scientific and engineering problems that computing systems be designed with maximum abilities in all computational modes. In other words, sequential, vector and parallel computation may be regarded as the three dimensions describing the space of the computations that we wish to execute. Neglecting any component will severely degrade the solution of a large subset of problems of interest today.

References

1. a) *International Conference on Parallel Processing* (August, 1981-84), Bellaire, MI.; (1985-86), St. Charles, IL.

b) Hockney, R. W., Jesshope, C. R. (1981). *Parallel Computers: Architecture, Programming and Algorithms.* Adam Hilger, Lts., Bristol.
c) *Parallel Processing Systems* (1982) (J. Evans, ed.). Cambridge University Press, Cambridge, NY.
d) Wallach, Y. (1982). "Alternating Sequential/Parallel Processing," *Lecture Notes in Computer Science* 124. Springer Verlag, Berlin, NY.
e) Corongiu, G. and Detrich, J. H. (1985). "Large Scale Scientific Applications in Chemistry and Physics on an Experimental Parallel Computer System," *IBM Journal Res. and Dev.* **29**, 422.

2. Wilson, K. R. (1975). In "Computer Networking and Chemistry" (P. Lykos, ed.), *ACS Symposium Series* 19, American Chemical Society.
3. We refer to work by Prof. C. C. J. Roothaan on this matter.
4. Flynn, M. J. (1972). "Some Computer Organizations and Their Effectiveness," *IEEE Trans. Comp.* **C-21**, 948.
5. *Virtual Machine/System Product System Programmer's Guide,* Third Edition (August 1983). Publication No. SC19-6203-2, International Business Machines Corp.
6. a) *FPS-164 Operating System Manual,* **Vols. 1–3** (January, 1983). Publication No. 860-7491-000B, Floating Point Systems, Inc.
b) Dongarra, J. J. (1985). "Performance of Various Computers Using Standard Linear Equations Software in a Fortran Environment," Argonne National Laboratory Technical Memorandum **28**.
7. Meck, D. L. (1984). "Parallelism in Executing FORTRAN Programs on the 308X: System Considerations and Application Examples," IBM Technical Report POK-38. For another set of FORTRAN-callable communications subroutines to support parallel execution on the IBM 308x under MVS, see IBM program offering 5798-DNL, developed by P. R. Martin; the Program Description Operations Manual for this program offering is IBM publication number SB21-3124 (release date May 4, 1984).
8. Mudge, T. N. and Al-Sadoun, H. B. (1985). "A Semi Markov Model for the Performance of Multiple Bus Systems," *Proceedings of the Int. Conf. on Parallel Processing,* St. Charles, IL., p. 521.
9. Kleinrock, L. (1976). *Queueing Systems,* **Vols. 1 and 2.** John Wiley and Sons, New York.
10. Kobayashi, H. (1978). *Modelling and Analysis.* Addison-Wesley, Reading, Mass.
11. Sauer, C. H., MacNair, E. A., Kurose, J. F., Heidelberger, P., Jaffe, E., Tucci, S., and Welch, P. D. (1982). "The Research Queueing Package RESQ: Present and Future," *Proceedings 1982 Performance ITL,* NY.
12. Bucher, I. Y. (1983). "The Computational Speed of Supercomputers," *Proceedings of the ACM Sigmetics Conf. on Measurement and Modeling of Computer Systems.* Minneapolis, MN.
13. Axelrod, T. S. (1985). "Comparing the Performance of Parallel Computers," *Proceedings of COMPCON.,* San Francisco, CA.
14. Clementi, E., Corongiu, G., Detrich, J. H., Khanmohammadbaigi, H., Chin, S., Domingo, L., Laaksonen, A., and Nguyen, H. L. (1984). "Parallelism in Computational Chemistry: Applications in Quantum and Statistical Mechanics," In *Structure and Motion: Membranes, Nucleic Acids and Proteins* (E Clementi, G. Corongiu, M. H. Sarma and R. H. Sarma, eds.). Adenine Press, Guilderland, NY. Clementi, E. (1985). J. Phys. Chem. **89**, 4426.
15. Gazdag, J., Squazzero, P., and the Palo Alto IBM Scientific Center, CA USA. The Seismic Data Analysis Code PSPI; L. Domingo, E. Clementi, IBM Technical Report **KGN-17,** "Parallel Computation of Migration of Seismic Data on the LCAP." Gazdag, J., Squazzero, P. (1984). *Geophysics,* **49**, 2.

16. a) Bader, R. F. W., Nguyen, T. T., and Tal, Y. (1981). *Rep. Prog. Phys.* **44**, 926.
     b) Biegler-Koonig, F. W., Bader, R. F. W. and Tang, T. H. (1982). *Journal of Compt. Chem.,* **13**, 317.
17. Carminati, F., Mount, R., Newman, H., Pohl, M., CERN Technical Report L3-313/1984.
18. H. J. Lustig, R. Y. Cusson, and J. W. Stephenson from the Triangle Universities Computation Center in North Carolina, USA.
19. Clementi, E., Corongiu, G., Detrich, J., Chin, S. and L. Domingo (1984). *Int. J. Quantum Chem. Symp.* **18**.
20. Detrich, J. H., Corongiu, G., and E. Clementi (1984). *Int. J. Quantum Chem. Symp.* **18**, 701.
21. Nguyen, H. L., Khanmohammadbaigi, H., and Clementi, E. *J. Computational Chem.* to be published.
22. Kaski, K. Nieminen, J., and Gunton, J. D. (1984). *Phys. Rev. D.* **31**, 2998.
23. Chin, S. and Clementi, E., "Tertiary Structures of Proteins," IBM report **KGN-16**. Gibson, K. D., Chin, S., Pincus, M. R., Clementi, E., and Scheraga, H. (1986). *Lecture Notes in Chemistry* (M. Dupuis, ed.). 44, 198. Springer Verlag, Berlin.
24. Kolos, W., and Wolniewicz, L. (1968). *J. Chem. Physics.* **49**, 404.
25. Ortega, J. M., and Voigt, R. G. (1985). *Solution of Partial Differential Equations on Vector and Parallel Computers.* SIAM Press, Philadelphia.
26. *Shared Bulk Memory System Software Manual,* Version 2.0 (1987). Scientific Computing Associates, Yale, New Haven, USA.
27. *FPSBUS Software Manual,* Release G (1986). Publication 860-7313-004A, Floating Point System Inc., Beavertown, Oregon, USA.
28. Csanady, G. T. (1982). *Circulation in the Coastal Ocean.* Kluwer Academic Press, Reidel, Holland.
29. Capotondi, A., Signell, R., Beardsley, R., and Sonnad, V. (1987). "Time Induced Residual Circulation Simulated on a Parallel Computer," IBM Technical Report KGN-132.
30. Orszag, S. A. (1972). "A Comparison of Pseudo Spectral and Spectral Approximations," *Studies in Applied Mathematics.* 51, 253.
31. Christidis, Z. D., and Sonnad, V. (1987). "Parallel Implementation of a Pseudo Spectral Method on a Loosely Coupled Array of Processors," IBM Technical Report KGN-143.
32. Christidis, Z. D., Sonnad, V., and Logan, D. (1987). "Parallel Implementation of a 2D Fast Fourier Transform on a Loosely Coupled Array of Processors," IBM Technical Report KGN-68.
33. Hackbusch, W. (1985). *Multi-Grid Methods and Applications.* Springer Verlag, Berlin.
34. Clementi, E., Logan, D., and Sonnad, V. (1987). "Parallel Solution of Fundamental Algorithms Using a Loosely Coupled Array of Processors," IBM Technical Report KGN-105.
35. Van Loan, C. (1986). "A Block QR Factorization Scheme for Loosely Coupled Systems of Array Processors," *Proceedings of Algorithms for Modern Parallel Computers.* University of Minnesota, MN., USA.
36. Bischof, C. (1987). "Computing the Singular Value Decomposition on a Distributed System of Vector Processors," Cornell University Computer Science Technical Report TR86-798, Ithaca, NY.
37. Opik, E. J. (1976). *Interplanetary Encounters.* Elsevier Publishing Co., N.Y.
38. Milani, A., and Nobili, A. M. (1983). "On the Stability of Heirarchical Four Body Systems," *Celestial Mechanics,* 31, 241.
39. Milani, A., Carpino, M. and Logan, D. (1987). "Parallel Computation of Planet Crossing Orbits," IBM Technical Report KGN-161.

6 Design and Implementation of the Delft Molecular-Dynamics Processor

A. F. BAKKER AND C. BRUIN

Faculty of Applied Physics
University of Technology
Delft
The Netherlands

I. Introduction

A. Molecular-Dynamics Simulation

The subject of this chapter is molecular-dynamics simulation with a special-purpose computing device. The general background for the subject is sketched in this introduction.

The increasing availability of computational power for scientific investigation has widened the role of computational physics. This is particularly true for computer simulations in the wide field of many-body systems. In such systems the macroscopic behavior is obtained from the microscopic interactions between the constituent particles.

A computer simulation acts as a bridge between experiment and theory. A simulation can be considered as an ideal experiment, performed on a precisely defined model system. By simulating a model, quasi-experimental estimates can be obtained for certain properties of the model. These can be compared to experimental data on the one hand and to the results of (approximate) analytic solutions on the other hand. Moreover, in a simulation systems can be studied under circumstances that would not, or would only with great difficulty, be accessible in a real experiment. The disadvantages of a simulation are the restrictions on system size and system observation time; because of obvious limitations these differ by orders of magnitude from physical experimental situations.

This chapter will be concerned only with classical model systems consisting of many particles as studied in statistical mechanics. Most often, the basic equations describing such systems are for continuous space and time, and they have to be made discrete before numerical solution is possible. In a molecular-dynamics (MD) simulation, both the positions of the particles and their momenta are taken into account, and the trajectories of the particles are calculated in space, discrete in time, through their equations of motion (see e.g. [1]). The time-averaged quantities of MD are equal to the ensemble averages of statistical mechanics, by the ergodic theorem (see e.g. [2]).

B. Computational Tools for Molecular Dynamics

If the simulation on an ordinary general-purpose computer with the aid of a high-level language is not fast enough for the user, attempts can be made to speed up the simulation by using a machine-oriented language, mainly to accelerate the time-consuming inner loop of a program. In general, the speed increase gained by using a machine-oriented language is modest. The efficiency of the used algorithm is the major factor in the computational speed. Even though the chance to find a new and better algorithm is small, speedup factors of up to several orders of magnitude are sometimes feasible (e.g. by making use of fast Fourier transforms, or of special coding techniques). Ultimately, the performance of a computer is restricted by its hardware limitations.

Three types of computers are identified. *General-purpose computers* are designed to have an average efficiency for all types of problems. They are not tailored to a fast computation of molecular dynamics or other algorithms. To compensate for the lack of specialization, more powerful *operation-oriented processors* that are commercially available can be attached to the computer (e.g. AP 120B, STAR 100). The algorithm used in the general-purpose computer has to be adapted to the available vector operations in the attached processor. This can speed up significantly the execution of programs that can be fully vectorized. When only part of an algorithm can be vectorized, the total result may be disappointing. Whenever frequently occurring simple operations are the major part of the algorithm execution, adaptation of the processor architecture to the particular algorithm involved may be far more efficient. This means designing an *algorithm-oriented processor*. This processor is then exclusively at the disposal of the user for solving the problem to which it is dedicated. Clearly, the design of such a special-purpose machine only pays off if the class of problems in the particular application is wide enough to run the machine for a long time.

The advantages of this algorithm-oriented processor approach are that (operation) wordlengths, the memory organization and the instruction set can be adapted to the problem involved. Moreover, parallel and pipelined operations can be applied wherever this is allowed in the algorithm. In addition, "measurements" can be carried out in parallel with the simulation calculations. The result will be a low-cost high-speed processor.

For MD simulations, where particle positions and velocities are kept as 32-bit fixed- or floating-point numbers, the advantage of algorithm-oriented processors is not obvious. The commercial availability of floating-point vector and scalar processors appears to be an effective solution for speeding up MD calculations. A special-purpose approach would seem to mimic such a processor. However, a closer study of such a processor, as described in the following chapters, shows otherwise; a low-cost special-purpose molecular-dynamics processor has been designed and constructed, with an uncommon architecture adapted to the MD algorithm that operates at a speed comparable to supercomputers.

II. Computational Aspects of Molecular Dynamics

A. Molecular Dynamics of a System with Pair Interactions

We consider a classical system of N particles (atoms) occupying positions $r_1, r_2, \ldots, r_n$ in space. With each configuration a potential energy E_p is associated, which is the sum of pair energies:

$$E_p(r_1, \ldots, r_N) = \sum_{j=1}^{N-1} \sum_{i=j+1}^{N} V(r_{ij}), \tag{1}$$

where $r_{ij} = |r_i - r_j|$, i.e. a spherically symmetric potential V is assumed. Different choices of the potential V enable the simulation of a variety of physical systems. In calculations or simulations often a $V(r)$ is used of the form

$$V(r) = 4 \epsilon \left\{ \left(\frac{\sigma}{r}\right)^{12} - \left(\frac{\sigma}{r}\right)^{6} \right\} \tag{2}$$

which is called the Lennard–Jones potential. The molecular-dynamics method for this system amounts to solving Newton's equations of motion for all N particles,

$$m \frac{d^2 \mathbf{r}_i}{dt^2} = -\frac{\partial E_p}{\partial \mathbf{r}_i}, \tag{3}$$

where m is the particle mass and t denotes time.

The equations of motion for the particles can be rewritten in the form

$$m \frac{d\mathbf{r}_i}{dt} = \mathbf{p}_i, \tag{4}$$

$$\frac{d\mathbf{p}_i}{dt} = \mathbf{F}_i, \tag{5}$$

where $\mathbf{p}_i$ is the momentum of the i-th particle and $\mathbf{F}_i = -\partial E_p/\partial \mathbf{r}_i$ is the force acting on it. There are many ways in which the differential equations Eqs. (4) and (5) can be made discrete. A simple and computationally efficient time-integration scheme is the leapfrog scheme [3]. The leapfrog scheme is characterized by defining the positions at integral timelevels and the momenta at half-integral timelevels:

$$m \frac{\mathbf{r}_i(n) - \mathbf{r}_i(n-1)}{\Delta t} = \mathbf{p}_i(n - \tfrac{1}{2}), \tag{6}$$

$$\frac{\mathbf{p}_i(n + \tfrac{1}{2}) - \mathbf{p}_i(n - \tfrac{1}{2})}{\Delta t} = \mathbf{F}_i(n), \tag{7}$$

where n denotes the timelevel and Δt the time-increment. This scheme meets the following important requirements:

Consistency. The difference schemes of Eqs. (6) and (7) are consistent with the differential equations Eqs. (4) and (5), since for infinitely small timesteps Eqs. (6) and (7) give Eqs. (4) and (5). The differential equations Eqs. (4) and (5) are time reversible, which is also true for the difference scheme because of the time-centered derivatives.

Accuracy. Apart from blunders, the accuracy depends on roundoff errors and truncation errors [4]. Truncation errors arise from the representation of continuous quantities by discrete sets of values and are proportional to Δt^p in a p-th order difference scheme. The leapfrog scheme is a second-order method. Roundoff errors result from the finite wordlength of number representations in the computer. Provided the scheme is stable, roundoff errors can be kept smaller than truncation errors if computers with an appropriate wordlength are selected.

Stability.   Stability is concerned with the propagation of errors. The leapfrog scheme is stable when the condition

$$\frac{1}{m}\left|\frac{dF}{dr}\right|_{max} < \frac{4}{(\Delta t)^2} \tag{8}$$

is met [1]. This can be obtained by a suitable choice for Δt, for a given F.

Efficiency.   The leapfrog scheme is an efficient time-integration scheme. The cost in storage is minimal, since only one timelevel of the particle positions and momenta is to be kept in memory during the simulation. Higher-order schemes need those values at several timelevels. The computational costs are minimal since the number of operations per particle and per timestep is minimal. So-called "higher-order" schemes (see e.g. [5]) require more storage and more operations for a time-integration that, in absence of roundoff, gives identical trajectories.

Finally, it is noted that with this scheme some caution is required when calculating mixed velocity–position correlations, because of the out-of-phase treatment of these quantities. This problem is usually resolved by an interpolation of the velocities.

B. Strategies in Particle-Interaction Computations

Three simulation methods for particle systems can be distinguished. They differ in how the force in Eq. (7) is calculated.

Particle–Particle (PP) method.   The total force on a particle resulting from the interactions with other particles is calculated directly by summing all force contributions. This is an accurate but computationally intensive method. It is suited for systems with short-range interactions only.

Particle–Mesh (PM) Method.   The forces on the particles are computed via an auxiliary field obtained by solving the Poisson equation using a mesh. This method is fast compared to the PP method, but is accurate only for force fields that have negligible harmonic content beyond wavelengths shorter than two mesh spacings. When long-range interactions are dominating (collisionless phase fluid limit), the PM method is efficient, e.g. in plasma calculations and galaxy simulations (see e.g. [6] and [7]).

Particle–Particle–Particle–Mesh (PPPM or P^3M) Method.   This method is a compromise between speed and accuracy, and uses both PP and PM schemes [1]. Simulations with both long- and short-range interactions (e.g. for molten salts) are most efficiently carried out by the PPPM method.

This chapter is restricted to short-range interactions and hence to the PP method.

C. The Cutoff Radius of the Potential and Linked-List Method in the PP Method

The total force on a particle i at position $\mathbf{r}_i$ is given by the sum of the interparticle forces

$$\mathbf{F}_i = \sum_{\substack{j=1 \\ (j \neq i)}}^{N} f(r_{ij}) \mathbf{r}_{ij}, \tag{9}$$

where $f(r_{ij})$ is the scalar part of the force exerted by particle j on particle i, and is given by

$$f(r) = -\frac{1}{r} \frac{dV(r)}{dr}. \tag{10}$$

All particles are located in a "computational" box. Periodic-boundary conditions are used; when a particle leaves the box its image will enter from the opposite side with the same velocity. Hence the number of particles is conserved. The minimum image convention is used, according to which a given particle interacts at most once with each particle. While it is true that, for potentials similar to that in Eq. (2), the interparticle force f_{ij} does not completely vanish with increasing distance r_{ij}, $V(r)$ is safely approximated by zero for r, larger than a cutoff radius r_c, without distorting the results and with a considerable increase in calculational efficiency. A straightforward method of evaluating $\mathbf{F}_i$ for a particle i is then to consider all other particles $j = i + 1, \ldots, N$ and compute f_{ij} only if $r_{ij} = |\mathbf{r}_i - \mathbf{r}_j|$ is less than r_c. Moreover, the contribution of each f_{ij} to $\mathbf{F}_j$ is taken into account. Nevertheless, the computational cost of all r_{ij} calculations is proportional to N^2 and makes this method impractical for large N. An efficient approach is to order the particle coordinates such that most of the noninteracting particle pairs are excluded from the r_{ij} calculations in advance. This is done by the linked-list method.

The computational box is divided into a number of subboxes [1], viz. a regular array of linked-list (LL) cells. The sides of the cells are chosen to be not smaller than r_c so that a particle located in a given LL-cell can only interact with the particles located in that same cell and with the particles located in the directly neighboring cells (26 cells in three dimensions and 8 cells in two dimensions).

The purpose of the linked-list method is to obtain the particle attributes directly without searching. To this end, a presorting mechanism, chaining the addresses of the particles in a cell, is applied. This mechanism makes use of a linked-list array $LL\{i\}$, $i = 1, \ldots, N$, and a Head-Of-Chain array $HOC\{j\}$, $j = 0$, . . . $N_c - 1$. Here N is the total number of particles and N_c is the total number of LL-cells (subboxes).

All particles located in a given LL-cell, for example LL-cell number q, are chained together by pointers. $HOC\{q\}$ points to the first particle, number m, in the chain (head of chain) and, hence, $HOC\{q\} = m$. The next particle in the chain, number 1, is linked to m through LL; $LL\{m\} = 1$. The end of the chain is represented by zero; e.g. $LL\{j\} = 0$.

The linked-list method reduces the number of r_{ij} calculations drastically; the number of operations is now proportional to N. The overhead in maintaining the lists is small.

D. *PP Algorithm Procedure*

In general, a single timestep in a simulation using the PP method includes the following three actions:

- set up linked-list

> set $HOC\{q\}: = 0$ for all q
> do for all particles i
> $\quad q: = number\{LL - cell(\mathbf{r}_i)\}$
> $\quad LL\{i\}: = HOC\{q\}$
> $\quad HOC\{q\}: = i$
> enddo

- update the momenta

> do for all LL-cells, I
> $\quad$ do for all (neighboring) LL-cells, $J \geq I$
> $\quad\quad$ do for all combinations, i and j; $\{i\} = I$, $\{j\} = J$
> $\quad\quad\quad$ update momenta of particles i and j [Eqs. (7) and (9)]
> $\quad\quad$ enddo
> $\quad$ enddo
> enddo

- update the positions

> do for all particles i
> $\quad$ update positions of particle i [Eq. (6)]
> enddo

E. Reduced Quantities for a Lennard–Jones System

The Newtonian equations of motion, Eqs. (4) and (5), are usually formulated in reduced physical quantities. For Lennard–Jones 12–6 interaction (Eq. (2)), the natural units of length, energy and mass are the diameter σ, the potential well depth ϵ, and the particle mass m, respectively. Therefore the reduced quantities are defined by

$$\mathbf{r}_i^* = \frac{\mathbf{r}_i}{\sigma}, \tag{11}$$

$$\mathbf{p}_i^* = \frac{\mathbf{p}_i}{\sqrt{\epsilon m}}, \tag{12}$$

$$t^* = \frac{t}{\sigma\sqrt{m/\epsilon}}. \tag{13}$$

For the Lennard–Jones potential the quantity $f(r)$, defined by Eqs. (2) and (10), takes the form

$$f(r) = \frac{24\epsilon}{r^2}\left\{2\left(\frac{\sigma}{r}\right)^{12} - \left(\frac{\sigma}{r}\right)^6\right\}. \tag{14}$$

A function f^* of the reduced variable r^* is defined by

$$f^*(r^*) = \frac{24}{r^{*2}}\left\{\frac{2}{r^{*12}} - \frac{1}{r^{*6}}\right\}. \tag{15}$$

Hence the leapfrog scheme (Eqs. (6) and (7)) can be expressed in reduced quantities as

$$\mathbf{r}_i(n) = \mathbf{r}_i(n-1) + \mathbf{p}_i^*(n-\tfrac{1}{2})\Delta t^*, \tag{16}$$

$$\mathbf{p}_i^*(n+\tfrac{1}{2}) = \mathbf{p}_i^*(n-\tfrac{1}{2}) + \Delta t^* \sum_{j\neq i}^{N} \mathbf{r}_{ij}(n)f^*(r_{ij}^*(n)). \tag{17}$$

For completeness a few other quantities that will be used later are defined, namely the reduced temperature

$$T^* = \frac{1}{dN}\sum_{i=1}^{N}\mathbf{p}_i^{*2}, \tag{18}$$

where d is the dimension, the reduced density

$$\rho^* = N\left(\frac{\sigma}{L}\right)^d, \tag{19}$$

where L is the box length, the reduced box length

$$L^* = \frac{L}{\sigma},$$
(20)

and the reduced potential energy per particle

$$E_p^* = \frac{E_p}{N\epsilon}.$$
(21)

III. Design Considerations for a Special-Purpose Molecular-Dynamics Processor

A. Introduction

The art of designing an algorithm-oriented processor is to incorporate so many hardware operators, simultaneously active in parallel or in pipelines, that the cost/performance ratio for the total algorithm procedure is as small as possible. The freedom in the design is furthermore restricted by the minimum speed required and the maximum available budget. The design of the molecular-dynamics processor started with a feasibility study [8] in which a rough sketch of the parallel and pipelined operations was given for the data flow and control flow of the leapfrog algorithm. The aim was to estimate the cost and performance of such a processor. In comparison with commercially available solutions, the algorithm-oriented processor approach seemed to be attractive here: high speed at low costs.

B. System Partitioning

The main goal of using an algorithm-oriented processor is to speed up time-consuming operations rather than to replace a total program, or to replace a general-purpose computer. For frequently occurring simple operations involving multiplication, addition, subtraction, and function look-up tables, dedicated hardware can easily be built. However, the man–machine interface, incidental and complex operations, part of the data analysis, and the presentation of results can be done more efficiently by a general-purpose computer. Hence, the present computing apparatus consists of a dedicated processor, in which the main algorithm loop is executed, and a general-purpose computer (e.g. minicomputer) that performs the rest of the total simulation program and through which the user controls the attached dedicated processor. The combination has to be presented to the user as a user-friendly high-speed computer, carrying out the particular algorithm for which it was designed. Here a HP 1000 mini-computer is used for the general-purpose part of the apparatus. The dedicated part, called the MD processor, is linked to the HP computer by a 16-bit parallel input-output (I/O) channel, through which the flow of all data, instructions, etc., takes place.

C. Tasks of the MD Processor

The basic functions required from the processor are

- To calculate the forces and to update the momenta. These calculations are the core of the leapfrog algorithm and occupy a central place in the design of the total processor.
- To keep the particle momenta and positions in local memory. To avoid massive I/O overhead in the simulation execution, all particle attributes have to be kept locally in the MD processor by a large particle memory.
- To update the positions. The particle attributes are located in the MD processor, and this information is required for calculating the new positions at every timestep. Obviously, again to avoid I/O overhead, this simple operation is built into the MD processor.
- To do linked-list procedures. The linked-list method is used during the momentum-update phase and is inseparable from this section. Hence this bookkeeping function will be a part of the MD processor.
- To measure in parallel. With the aid of a little extra hardware all data required for a measurement (for example, the potential and kinetic energy, and the pair-correlation function) are tapped from the hardware during each timestep. These are fed to simple measurement hardware sections. Since these calculations are carried out in parallel with the simulation, no extra computing time is used.

D. User Requirements

Important user requirements for the MD processor are that the results be sufficiently accurate, that they be produced in a reasonable time, and that the processor be easy to operate.

1. Capacity An important parameter to be set in advance is the maximum number of particles whose simultaneous motions are to be simulated with the MD processor. A typical molecular-dynamics simulation on a general-purpose computer may involve a system of about 1000 particles. An algorithm-oriented processor should be able to study systems at least 10 times larger, if the construction of such a processor is to be worthwhile.

The maximum system size for the MD processor was chosen to be $2^{16} - 1 = 65,535$ particles. Such an extension of the maximum number of particles is useful in studying system-size effects.

2. Operational Speed   The user is interested in results and their statistical accuracy. The more particles and timesteps involved in a simulation, the better the obtained statistical accuracy will be. The number of timesteps in a typical simulation run is about 10^4 for a fixed temperature and density. The execution time of both a timestep and a measurement has to be shorter, or at least not much longer, than it would take on a large computer. Given the speed limits of commercially available hardware operators (typically 5 MHz throughput in 1978), this requirement can be met by arranging for an appropriate number of simultaneous operations in the processor.

3. Wordlength and Accuracy   Given the leapfrog algorithm, the accuracy of the results depends on the wordlength of the particle positions and momenta and on the size of the timestep used. It is difficult *a priori* to estimate wordlength effects because of the nonlinearity of the algorithm. Therefore the experience gained from simulations on general-purpose computers was used to determine the appropriate wordlength of the positions and momenta. In most MD simulations on general-purpose computers the particle positions and momenta are represented as floating-point numbers. However, there are two important arguments for using a fixed-point format in our case. In the first place, construction of floating-point operators is complicated and expensive, compared to the construction of fixed-point operators. Secondly, floating-point notation of the particle positions implies position-dependent accuracy, and the accuracy gives hardly any improvement in comparison with using fixed-point numbers. From simulations on general-purpose computers it was concluded that wordlengths of 24 bits for the positions and 32 bits for the momenta are enough for most applications. The extra eight bits are incorporated in the momenta to reduce roundoff effects caused by the accumulation of the momenta changes due to the interactions.

As in most software MD simulations, the forces are retrieved from a predefined force look-up table, rather than calculated by an analytic expression. The latter method could slow down the simulation dramatically when complex force expressions are involved. The number of entries in the table and a linear interpolation scheme between the entry values determine how close the looked-up values are to the force that is to be applied in the simulation. Again experience from simulations on general-purpose computers was used to decide the number of table entries. The look-up table was chosen to have 1024 entries, each of which contains a 32-bit fixed-point value. Moreover, a linear interpolation between the entry values is applied. In the table, the force is stored as a function of the square of the particle separation to avoid a square root operation.

Software simulations with wordlengths as mentioned above have been made and were found to achieve a satisfactory accuracy in comparison with the usual simulations on mainframe computers.

4. User Interface to the Processor The user should not be distracted from the problem he wants to solve by the architecture of the MD processor. He wants to run his simulation program as on a general-purpose computer and to communicate with the MD processor by subroutine calls. This requirement is met when the user is supplied with a subroutine package that makes full use of the operational speed of the MD processor. Fortran 77 is the supported high-level language on the HP 1000 and is used in this package.

E. Design Requirements

The design of a dedicated processor is almost straightforward when hardware components are used with an operational speed below 10 MHz. Above this frequency, power dissipation and wire-length effects become important problems. The most complete commercially available logic family is the TTL series, which meets the frequency requirement of 10 MHz. Being available in SSI, MSI, LSI and VLSI techniques, this family is most suitable for application in the MD processor. Operators like multipliers and adders can be constructed such that a 4-MHz operational speed is feasible for the MD processor.

1. Control Requirements There are three ways to control hardware operators and data flows:

- The predefined hard-wired control, which is fixed during the detailed design. Logic-state diagrams are implemented with random logic. Changes or additions in this type of control are only possible by hardware intervention and restrict the flexibility of the total system.
- The microprogrammed control, where the control sequence is generated by software rather than by hardware. A fixed microprogram (firmware) in programmable read-only memory (PROM) together with an appropriate controller (e.g. microprocessor) makes the control transparent and easy to design. Control modifications are made by replacing the PROMs.

- The microprogrammable control, which is identical to the microprogrammed control with the exception that the PROM is replaced by
read-write memory (random access memory or RAM). This control
memory has to be loaded by the general-purpose host computer, and
can be modified easily by compiling and loading the modified microprogram.

For the MD processor the microprogrammable control approach is
preferable to the first two possibilities. In the design stage only the control
lines need to be defined and immediate hardware implementation is possible. The control functions can be developed simultaneously in microprograms. For maintenance purposes, automatic test procedures can be incorporated at any level by additional microprograms, a feature that detects
failures efficiently.

F. Scaling the Physical Quantities for the MD Processor

The MD processor is designed to operate on fixed-point two's-complement
numbers ranging from -1 to 1, but excluding 1. Consequently all numbers
used by the processor must fall in this range. Hence, it is necessary to
introduce so-called normalized quantities that are suited for the MD processor.

In general, a normalized quantity is found by dividing the reduced
quantity by its maximum value. The maximum absolute value of the
particle positions is exactly known because periodic boundary conditions
are used; the normalized particle positions are then

$$r_i^+ = \frac{2r_i^*}{L^*}.$$
(22)

Note that the origin of the position coordinate system is located in the
center of the computational box.

When the momenta values have a Gaussian distribution, p_{max}^* has to be
chosen large enough so that there is only a negligible probability of finding
a particle with a larger reduced momentum value. Hence

$$p_{max}^* = f p_{average}^* = f\sqrt{T^*},$$
(23)

where f is a factor, typically taken to be between 4 and 8. This corresponds
to the approach taken on general-purpose machines where typically cutoffs
of three times the thermal velocity are used. For example, when $f = 8$, the
probability of finding a particle with $p^* > p_{max}^*$ is less than 10^{-12}.

An additional scaling factor, c, is introduced to allow the momenta values to be scaled down further to compensate for the scaling of the force values. Hence

$$\mathbf{p}_i^+ = \frac{c}{f\sqrt{T^*}} \, \mathbf{p}_i^*. \tag{24}$$

For an interaction potential like the Lennard–Jones potential, which increases rapidly with decreasing distances below σ, the maximum value of the potential and the force are determined by the minimum interparticle distance, r_{min}, possible for a certain density and temperature. It is assumed that the potential energy of two particles will never be larger than the maximum kinetic energy determined by p_{max}^*. For a two-dimensional system, that is

$$V_{max}^* = f^2 T^* = 4 \left\{ \frac{1}{r_{min}^{*12}} - \frac{1}{r_{min}^{*6}} \right\} \approx \frac{4}{r_{min}^{*12}}, \tag{25}$$

which gives

$$r_{min}^* \approx (f\sqrt{T^*})^{-1/6}. \tag{26}$$

Hence

$$f_{max}^* = f^*(r_{min}^*) \approx \frac{48}{r_{min}^{*14}} \approx (f\sqrt{T^*})^{7/3}. \tag{27}$$

The leapfrog equations (16) and (17) in normalized quantities read

$$\mathbf{r}_i^+(n) = \mathbf{r}_i^+(n-1) + \mathbf{p}_i^+(n-\tfrac{1}{2}) \frac{2f\sqrt{T^*}}{L^*c} \Delta t^* \tag{28}$$

and

$$\mathbf{p}_i^+(n+\tfrac{1}{2}) = \mathbf{p}_i^+(n-\tfrac{1}{2}) + \sum \frac{L^* \, \Delta t^* \, c}{2f\sqrt{T^*}} f^*(r_{ij}^*(n)) \, \mathbf{r}_{ij}^+(n). \tag{29}$$

A "move-factor" is introduced:

$$\Delta t^+ = \frac{2f\sqrt{T^*}}{L^*c} \Delta t^*, \tag{30}$$

which is the number used in the MD processor to multiply the momenta of the particles to calculate their new positions.

Using the linked-list method, the interparticle distance per direction will never exceed twice the LL-cell length, H_c. The maximal squared interparticle distance that is calculated in the MD processor is $3(2H)_{c^2} = 12H_c^2$, while the look-up table contains only nonzero values up to H_c^2. To minimize the number of entries in the tables, a test for values greater than H_c^2 is made and consequently, for larger values, the table values are forced to zero by a logical "and" operation. To avoid the overlap of neighboring LL-cells, at least four cells should be involved per dimension.

When only four LL-cells per dimension are involved, $H_c = 1/2$, and only values between 0 and 1/4 are used to address the tables. Larger values are treated as overflows, an indication to make the table output values zero.

Doubling the number of LL-cells per dimension implies that only the first quarter of the tables contain nonzero values. To avoid inefficient use of the tables a shift factor, I, is introduced that will be used to multiply the interparticle distance by 2^I for every direction, before it is used in further calculations. Hence, it follows that $2^I \leq N_c/4$.

With the definition of a shifted interparticle distance

$$\mathbf{r}_{ij}^{+s}(n) = \mathbf{r}_{ij}^{+}(n)2^I, \tag{31}$$

Eq. (29) becomes

$$\mathbf{p}_i^{+}(n + \tfrac{1}{2}) = \mathbf{p}_i^{+}(n - \tfrac{1}{2}) + \sum K(r_{ij}^{*}(n))r_{ij}^{+s}(n), \tag{32}$$

where the

$$K(r_{ij}^{*}) = \frac{L^* \Delta t^* c}{2f\sqrt{T^*}} 2^{-I} f^*(r_{ij}^{*}(n)) \tag{33}$$

are the table values for the force.

When the maximum value of $K(r^*)$ exceeds the value one, the factor c becomes important, and has to be chosen such that $K(r^*)_{max} = 1$. Consequently the momenta are scaled down further as well.

IV. Design of the MD Processor

The MD processor consists of a data part and a control part; supervised by the host computer they carry out the simulation calculations as a function of the input parameters and return the measurement results as output.

A. General Hardware Description

The basic functions of the MD processor as mentioned in Section III.C are housed in five hardware sections interconnected by a data bus (Figure 1). They are

- the momentum-update section (P), in which the momenta of particles are modified according to their interactions with other particles;
- the position-update section (X), in which the positions of the particles are modified according to the new momenta;

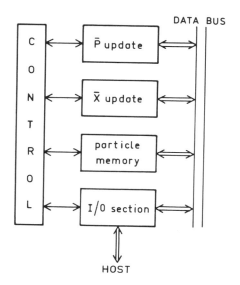

Figure 1. The main hardware sections of the MD processor.

- the particle memory, where the current momenta and positions of the particles and the linked-list array are kept;
- the input-output section, which handles the interface between the MD processor and the host computer;
- the control section, which controls the entire data handling and linked-list procedures.

The measurement sections are partly integrated in the momentum-update section but will be discussed separately in Section IV.D. Before focusing on a more detailed description of the hardware sections, a rough sketch of the data flows in a single timestep calculation will be given.

The starting point in a simulation is the loading of the initial particle positions and momenta from the host computer via the I/O section into the particle memory. One timestep in the leapfrog algorithm consists of two basic phases: the position-update phase and the momentum-update phase.

In the first of the two phases all HOC elements in the control section are set to zero and then the new positions of the particles are calculated from their momenta. The processor must transfer the position and momentum for each particle from the particle memory to the position-update section to apply Eq. (28), and then replace the old position in the particle memory by the calculated new position. At this point in the calculation sequence the new position is also brought into the control section to determine the LL-cell number in which this particle is located. This information is used to set up the linked-lists that will be employed in the next phase.

In the second of the two phases the new momenta of the particles are calculated, taking into account all their interactions with the other particles. Using the linked-list method all relevant particle-pair positions and momenta are selected for transfer to the momentum-update section. Here, Eq. (32) is applied and the resulting momenta replace the previous momenta in the particle memory.

B. Detailed Description of the Data Part

1. Momentum-Update Section   The momentum-update section handles Eqs. (32) and (33). These equations can be written in terms of basic operations, where Δx^2 is a shorthand notation for $(\Delta x)^2$ (Table 1).

In this calculation scheme the positions and momenta of two interacting particles are input and the new momenta of both particles are output. Since the momentum-update calculations are the major compute-bound part of the MD algorithm, a parallel and pipelined processor architecture was designed that focused on the speedup of that portion of the algorithm.

Parallel Operations   Nonsequentially dependent operations, such as those used in the calculation of the particle separations in the $x-$, $y-$ and z-direction (Ops. a,b,c), can be executed simultaneously in identical parallel hardware operators.

Figure 2 shows a generalized block diagram of a possible parallel hardware design. Here the three parallel planes represent identical operations for all three dimensions; the front plane illustrates the operation scheme for one dimension.

The procedure that is used for updating the momenta of two interacting particles, i and j, is to move the position and momentum values of particle i for all $x-$, $y-$ and z-directions from the particle memory into the **XI** and **PI** files and those of particle j into the corresponding **XJ** and **PJ** files. For the

Table 1. Basic Operations

$\Delta x = x_i - x_j$	$\Delta y = y_i - y_j$	$\Delta z = z_i - z_j$	(Ops. a, b, c)
$\Delta x^2 = \Delta x * \Delta x$	$\Delta y^2 = \Delta y * \Delta y$	$\Delta z^2 = \Delta z * \Delta z$	(Ops. d, e, f)
$\Delta r^2 = \Delta x^2 + \Delta y^2 + \Delta z^2$			(Op. g)
$F = f(\Delta r^2)$			(Op. h)
$\Delta p_x = \Delta x * F$	$\Delta p_y = \Delta y * F$	$\Delta p_z = \Delta z * F$	(Ops. i, j, k)
$p_{xi} = p_{xi} + \Delta p_x$	$p_{yi} = p_{yi} + \Delta p_y$	$p_{zi} = p_{zi} + \Delta p_z$	(Ops. l, m, n)
$p_{xj} = p_{xj} - \Delta p_x$	$p_{yj} = p_{yj} - \Delta p_y$	$p_{zj} = p_{zj} - \Delta p_z$	(Ops. o, p, q)

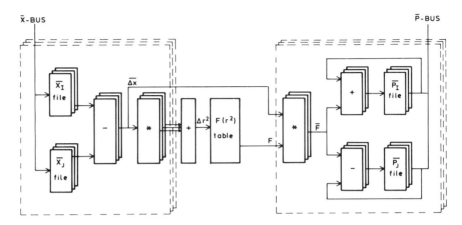

Figure 2. The parallel hardware structure in the momentum-update section.

moment these twelve files should be thought of as temporarily storing the position and momentum coordinates of particle i and j; their complete function will be explained later. For each $x-$, $y-$ and z-direction, a hardware subtract operation ("-") obtains the interparticle-distance component (Ops. a,b,c) and subsequently a hardware multiplier ("*") calculates the corresponding squared value (Ops. d,e,f). These values are then summed in a single hardware add-operator ("+") to yield the squared interparticle distance (Op. g). This squared value is used to address a predefined force look-up table (Op. h). For each x-, y- and z-direction the resulting table value is multiplied by the corresponding interparticle distance using a hardware multiplier ("*"). Thereby the change in momentum ($\Delta\mathbf{p}$) for all directions is found (Ops. i,j,k). These values are used to update the momenta values of both particles, i and j, available in the $\mathbf{P}I$ and $\mathbf{P}J$ files, by an appropriate hardware summation ("+") and subtraction ("-") for each direction. Note that these last six operations (Ops. l,m,n,o,p,q) are all performed simultaneously. The final step is then to store the new momenta of the two particles from the P files into the particle memory.

Each dimension is operated on in parallel as described above. For a three-dimensional model this speeds the calculations by a factor of three. The overhead in the data transfer between the particle memory and the files can be reduced if the particle memory allows a simultaneous access of both position and momentum for the x-, y- and z-directions, a feature that will be discussed in the next section.

Pipelined Operations   The simple calculational scheme of the momentum-update section allows the processing hardware to be divided into stages, which are separated by pipeline registers. These registers hold the intermediate pipe-state results that are generated each clock period. Roughly, the operational throughput increases by a factor p when p pipe stages are involved. The full power of this pipelined computing method is obtained only if the pipe is fed with new data every clock period.

To reduce the time required for the data transfer between the particle memory and the files, the **X** and **P** files are designed to hold the positions and momenta for all three directions of all the particles located in a single LL-cell. The position and momentum of all particles i located in LL-cell I are kept in the **X**I and **P**I files, whereas the position and momentum of all particles j, located in LL-cell J, are kept in the **X**J and **P**J files. The **X** and **P** files can be considered as basic vector memories. By dynamically addressing these files, six vectors are generated that are then passed to the pipelined hardware operators in the momentum-update section. These vectors contain all relevant particle-data combinations of cell I and cell J; the change in momentum is updated in the basic vector memories **P**I and **P**J. Clearly, the data transfer between the register files and the particle memory entails an overhead, but it will be small when the basic vectors are large.

The total effect of pipelining the momentum-update section, including parallel operations, provides a speed-up factor of 25 over a sequential calculation.

The detailed block diagram of the pipelined momentum-update section (Figures 3, 4 and 5) shows the hardware design for just one of the three directions, namely for the x-direction. The hardware block diagrams of the additional two directions are replicas of Figure 3 and Figure 5, where X is

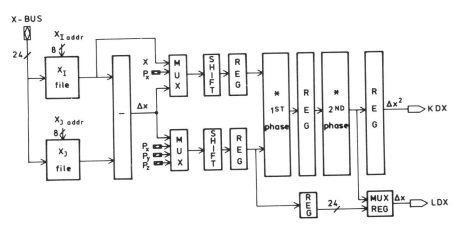

Figure 3. The pipelined hardware for the calculations of the squared interparticle-distances in the x-direction.

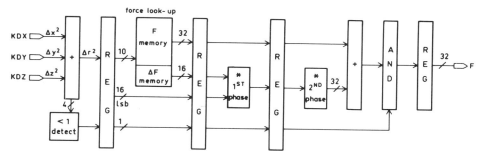

Figure 4. The pipelined hardware for the force look-up, and the linear interpolation calculations.

replaced by Y and Z. The "REG"-blocks are the pipeline registers (edge-triggered D-flip-flops).

The **X** bus provides input for both the **X***I* and **X***J* files (256-word by 24-bit, high-speed memories) which can be loaded with the positions of particles (see Figure 3). After subtraction the interparticle distance in this direction, Δx, is fed to two multiplexers ("MUX") and then to a shifter ("SHIFT") and a pipeline register before being input to the multiplier. The multiplexers are designed to allow a variety of possible usages of the multiplier, e.g. the measurement of the kinetic energy (see Section IV.D.2). The additional possible inputs for the multiplexers include the position coordinate and the momenta in all directions. A hardware shifter

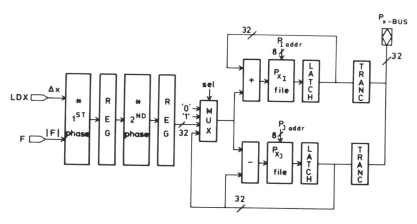

Figure 5. The pipelined hardware for the calculations of the momentum change and for the momentum update in the x-direction.

("SHIFT"), allowing a blockscale operation of 2^n, $n = 0,1, \ldots, 15$, is used to optimize the table look-up usage as was shown in Section III.F.

The squaring operation is carried out in a two-stage multiplier. In the first stage the partial products are calculated (by 8*8 multiply components), whereas in the second stage these products are added (full-adders). The result is the squared distance in the direction being examined, Δx^2. The value of the interparticle distance, Δx, is passed through the pipeline registers, and multiplexed with Δx^2 to allow calculations of the virial pressure.

The squared interparticle distances of each direction, which are calculated for the three dimensions in parallel, are fed to the next stage (Figure 4). Here these results are summed and tested against r_c^2; the effect of this test is to control the output of the table look-up by the "AND" operator (i.e. the force look-up table value will become zero whenever r^2 is greater than r_c^2). The resulting 10 most significant bits of the squared interparticle-distance value, Δr^2, are used to address the force look-up table. Both the initial table entry for that value, F, and the difference between that entry and the next entry in the table, ΔF, are stored in the memory to be able to linearly interpolate on the force. ΔF is multiplied in a two-stage multiplier by the remaining 16 bits of the squared distance and the result of this multiplication is added to the initial value. For each x-, y- and z-direction (Figure 5) a two-stage multiplier provides the force in the three dimensions by using their interparticle distances Δx, Δy and Δz. The updating of the momenta in the **P** files is enabled by latches ("LATCH") to protect the old momentum values while writing the new momenta. The multiplexer ("MUX") in Figure 5 is designed for zeroing the *PJ* files if the forces of particles in the same LL-cell are being determined, and of summing the total change in momentum. In addition, storage of the momentum values from the particle memory is then possible via the add and subtract operators. Transceivers ("TRANC") allow a bidirectional data transfer between the **P** files and the **P** bus.

Control Requirements   The calculating pipe for the momentum-update section is driven by the system clock. The method used to collect the proper data from the pipe is to control the register files *I* and *J* by applying appropriate addresses (8-bit wide) and read/write control. In addition the multiplexers, shifters and I/O to the buses must be controlled. The method will be discussed in Section IV.C.4.

2. Particle-Memory Size   The particle memory of the MD processor contains all the information about each particle: the positions and the momenta ($d*24 + d*32$ bits per particle in d dimensions), the linked-list addresses (16 bits) and a particle identification number (4 bits), which provides the option of using different types of particles in the simulation. Often both the position and momentum information are involved in the calculations. If all the required quantities for three dimensions are stored in one addressable word in the particle memory, a read/write operation for all the particle attributes will be effectuated by just one memory access. This is critical for efficiently writing and reading the register files in the momentum-update section. The maximum wordlength required for the particle definition is then calculated to be 3*24-bit position + 3*32-bit momentum + 16-bit linked-list address + 4-bit type code, resulting in 188-bit width (Figure 6). The 16-bit linked-list element corresponds to a maximal addressable memory size of $2^{16} = 65,536$ words, each containing 188 bits. For reasons of chip count, cost and power consumption, the large particle memory is built with 16k-bit dynamic-memory components rather than with 4k-bit static-memory components.

Memory-Control Requirements   There are two modes in which the particle data have to be accessed:

- the incremental mode, in which the particle addresses are generated in their successive order. This mode is used during both the position-update phase and the linked-list setup phase;
- the linked-list mode, in which all particles located in a LL-cell are addressed one after another, using their linked-list address. During the momentum-update phase all particles in a LL-cell are addressed to either load or to rewrite the particle memory into or from the files. The particle memory control will be described in Section IV.C.3.

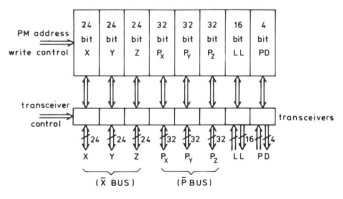

Figure 6. The particle-memory section.

3. Position-Update Section   The number of operations involved in the position-update part of the algorithm is proportional to the number of particles, and is considerably smaller than the number of operations in the momentum-update section. Parallel operations in all dimensions would only slightly increase the speed of the total algorithm, but would require an additional separate hardware operator for each dimension. For that reason this section was provided with only one operator that sequentially executes the position-coordinate updating for every dimension. The momentum and position coordinates are fetched in parallel from the particle memory, the new positions are calculated sequentially one after another and finally the position coordinates are written back to the particle memory. The hardware implementation is straightforward; a block diagram is shown in Figure 7. The predefined "move factor," stored in the constant memory, is multiplied by the momentum coordinates one after another using a hardware multiplier; the result is added to the old position coordinate to give the new position coordinate. This is stored in the appropriate position output register.

The same multiplication hardware is also used to modify the momentum coordinates of the particles by another prescribed factor in the con-

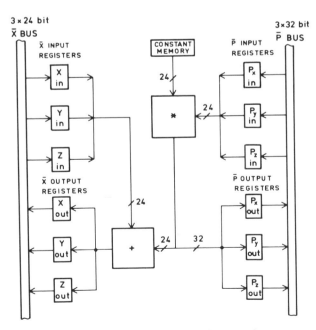

Figure 7. The position-update section.

stant memory. For those calculations additional momenta output registers were designed. This scaling operation is used for simulating the heating or cooling of the model system.

Control Requirements The position-update section communicates only with the particle memory. Consequently the input and output of the positions and the momenta is controlled by the same controller that is used for the particle memory.

4. Input/Output Section The MD-processor interface to the host has to take care of all data and control transfer between the special-purpose part and the general-purpose part of the simulation apparatus. The restriction to a 16-bit data channel, the usual size in a minicomputer, forces the multiplexing of all data buses in the MD processor to this single channel. So a bidirectional 16-bit common bus (ITD bus) was designed for the whole processor. All 16-bit portions of the data flow through the buses can be connected to this shared bus under control of an 8-bit control word (ITC bus). An additional 16-bit address bus (ITA bus) controls the memory module when it is selected for I/O transfer.

Figure 8 shows one connection to the bus. A decoder in both the I/O section and the data module controls the ITD bus transceivers by the flow direction ("dir") and the output enable ("oe") lines. The data module is selected by a unique code on the ITC bus, which activates the connection.

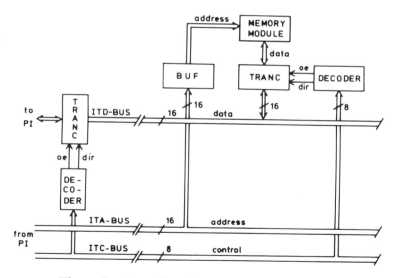

Figure 8. A load interface with the I/O section.

When a memory is involved, the ITA bus submits an address through a tri-state buffer, which functions as a multiplexer.

In Section IV.C.1 the control of the I/O section will be described.

C. Processor Control

The control part of the MD processor consists of four independent programmable bit-sliced microprocessor systems (Figure 9):

- The interface processor, PI, a 16-bit microprocessor system, which controls the interface section, receives data and instructions from the minicomputer and forwards them to the other processors;
- The memory processor, PM, a 16-bit microprocessor system, which generates addresses and control signals for both the particle memory and the position-update section;

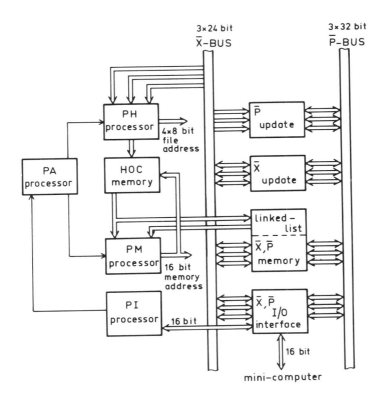

Figure 9. The data and control sections of the MD processor.

- The HOC processor, PH, a 32-bit microprocessor system, which generates four addresses for the register files in the momentum-update section, and calculates the LL-cell numbers of the particles during the linked-list setup;
- The arbiter processor, PA, a 16-bit microprocessor system, which receives all instructions from PI and generates instructions and synchronization signals for both PM and PH.

Between all processors, handshake signals are used for the internal synchronization of independent microprogram processes.

In general, the microprocessor control sections in the MD processor consist of a control part and an arithmetic part (see Figure 10). The arithmetic part is mainly responsible for the memory-address calculations, whereas the control part supplies the arithmetic part with instructions and the hardware operators with appropriate control signals.

The arithmetic part is constructed from 4-bit slices (AM2901), which,

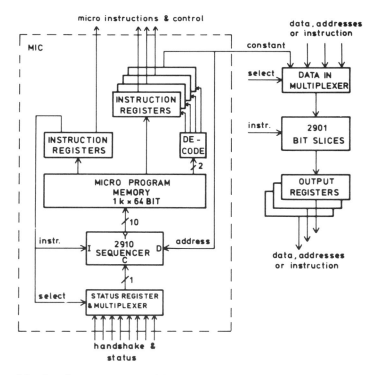

Figure 10. A microprogrammable control section used in the MD processor.

linked together, behave like a $4n$-bit arithmetic processing unit. A multiplexer is used to allow more than one input path to the single input port, whereas multiple output registers at the single output port allows more than one output path. The 17 internal registers provide temporary storage of data, and an ALU and shifter allow a variety of data manipulations (see e.g. [9]).

The control part consists of a microprogram memory, which contains all microinstruction codes, and a sequencer, which generates the addresses of the microprogram memory. The addressed microinstructions are stored in a microinstruction register at the end of every system-clock period. This pipeline register allows an overlap of instruction fetch and instruction execution. The microprogram memory is designed to contain 1024 words of 64-bit microcode and is constructed from 4k-bit fast static memory components. A portion of the microcode can be stored in one of the possible four instruction registers, under control of two bits in the microcode. This method of using multiple instruction registers enables the use of more than 64 bits of microcode.

The microprogram sequencer used, the AM2910, produces a next address as a function of a 3-bit instruction and a 1-bit test input. A direct address input, a microprogram counter, a direct input register and a stack are the sources from which the sequencer selects an output that addresses the microprogram memory. A multiplexer connected to the test input allows multiple test inputs such as the status of the arithmetic part of the control processor and the handshake signals from the other processors. The microinstruction control (MIC) part is identical for all the processors and is represented by a MIC-block in the block schemes of all four control sections.

1. Interface Processor PI   The tasks of the PI processor are

- to decode the instruction and fetch operands from the minicomputer;
- to pass the instruction and operands to PA;
- to load the microprograms in the processors PA, PM and PH;
- to load the look-up tables and the constant memory in the position-update section;
- to load the particle memory from the minicomputer and vice versa;
- to transfer the simulation results to the minicomputer;
- to calculate the "checksum" of all data transfers with the minicomputer.

To meet the requirements for instruction and data flow, the input of the 16-bit arithmetic part of PI is tapped from a bus rather than using an input multiplexer (see Figure 11). This enables the microprocessor to calculate the checksum for both input and output data. Tri-state driven devices

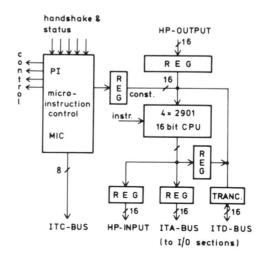

Figure 11. The block scheme of the interface processor PI.

connect the ITD bus, the minicomputer output channel, a constant from the WCS and the output registers of the microprocessor to this bus. The output registers are the address register (ITA bus), HP input register and data output register, the output of which is connected to the input bus.

The connection between the PI and all data buses in the MD processor during an input or output operation is achieved by an 8-bit code, one bit of which determines the direction of the data flow (e.g. input or output). For each 16-bit portion of a data module a unique 8-bit code is reserved. By locally decoding the 8-bit control word in both the PI and the data module, a data link will be established with the proper direction. For modules containing the data of more than one 16-bit word, e.g. a memory module, a 16-bit address is applied to access one of the memory words. The PM provides that address for the particle memory, and the PI, by its 16-bit address register, addresses all other modules such as the microprocessor memories, look-up tables and measurement memories. During an input, data are received from the minicomputer and brought into the PI, which both updates the checksum and stores the data in the data register. The appropriate 8-bit code is fed to all modules, one of which will respond. The PI address register addresses that module, and its data are transferred via the ITD bus. During an output, the selected data are stored in the micro-processor, which updates the checksum and sends the data to the mini-computer through its data register.

When no data I/O is in process, the ITD bus is free to be used for the instruction flow from PI to PA. PI waits for an instruction from the minicomputer. Then the instruction is decoded, and depending on the instruction, operands are fed to PI. When neither PM nor PH are involved with the operation to be executed (e.g. for loading microprograms, and look-up tables), PI executes the instruction independently, by using the 8-bit control word and address register. In other cases PI sends appropriate instructions to PA via the ITD bus and waits for PA to complete.

2. Arbiter Processor PA   The tasks of the PA processor are

- to decode the instruction and fetch operands from PI;
- to generate instructions and operands for both processors PH and PM;
- to synchronize the program flows in processors PH and PM;
- to inform processor PI about the status of processors PH and PM.

The input of the 16-bit arithmetic part of the PA processor is multiplexed with a constant from the WCS and the ITD bus, which functions here as an instruction bus from the PI processor during the simulation (see Figure 12); an instruction for both PM and PH is output.

The timestep loop of the leapfrog algorithm is mainly controlled by the PA processor, which distributes subtasks to PM and PH.

3. Memory Processor PM   The tasks of the PM processor are

- to decode the instruction and fetch operands from PA;
- to address the particle memory;
- to submit the start address of a particle in a linked-list cell to the HOC memory.

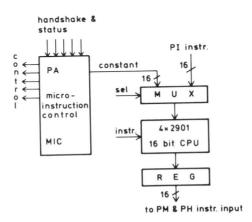

Figure 12. The block scheme of the arbiter processor PA.

The input of the 16-bit arithmetic part of the PM processor is multi-plexed with a constant from the WCS, the output of the HOC memory, the linked-list address from the particle memory and the instruction from PA (see Figure 13). The output is fed to the address input of a dynamic memory controller, which controls all the functions of the particle memory. In addition to this, the data input of the HOC memory is provided with this address, a requirement for the linked-list method.

4. Head-of-Chain Processor PH   The tasks of the PH processor are

- to decode the instruction and fetch operands from PA;
- to calculate the linked-list cell number from the positions during linked-list setup and to use this number as the address of the HOC memory;
- to generate addresses for the HOC memory, which contains the start address of a particle in the cell, and to pass that address to PM;
- to address and control the four register files in the momentum-update section;
- to address and clear the HOC memory before a new linked list is set up.

The arithmetic part of the PH processor is divided into four 8-bit sections (see Figure 14). A common constant from the WCS is fed to all four input multiplexers. The other inputs for the multiplexers are the most

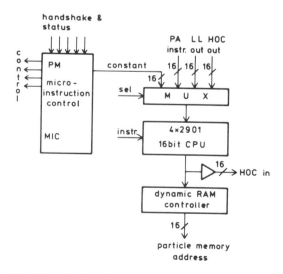

Figure 13. The block scheme of the memory processor PM.

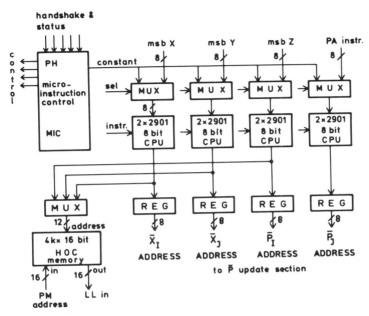

Figure 14. The block scheme of the head-of-chain processor PH.

significant bits of the three position coordinates from the buses for the first three sections, and an 8-bit instruction from PA for the fourth section. For each section an 8-bit file address register is connected to its output. They address the files XI, XJ, PI and PJ in the momentum-update section. The outputs of the first three arithmetic sections are also fed to a multiplexer that selects either a two- or a three-dimensional address for the HOC memory. This feature is used in the linked-list method.

D. Measurement Sections

1. Potential Energy and Potential Part of the Pressure During the momentum-update phase the forces, the potential energy and the potential part of the pressure between two interacting particles are simultaneously determined. This is accomplished by having separate force, potential energy and pressure look-up tables. An accumulator sums all the contributions during a timestep. The final sum can be transferred to the minicomputer in three 16-bit portions via the ITD bus (see Figure 15).

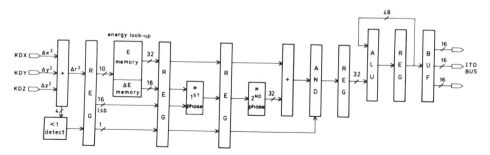

Figure 15. The block scheme of the potential-energy calculations.

2. Kinetic Energy During the position-update phase the momenta of the particles are available on the P-data bus and are fed into the momentum-update section. The input of the square operators is multiplexed with both particle distance and particle momentum. By selecting the momenta as input, the kinetic-energy contributions are obtained at the KDX, KDY and KDZ output ports. These values are summed and then accumulated to give the total kinetic energy as the positions are being updated (see Figure 16). The result can be transferred to the minicomputer via the ITD bus.

3. Radial Distribution Function During the momentum-update phase the squared distances between the particles are tapped and used as an address of a memory module (see Figure 17). For every particle pair that passes the momentum-update section during a timestep, the content of the addressed memory location is incremented by one. This yields a histogram of the radial distribution function. This information can be used in the minicomputer to calculate thermodynamic quantities such as the pressure and potential energy. Moreover, the radial distribution function is itself a quantity of interest.

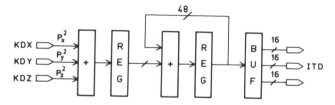

Figure 16. The block scheme of the kinetic-energy calculations.

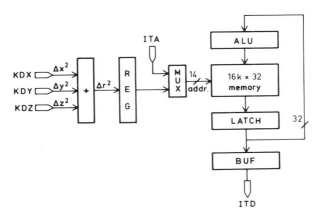

Figure 17. The block scheme of the radial-distribution tabulation.

E. Detailed Simulation-Step Procedure Description

The startup procedure of the MD processor is the loading of the microprogram codes for PA, PH and PM. From the minicomputer, 16-bit portions of these codes are transferred via the MD I/O section to PI. Here a checksum is maintained and the data is passed to the ITD bus. An appropriate code on the ITC bus connects the ITD bus with the required microprogram memory part, whereas the ITA bus supplies the memory address to store that 16-bit portion. The final step in the loading procedure is to send the checksum via the HP-input register to the minicomputer for verification.

Similarly, the table values are loaded. These include the force values, the potential-energy values, the potential part of the pressure values and the move factor.

The next step (see Figure 18) is to load the initial particle positions and momenta coordinates into the particle memory. The 16-bit portions of all the coordinates of a particle are transferred from the minicomputer via the PI and ITD bus to the appropriate transceiver input register before they are written to the memory. This procedure is started by a "load particles," LP, instruction, which is decoded in PI and passed to PM via PA. In addition, a parameter is passed, which gives the total number of particles to be loaded.

Once all particle coordinates are transferred to the input registers, PM addresses the particle memory and stores the particle attributes. When all particles are stored, PM flags PA, and PA in its turn flags PI, which then waits for the next instruction from the minicomputer.

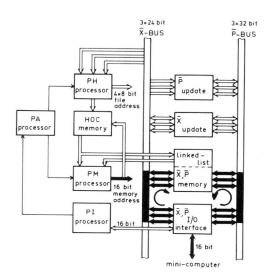

Figure 18. The particle memory is loaded from the minicomputer.

The first of the two phases in a single timestep is the position-update phase. During this phase three important actions take place:

- the position update;
- the setup of the linked-list, using the new positions;
- the total kinetic-energy calculations.

Via PI, the instruction "timestep," TS, and operands containing the total number of particles, the number of dimensions involved, the number of LL-cells per dimension and the number of timesteps are passed to PA. This processor will generate all instructions for PM and PH and will receive flag signals from them to synchronize their flow control by sending control signals to them.

The following procedure is carried out sequentially for all particles i (see Figure 19): PM addresses the particle memory, and all coordinates of particle i are transferred to the position-update input registers. Simultaneously, the momenta coordinates are fed to the momentum-update section, which will produce the squared momenta coordinates at the KDX, KDY and KDZ outputs after four system cycles. For this purpose PH changes the multiplexer input mode to allow the momenta to enter the squaring operation in the multiplier section (Figure 3). These results are accumulated in the kinetic-energy measurement section (see Section IV.D.2). After the sequential calculations in the position-update section, the new positions are transferred to both the particle memory and to PH.

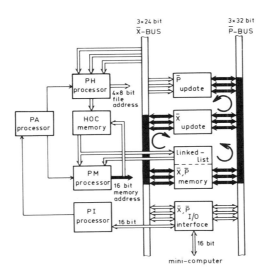

Figure 19. The position-update phase: the particle coordinates are moved to the position-update section and E_k is calculated in the momentum-update section.

The latter forms the address of the HOC memory from their most significant bits. This address is identical to the LL-cell number in which the particle is located. The addressed HOC location contains either the address of a previously detected particle in the LL-cell or zero, indicating that particle i is the first particle found in the LL-cell. That information is fed to the linked-list portion of the particle memory and is stored in that memory together with the new position coordinates (see Figure 20). The remaining step is to store the address of particle i, i, in the addressed HOC memory. Hence the HOC memory will contain the addresses of the particles that were found last in their respective LL-cell during the linked-list setup. These particles are used as the head-of-chain in the linked-list procedure to directly find all particles in a given LL-cell (see Figure 21). The linked-list is used in the second phase of a single timestep. The first particle in a chain of a LL-cell I is found by submitting address I to the HOC memory. PH generates the head-of-chain address for the HOC memory, the content of which is an input of PM. This address is passed to the particle memory and the address contents, and the particle position and momentum coordinates are transferred to the momentum-update section, whereas the linked-list address is passed to PM. PH addresses the I files to store the particle attributes. PM reads the linked-list address, and tests for a zero value. A nonzero value gives the next particle in that LL-cell, the attributes of which

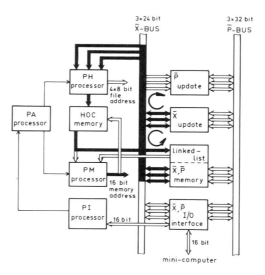

Figure 20. The position-update phase: the particle position coordinates are restored in the particle memory and the linked-list is set up.

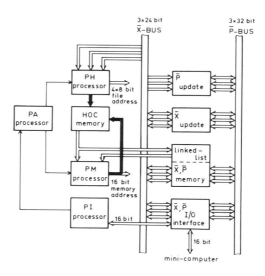

Figure 21. The position-update phase: the particle becomes the new head-of-chain.

are stored in the next location of the *I* files. This procedure is continued until a zero address is detected.

The *J* files are loaded similarly (see Figures 22 and 23). Then all relevant particle-data combinations are fed to the calculating pipe. PH generates appropriate addresses for the X*I*, X*J*, P*I* and P*J* files. These can be considered as a vector set for the pipe. The two addresses for the P files are delayed 10 cycles with respect to the two addresses for the X files to compensate for the pipeline delay.

The next step in the I–J cell calculation is to overwrite the old momenta in the particle memory with the just-calculated new momenta for all particles *i* and *j*. The new momenta are stored into the particle memory using the linked-list method, similarly to filling the files (see Figures 24 and 25).

A special case occurs for interactions within one LL-cell. Then the procedure is to fill the X*I* and X*J* files, the P*I* files, and zero the P*J* files. After the pipe calculations of all relevant combinations, the contents of the P*I* files are added to the P*J* files to find the total new momenta of the particles in cell *I*. This enables one to handle this special case similarly to the general case. This summation is achieved by selecting the appropriate input of the multiplexers at the end of the calculation pipe.

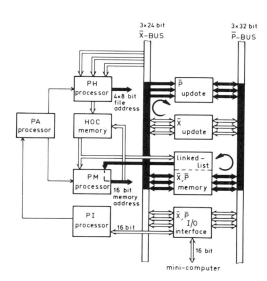

Figure 22. The momentum-update phase: the register files in the momentum-update section are filled with the coordinates of the first particle in the linked-list.

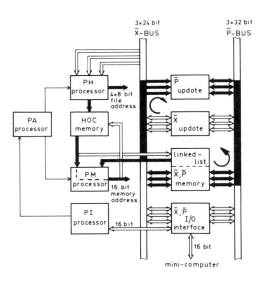

Figure 23. The momentum-update phase: the register files in the momentum-update section are filled with the coordinates of the next particle in the linked-list.

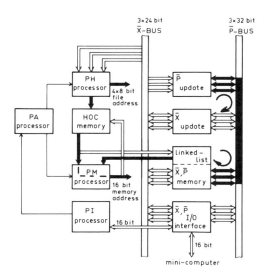

Figure 24. The momentum-update phase: the momentum coordinates of the first particle in the linked-list are stored back in the particle memory.

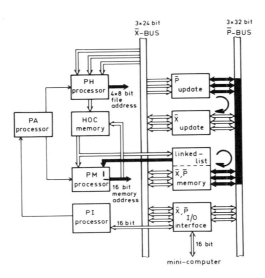

Figure 25. The momentum-update phase: the momentum coordinates of the next particle in the linked-list are stored back in the particle memory.

For all relevant cell I–cell J combinations, PH will generate the HOC addresses. The result will be that the momenta of all particles are updated and PA will flag PI, which then will wait for the next instruction from the minicomputer.

During the momentum-update calculations the measurement of potential energy, the potential part of the pressure and the radial distribution function is performed.

At the end of a timestep the potential energy, the potential part of the pressure, the kinetic energy and the radial distribution function are transferred to the minicomputer, for tests or for further calculations.

V. Implementation

A. Assembly Method

The MD processor is both a prototype and a final product because only one has been planned. Often, prototypes differ from series products in the method of interconnecting the individual components; the final product, containing printed-circuit boards, is usually preceded by prototype boards, constructed with the help of an easy-to-modify assembly technique. The wirewrap method was used in the MD processor. This method is exceptionally well suited for hardware development and test purposes; modifications are easily rewired. All wirewrap pins are testpoints, easily connectable to testing devices. A low-impedance power distribution on the boards has been achieved by using double-layer bus-bars.

B. Component Choice

The MD processor is realized with TTL-compatible components. A wide choice in this logic family is commercially available and is second-sourced by many manufacturers. A higher-speed alternative, the ECL logic, would be far more difficult to use, since line-length effects, line-termination and power-dissipation problems have to be carefully taken into account. TTL components can be interconnected without many problems as long as the line lengths are kept short (< 40 cm) and the applied clock frequency is less than 16 MHz. For power-dissipation reasons the low-power Schottky (LS) version of TTL is used in the construction of the MD processor. The larger-scale integration techniques (LSI, VLSI) allow higher circuit complexity; hence, fewer components are required to build in certain functions such as memory and multipliers. Reliability increases since the hardware failure rate is related to the number of chips rather than the number of gates in a design. The hardware implementation of memory, multipliers and microprocessor control in the MD processor will be illustrated in the next three sections.

C. Memory Implementation

1. The Particle Memory   The particle memory in the MD processor is the largest memory in the system (maximum 64k-word by 188-bit), and is constructed from dynamic memory components for reasons of cost, power dissipation and bit density. Dynamic memories, in contrast with static memories, need to be refreshed every 2 ms, the control of which requires special care. For this purpose a dynamic-RAM controller (Intel 8203) is used, which handles both memory requests and automatic refreshing. A refresh indication is brought into the memory control section, which, when a refresh operation is in progress, will delay a memory request. The total refresh procedure adds about 5% overhead in time. A normal read or write operation takes 330 ns, which is fast enough to be carried out within two system cycles. A memory operation delayed by a refresh takes four system cycles. The basic memory components are the 16k-word by 1-bit components with a cycle time of 330 ns. Bus transceivers (AM2917A) are used to interface the memory with the appropriate buses.

2. The Microprogram and Table Look-Up Memory Fast memory is required for the microprogram and table look-up memories since they are accessed every clock cycle. TTL-compatible MOS memory, available in 1k-word by 4-bits components (AM9144), meets that speed requirement of 250 ns. The shared input and output pins require special interfacing to the ITD bus to electrically separate the input and output function of that memory. For loading, a write operation disables the memory output and enables the data of the ITD bus to be written in the memory. In the operational mode the memory is connected to the I/O pins, while the ITD-bus connection is disabled.

3. Register Files In the momentum-update section, the register files have to carry out a read–modify–write cycle within one clock cycle. Separated input and output pins are required for this purpose. A 256-word by 4-bit memory component, the MMI91L422, is used. A latch at the output port holds the selected output during the writing.

D. Microprocessor Control

To control all dedicated functions in the MD processor during every system-clock cycle, components of the AM2900 bit-sliced family are used in the construction of the control microprocessors. The data path consists of cascaded AM2901 slices, which can perform simple arithmetic operations such as addition, subtraction, shifting and logical operations. It is able to control the continuous address generation for the memories in the MD processor, to decode instructions received from the input port and to keep loop counters. The control path consists of a microprogram memory and a microprogram address sequencer, the AM2910. The inputs of this sequencer are the instruction and a constant or a jump address from the microprogram, and also a test input for conditional jumps. A multiplexer in front of this test pin allows multiple test conditions, one of which can be selected by the microprogram. The test inputs are the handshake signals from other processors and data-path status (e.g. sign, carry, zero detect, etc.) A one-level pipelined microprogram-instruction register allows simultaneous execution of a microinstruction and the fetching of the next microinstruction; this enables the control section to operate at 4 MHz.

E. Multipliers

Two acceptable fast multiplier components were the 4*2-bit AM2505 and the 8*8-bit MMI67558. Both types met the speed requirements of 250 ns, but the component count of the latter was smaller. Therefore the MMI67558 was selected. The total 24*24-bit multiplier was built from 16-bit partial products, which are fed to an array of full-adders, resulting in a 48-bit result. For speed reasons a pipeline register breaks up the operations into two equal time-consuming parts to meet the speed requirement (see e.g. [10]).

F. Functional Division

The choice of the board size depends heavily on the number of pins required for board interconnections. A good backpanel design, preferably with straight buses and control signals, is imperative. Given the number of functions to be built in and the number of interconnections to be made, we decided on a triple Euro-board 28 cm. long, allowing three 96-pin connectors to the backpanel. This exceptionally large board size made a modular and structured functional division possible in which the number of identical boards was maximal. Three sets of identical boards are used for the squared-distance calculations for one dimension, the momentum-update calculations for one dimension, and the particle memory for one dimension. The force look-up board on the one hand and the energy and pressure look-up boards on the other hand differ only in the accumulation part. For each control section one board is used. Furthermore there is a board for the linked-list memory, for the I/O section, for the radial-distribution function calculations and for the kinetic-energy calculations.

G. Microprogram and Hardware Test Equipment

The microprograms for the control sections in the MD processor are developed in the minicomputer (see also Section VI.E.). The resulting 64-bit microcodes are loaded into the microprogram memories of the PA, PM and PH control sections under control of the interface processor PI. The latter processor was designed to have a permanently stored microprogram in its microprogram memory to carry out the load function. In general, a programmable read-only-memory (PROM) is used for this purpose.

For the development and test phase this solution would be expensive. Furthermore, it is difficult to test this processor's proper functioning. To solve these problems a special test device has been built, the "ROM-simulator." Its major function is to take over the function of the PROM. For that purpose, a fast 1k 64-bit RAM section has been included in the ROM-simulator, which can be loaded by the minicomputer through an additional data channel. Flat cables connect this RAM section with the PROM sockets in the PI-control section.

Additional functions of the ROM-simulator feature microprogram debug facilities. Three sets of 16-bit probes can be used for test inputs, such as the microprogram addresses of the other control sections. One of the three probe sets or the microprogram address of PI can be selected for comparison with a predefined 16-bit code. When a match occurs, the system clock of the MD processor will be disabled and all 48 bits of the probes in addition to the microprogram address of PI are displayed for inspection. A single-step option makes it possible to follow the control sequence step by step.

An additional display panel shows the values of all four microprogram addresses and the output of the arithmetic part of all four control sections. This survey of the status of the four control sections appeared to be a helpful feature for testing the simultaneously operating microprogram sequences.

A logic analyzer (K100D) and high-speed oscilloscope have been used to test the dynamic behavior of the MD processor, or to trace selected parts of the control sequences.

H. Cost and Performance

Many students were involved in the construction of the MD processor. In the last two years of their final degree, as a part of the educational aspect of this project, they were trained to build and test subsections of the processor, or they specialized in microprogramming the control sections. It took about three years to build the machine, including the software required to run the processor with the minicomputer. To build a copy of the processor would take less than one man-year.

The hardware components, including the development overhead, cost about 100,000 Dfl., whereas a copy would now cost half that amount. In addition, the usage of the minicomputer (150,000 Dfl.) should be mentioned, as the MD processor consumes about 10% of its time and storage. However, the numbers mentioned above are negligible compared to the power of the system. Although it is difficult to compare the performance of the MD processor with commercially available (super)computers by some characteristic number (see e.g. [11]), the speed of the MD processor is of the same order as the speed of the CRAY-1 when simulating the same system. To be more specific, the theoretical speed of the MD processor is $4*10^6$ particle-pair calculations per second, including the standard thermodynamic calculations. In practice, it takes less than 0.1 sec. to simulate one timestep per 500 particles, which is at least three times faster than conventional mainframes such as the CDC7600 and comparable to CRAY-1 [12]. Furthermore the MD processor has an enormous advantage in the cost/speed ratio.

The measured Mean-Time-Between-Failure (MTBF) was dominated by the failure of the minicomputer or a power failure, and demonstrates the reliability of the processor.

I. Test and Maintenance

The modular setup and microprogrammable control of the MD processor allow for testing the hardware and software to any desired level. However, the amount of time needed to develop and test these test microprograms would stop the MD processor from running for a disproportional time. A more efficient approach that was used is to build in certain checkpoints in the simulation software:

- Energy conservation test. When no temperature adjustment is performed, the total energy must be constant with a predefined tolerance. This test, carried out with the help of user instructions in a command file, detects both a hardware failure and a program error in the command file. Auto restart procedures allow continuation after a power failure.
- Microprogram synchronization test. Whenever the control flow of microprocessors is "out of phase," the control flow of the other microprocessors will be trapped and will halt the processor.
- The maintenance of the dynamic files can be used to monitor the behavior of the kinetic energy, the potential energy and the pressure during a simulation.
- Total-momentum conservation test. Molecular-dynamics simulations are usually performed with a system at rest: the total momentum in the x-, y-, z-direction is initially set to zero. As the total momentum is a constant of motion, it should remain zero.
- Time-reversal test. A special feature of the MD processor is its exact time-reversibility, which results from the fixed-point data representation and the careful roundoff applied in updating momenta and positions. This also means that the total momentum can be exactly set to zero, and should remain so during a constant-energy simulation.
- The data transfer between the minicomputer and the processor is verified by a checksum. An error message will be given whenever such an error occurs.

Whenever an error of the above-mentioned type is detected, a more detailed test is required to trace the error source. Depending on the cause of the failure, one of the following test procedures helps to find the failing part of the MD processor:

- Memory tests. By writing to and reading from the memories in the MD processor, the minicomputer can detect failures in those memories.
- Symmetry tests. A set of particle configurations for symmetry tests in the x-, y- and z-directions discriminates a hardware failure in one of the three boards. In addition, swapping the equal boards for x-, y- and z-directions may be of use to determine which one of the sections fails.
- By loading the force and the energy table with special values, the force- and energy-calculating sections can be tested in detail.
- Special configurations and tables can be used to detect failures in a section of the processor.
- As a final test all runs should be reproducible.

VI. Software

A. Introduction

Using an algorithm-oriented processor in a computer experiment does not reduce the size and complexity of the software required to carry out the simulation. The dedicated processor carries out only the frequently occurring inner loop operations of the algorithm involved and replaces just a small, albeit the most time-consuming, part of the total simulation program.

A top-down planning and design technique was used to create the software that integrates the MD processor into an MD-simulation program.

B. User Requirements

The typical user of the MD processor will be a physicist or a chemist rather than a computer scientist. He is primarily interested in the physical content of the simulation and should not be bothered with software or hardware details. His specialty is to set up a computer experiment, run it and finally interpret the outcome. The total simulation program is a fully tested black box to him, supported with a wide choice of high-level language user instructions. However, he should be able to add new instructions to the system, to satisfy his special simulation requirements. Hence, the basic software has to be easy to read and easy to adapt, so that new software can easily be incorporated into the total software structure.

The user does not want to be distracted from his experiment by the worry of data bookkeeping. He wishes the resulting data from the simulation to be automatically stored in an easy-to-use data base on disc. These data can be used later for further calculations, such as the calculation of time-correlation functions.

A reference user manual that describes the functions of all possible user instructions in detail, and a comprehensive error-message manual, are additional requirements to guarantee a user-friendly environment.

C. MD Processor Host Software

The software package that is needed for the MD processor is a set of Fortran programs that run in the minicomputer. One program, the simulation program, controls the simulation in the MD processor and collects the results. The input of this program is high-level user instructions and additional parameters, whereas the output is stored in a file data base on the disc of the minicomputer.

The other programs use that same data base for further manipulation of the results, such as the calculation of the correlation functions. When time-consuming calculations are involved, e.g. calculating the orientation-correlation function or time-correlation functions, an array processor (AP120B) is used. The AP120B is attached both to the minicomputer for control and to the DMDP by a fast data-link.

1. The Simulation Program   There are two ways to supply the simulation program with instructions. In the *interactive* mode, the user has to type in an instruction and its parameter values every time a prompt occurs. The prompt indicates that the program waits for input.

The user can prepare a "command"-file, in which the instructions to be executed are collected, and he can switch from the interactive mode to the *interpreter* mode that uses the command-file now as input for the simulation program. Additional control-flow instructions can be used to allow conditional jumps in the command-file on a wide range of tests. For this purpose global parameters can be used. They can either be set to a constant value or to a current value of a dynamics quantity, such as the potential, the kinetic and the total energy, and the pressure. In addition, arithmetic operations on the global parameters are possible, whereas Fortran-like "IF () GOTO" instructions can be used for the conditional jumps.

2. Data Base   The data base in the simulation program distinguishes different types of files. They are

- the system information (S) file, in which all relevant information of the current simulation is kept;

- the particle (P) file, that keeps records of particle configurations;
- the writable control store (W) file, which contains the microcodes of the control processors in the MD processor;
- the table (T) file, which keeps all look-up table values for the MD processor;
- the dynamics (D) file, which keeps the records of the values of the pressure, the kinetic and potential energies and the corresponding time-step number;
- the block-sum (B) file, which keeps the record of both the values and the squared values of the quantities in the dynamics file, but summed over a number of timesteps;
- the radial-distribution function (R) file, which contains the records of radial-distribution functions;
- the averaged radial-distribution function (G) file, which keeps the records of radial-distribution functions, summed over a number of timesteps.

All B, D, G and R files contain the S file as a header, whereas all particle records in the P file are preceded by this header. In general, "user-files" can be assigned to be the S, B, D, G, P, or R files and are called "work-files." One set of S, B, D, G, P and R files is standard on disc, called "standard-files," and comprises default files for the system. User-files are involved whenever a filename "filnam" is specified in an instruction, whereas the work-files are selected if no filename specification is given.

D. User Instruction Set

A user instruction consists of an operation code, namely a two-letter mnemonic shorthand, followed by a set of variables separated by commas. In general, the first letter in the operation code describes the operation and the second letter denotes the object to operate on. The variables are filenames, numbers or additional codes, depending on the instruction. There are initialization instructions, I/O instructions, simulation instructions, measurement instructions, file instructions and interpreter control instructions.

E. Microprogram Software

A general-purpose cross microassembler has been designed and implemented in the minicomputer for efficient development of the microprograms that are required for the control sections in the MD processor. A code-definition file and a microprogram source file are input and a microcode object file is output. The cross microassembler handles labels and multiformats to satisfy the use of multiple instruction registers in the control sections. Furthermore, a microcode column shuffle program allows that the software bit sequence may differ from the hardware control bit sequence for every format.

VII. Conclusions

The MD processor has been constructed and tested for simulations of up to 16,383 particles in one, two or three dimensions of up to two different species of particles and for any short-ranged force law. Since 1982 it has run as planned, giving CRAY-1 speed for 24 hours per day. Theoretically it handles four million particle-pair calculations per second, which in practice gives 0.2 sec. per timestep per 1000 particles.

While the speed of the MD processor is comparable to that of the CRAY-1, its costs are not: it only cost Dfl. 100,000 to build and has negligible running costs. This amounts at commercial rates to about 10 hours CRAY-1 time or less than 1% of the CRAY-1 hardware cost, which means a cost/speed improvement of a factor greater than 100.

Usage of the MD processor is made simple by the software package and the data base in the minicomputer. Flexibility and ease of use is achieved by additional programs that use the data base for calculation of final results on the host minicomputer.

The MD processor was designed for, and can easily be extended to, simulations of 65,535 particles for up to four species of particles. The modular setup and microprogrammable control of the processor allow hardware functions to be added for special measurements. Furthermore, by linking the processor to the AP120B, the P^3M algorithm for systems with long-range forces can be implemented.

The MTBF of more than three months reflects the processor reliability. Maintenance and fault searching can be carried out by test-microprograms.

Simulations with the DMDP started with the study of the low-temperature two-dimensional solid phase as a test case [13]. Afterwards extensive simulations were performed on two-dimensional melting [14] exploiting the large number of particles possible.

A short study has been done on the two-dimensional equation of state [15]. For three-dimensional fluids the dynamic structure factor and the current–current correlation function have been determined for some thermodynamic states. The disappearance of the sound propagation gap has been observed for high-density fluids [16].

For two-dimensional Lennard–Jones systems, capillary waves have been studied both without [17] and with [18] a gravitational field.

The wetting transition has been studied extensively, where the possibility of two different types of particles could be used to incorporate a realistic substrate [19]. Partly finished are simulations regarding prewetting, collapsing systems and diffusion at low densities for large systems.

Nowadays, an algorithm-oriented MD processor would look much different from the one described here. The progression of technology since 1978 enables one to build a processor that is faster and much more flexible. More complex interactions may be involved, the usage of pairlists next to linked lists is feasible and more complex measurements can be incorporated. More computational power can be achieved by using a multiprocessor architecture — a set of parallel computing nodes interconnected by a network, where both nodes and the network are designed to efficiently carry out the algorithm involved.

The successful development and application of the algorithm-oriented MD processor described here provides a pointer to exciting future possibilities. The large cost/speed gains demonstrated may be used to open up regions of parameter space hitherto beyond reasonable cost bounds. For instance, fluid-flow simulations span a wide range of science and engineering disciplines. Already calculations in aeronautics, weather prediction, oil-reservoir simulations, tidal- and storm-surge prediction, astrophysical gas flows and shock modelling consume a lot of computer time; their enormous costs could be dramatically reduced by suitable algorithm-oriented processors. Similar instances may also be found in civil and mechanical engineering, quantum physics, plasma physics, structural chemistry and so forth.

References

1. Hockney, R. W., and Eastwood, J. W. (1981). *Computer Simulation Using Particles.* McGraw-Hill, New York.
2. Isihara, A. (1971). *Statistical Physics.* Academic Press Inc., New York.
3. Buneman, O. (1967). *Comput. Phys.* **1**, 517.
4. Ralston, A. (1965). *A First Course in Numerical Analysis*, pp. 3–5. McGraw-Hill, New York.
5. Beeman, D. (1976). *J. Comput. Phys.* **20**, 130.
6. Hockney, R. W. (1970). *Methods Comput. Phys.* **9**, 135.
7. Langdon, A. B., and Lasinski, F. (1976). *Methods Comput. Phys.* **16**, 327.
8. Bakker, A. F. (1978). *Internal Report SV 78-1.* Department of Applied Physics, Delft University of Technology.
9. Mick, J. and Brick, J. (1980). *Bit-Slice Microprocessor Design.* McGraw-Hill, New York.

10. *MMI Bipolar LSI Data Book* (1979).
11. Hockney, R. W., and Jessehope, C. R. (1981). *Parallel Computers*. Adam Hilger Ltd., Bristol.
12. Fincham, D., and Ralston, B. J. (1981). *Comput. Phys. Comm.* **23,** 127.
13. Bakker, A. F., Bruin, C., van Dieren, F., and Hilhorst, H. J. (1982). *Phys. Lett.* **93A,** 67.
14. Bakker, A. F., Bruin, C., and Hilhorst, H. J. (1984). *Phys. Rev. Lett.* **52,** 449.
15. Bruin, C., Bakker, A. F., and Bishop, M. (1984). *J. Chem. Phys.* **80,** 5859.
16. van Rijs, J. C., de Schepper, I. M., Bruin, C., van Delft, D. A., and Bakker, A. F. (1985). *Phys. Lett.* **111A,** 58.
17. Sikkenk, J. H., Hilhorst, H. J., and Bakker, A. F. (1985). *Physica.* **131A,** 587.
18. Sikkenk, J. H., Vossnack, E. O., van Leeuwen, J. M. J., and Bakker, A. F. (1987). *Physica.* **146A,** 622.
19. Sikkenk, J. H., Indekeu, J. O., van Leeuwen, J. M. J., and Vossnack, E. O. (1987). *Phys. Rev. Lett.* **59,** 98.
20. Sangster, M. J., and Dixon, M. (1976). *Adv. Phys.* **25,** 247.
21. Fisher, M. E., and Selke, W. (1980). *Phys. Rev. Lett.* **44,** 1502.

Acknowledgments

The authors wish to thank Prof. B. P. Th. Veltman for initiating the project of special-purpose computers in his group on Signal Processing and in particular for his efforts for over more than a decade in searching for a realization of a molecular-dynamics special-purpose computer.

They are also grateful to Prof. H. J. Hillhorst for his fruitful collaboration in the project.

They are indebted to Prof. J. M. J. van Leeuwen and Dr. A. Compagner for their support and many enlightening discussions.

The contributions of many students, who participated in the project and spent part of their youth in building the processor, can hardly be overestimated.

7   The Delft Ising System Processor

A. HOOGLAND, A. COMPAGNER, AND
H. W. J. BLÖTE

Faculty of Applied Physics
University of Technology
Delft
The Netherlands

I. Introduction

Numerical simulation by means of general-purpose computers is a standard technique in statistical mechanics. In principle, the method is straightforward, but in practice (particularly in the field of phase transitions and critical phenomena) it may be difficult to produce sufficiently accurate results within reasonable limits of time and money. The use of supercomputers alleviates the first of these restraints but is detrimental for the other.

Most simulations have in common that the bulk computational effort is concentrated in relatively simple elementary algorithms which have to be repeated a great many times. This situation is ideally suited for the use of special-purpose or algorithm-adapted processors [1, 2, 3], dedicated to one particular task only. As we will try to show in this contribution, such special-purpose machines may still be flexible enough to tackle a wide range of problems, while being both simpler and faster than general-purpose computers of a comparable technological level. In addition, they are continuously available and their costs of operation are much lower. Their main drawback of course is that one has to design and build these machines oneself.

The stochastic algorithm used to simulate Ising spin systems with short-range interactions is a perfect test-case for the construction of a special-purpose computer, because of the binary character of the main variables involved, i.e. the spin values, and because of the extremely long relaxation times and correlation distances in the critical region, which necessitate very long calculation times. It is for this algorithm that the Delft Ising System Processor, the DISP, was built in the years 1979–1981. Design, construction and operation of this machine will be described in this contribution.

We will begin with a few words about the history of the subject in Delft, where the idea of building special-purpose processors for simulation problems was originated by Veltman [4]. Predecessors of the DISP [2] were a small Monte-Carlo (MC) machine (handling 32×32 Ising spins with nearest-neighbor interactions only), a counting machine for the determination of the combinatorial factor for Ising systems of up to 6×6 spins, and an MC machine for the simulation of crystal growth according to the solid-on-solid model for a square array of 128×128 atoms [4]. In parallel with the development of the DISP, a special-purpose machine for the simulation of solid–fluid–gas systems by means of the molecular-dynamics method was constructed in Delft by Bakker [3, 5].

This contribution is arranged in the following manner. The design desiderata, i.e. the desired scope of the DISP in terms of its calculational possibilities and the Hamiltonians that it can handle, are set out in Section II. The chosen realization in hardware, key to the low-cost calculational efficiency and flexibility of the DISP is described in Section III. Considerable effort was invested in the hardware random-number generator to be employed; this is the subject of Section IV. Section V is dedicated to the performance of the DISP in comparison with general-purpose computers. A short survey is given in Section VI of the software written for the host computer, necessary for initialization of the DISP, for data acquisition and for the determination of results. Section VII contains a brief review of the results obtained with the DISP up to the moment of writing. Finally, Section VIII is a discussion devoted to a next-generation MC machine for Ising systems, which (due to recent and expected progress in the field of hardware components) can be considerably faster than the DISP.

II. Design Characteristics

The development of the DISP aimed at the construction of a cheap processor (necessary hardware investment less than 10^4 US\$) with a speed of at least one elementary MC step per microsecond for Ising systems of up to a few million spins in two and three dimensions (2-D and 3-D respectively), with as wide a range of Hamiltonians as is expedient.

The Ising systems that we want to study do not just contain pair interactions and interactions with an external field. Rather, the design to be selected should enable us to perform MC calculations including at least four different interactions of any type, though restricted to a certain range. We chose, quite arbitrarily, this range to be a square area of 8×8 spin sites in 2-D or a cubic volume of $4 \times 4 \times 4$ spin sites in 3-D. The number of spins within a range, 64, is small enough to be manageable while being sufficiently large to allow many different Hamiltonians.

To further explain this point, which is basic for the structure of the DISP, we use the following terminology. The spin that at some moment in the MC simulation is selected for the MC process is called the central spin. The collection of spins with which the central spin through terms in the Hamiltonian is interacting is called the local configuration (including the central spin). In the elementary MC process, the new value of the central spin is determined by means of the Boltzmann factors p_+ and p_- valid for the given local configuration with the central spin "up" or "down" respectively. These Boltzmann factors (or rather the related transition probabilities) can be stored in advance in a look-up table, the addresses of which must be determined from the local configuration. For fast simulation, the spin values of the local configuration must therefore be readable simultaneously, which implies that they should be contained in separate parts of the memory in which all spin values are stored, these parts (or memory banks) being simultaneously addressable and readable. If, as we chose, the local configuration will never extend beyond the (square or cubic) range of 64 spins, we will never need more than 64 separate memory banks. Each spin within this range can then be accommodated on a separate memory bank. Which spins on which memory banks should be read is completely determined by the addresses of the spins within the local configuration; in the chosen structure this information is available simultaneously.

Less drastic for the structure of the DISP are two other features that were adopted. Periodic boundary conditions of the toroidal type without helical shifts were chosen. In addition it was desired that the selection of the central spin, i.e. the spin to be subjected to the MC process, could be chosen either randomly or by going through the lattice in a sequential manner.

A typical Hamiltonian to be studied is

$$\mathscr{H} = K_1 \, \Sigma_{i=1}^N \, s_i + K_2 \, \Sigma_{\langle i,j \rangle} \, s_i s_j + K_3 \, \Sigma_{\langle i,j,k \rangle} \, s_i s_j s_k + K_4 \, \Sigma_{\langle i,j,k,l \rangle} \, s_i s_j s_k s_l, \quad (1)$$

where N is the number of spins, while K_i denotes the coupling constants and $s_i = \pm 1$ the spin values. The notation $\langle i,j,k \rangle$ indicates that the corresponding lattice sum must be taken over all translations over the lattice of one or more (e.g. up and down triangles) particular triples, selected from the (square or cubic) range of 64 spins discussed above; a similar remark applies to $\langle i,j \rangle$ and $\langle i,j,k,l \rangle$. It is very well possible to choose these sets of interacting neighbors such that the symmetry of the Hamiltonian is different from simple quadratic or simple cubic. For instance, in two dimensions one can define $\langle i,j \rangle$ to include, in rectangular coordinates, the neighbors at $\pm (0,1)$, $\pm (1,0)$ and $\pm (1,1)$. This choice leads to a triangular Ising model with nearest-neighbor interactions. Analogously face- and body-centered cubic models can be defined in 3-D. The expression (1) does not exhaust the possibilities of the final realization of the DISP. For instance, modifications in which the terms with K_3 and K_4 are replaced by further pair interactions, e.g. with second and third neighbors, are also allowed. Often, these modifications can be realized by means of software adaptations; in some cases, minor hardware modifications would be necessary. However, practical considerations cause certain additional (though not very restrictive) constraints on the Hamiltonians to be studied on the DISP; these constraints will be discussed later.

The summation in each term of the chosen Hamiltonian is performed by accumulation in lattice-sum registers. When necessary, other terms can easily be added to the four included in the above Hamiltonian, by implementation of more lattice-sum registers and by extending the size of the look-up table in which the Boltzmann factors (or rather the transition probabilities) are stored for the spin–flip mechanism.

The random-number generator was chosen to be of the linear 2-bit feedback shift-register type. In order to enable us to investigate its quality, a high degree of flexibility with regard to shift-register length and feedback position was implemented.

At a later stage, the design of the DISP has been extended in order to perform Monte Carlo Renormalization Group (MCRG) calculations. This means that the processor must not only be able to simulate Ising systems by means of the MC method; it must also be able to calculate many different multispin correlations. Furthermore it has to be able to renormalize the spin configuration, i.e. it has to map the spin configuration on a renormalized lattice which is smaller by a factor two in linear size. As it turned out, these extensions could easily be incorporated into the design of the DISP. Details concerning these extensions are given in Section III.F.

III. Hardware Architecture

A. Functional Organization

A shown in Figure 1, the DISP is composed of a number of hardware sections, each carrying out one or more operations that are part of the elementary spin–flip mechanism.

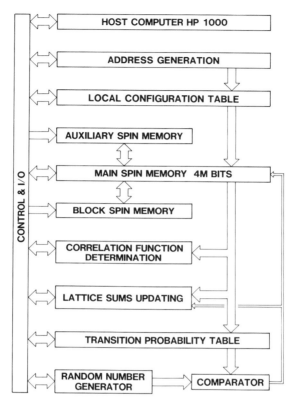

Figure 1. The functional organization of the Delft Ising System Processor.

The address-generation section consists of a number of separate address generators: one for the selection of random sites for the central spin, one for sequential selection, others for loading and reading look-up tables and the main spin memory, and still others for the MCRG block-spin generation and correlation function determination process. Which generator is used is decided in advance of a particular operation by means of software instructions for the host computer, for which we have a HP 1000 system available. The address of the central spin selected is passed on to the section which determines the local configuration; this section is programmed by the host computer to generate the spin addresses of the local configuration (taking into account the details of the Ising system to be studied: dimensionality, lattice structure, Hamiltonian, block-spin generation). The spin values of the local configuration are read simultaneously from the main spin memory (consisting of 64 different memory banks) and determine the address in the look-up table where the relevant transition probability is found. This transition-probability (TP) table is filled as part of the initialization procedure by means of the HP 1000; the value stored in a particular entry pertaining to a particular local configuration is

$$P = \frac{p_+}{p_+ + p_-}, \qquad (2)$$

where p_+ and p_- are the Boltzmann factors for the particular local configuration with the central spin "up" and "down" respectively. This corresponds with the transition probabilities for the MC simulation of Ising sytems used first by Yang [6]; alternatively, the DISP can also be run with the transition probabilities used by Fosdick [7]. On the other hand, when in the renormalization process a block-spin configuration must be determined, the TP table is filled with values that correspond with the particular rule (e.g. the majority rule) with which the block spins are defined.

The value P found in the TP table for the actual local configuration is compared with a random number R (uniformly distributed between 0 and 1) in the comparator section; if $P > R$ holds, the central spin is given the value $+1$, otherwise -1. If the new value of the central spin differs from the old one, the main spin memory must be corrected and the four different lattice-sum registers (one for each term in the Hamiltonian (1) or a similar one) must be updated. The contents of these registers can be used to calculate the thermodynamic quantities of the system under investigation, either at the end of a complete MC run or at certain predetermined moments during a run.

The other sections of the DISP shown in Figure 1, i.e. the auxiliary spin memory, the block-spin memory and the block-spin correlation function section are needed for MCRG calculations and will be discussed below. In general, the remainder of this section is concerned with further details of the hardware structure.

B. Bus Structure

The sections of Figure 1 are actually interconnected by means of four data buses: the C(ontrol)-bus, the A(ddress)-bus, the D(ata)-bus and the S(pin)-bus. The C-bus is a 16-bit data path that contols the function of the hardware sections of Figure 1 and the opening and closing of data paths within the DISP. The A-bus is 22 bits wide and carries the addresses for selection of central spin sites during the MC process, next to the transfer of addresses for loading and reading look-up table values, register values, etc. The 16-bit wide D-bus is used for data flow from the host computer to the different sections of the DISP and vice versa; in addition, the D-bus is used for some data transfers within the DISP. Finally, the main task of the 31-bits-wide S-bus is to carry central and neighboring spin values from the main spin memory to the look-up table, but it can also be used for data I/O with the host computer. The bus structure is shown in Figure 2, in which most available functions of the DISP are included.

C. Spin Memory Organization and Neighbor Determination

The main spin memory has a size of 2^{22} (4M) bits in which (or in part of which for smaller lattices) the momentary spin configuration is stored. This configuration is generated by the MC process or, at the start of an experiment, initiated by the host computer. The neighbor determination section is interwoven with the spin memory. Given the central-spin address, it produces the addresses of all spins of the local configuration simultaneously and directs the spin values to the S-bus. The method uses a subdivision of the lattice in 64 separate memory banks, each having a single-bit output. Thus, theoretically 64 spins can be produced simultaneously. However, the hardware demultiplexing scheme only allows for processing a local configuration of up to 31 spins, which was considered to be sufficiently large; this of course restricts the Hamiltonians that can be studied with the DISP.

In line with the addressing scheme of the overall memory, the lattice can be thought to be subdivided in an array of cells, each containing 64 spins. Each spin within one such cell is residing in a different memory bank,

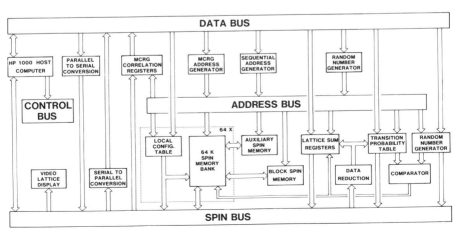

Figure 2. Bus structure and hardware units of the DISP.

while each memory bank contains the spins on one particular location in all cells. The cell size, being the number of memory banks, is conveniently chosen to be 64, which is both square and cubic. Thus a 2-D lattice is represented by an array of square blocks of 8×8 spins, a 3-D lattice by an array of cubic blocks of $4 \times 4 \times 4$ spins. This way the hardware needed for switching between 2-D and 3-D lattices is simplified considerably. Comparison with the discussion in Section II will show that the range in which the local configuration of spins can be defined is identical with the cell size (i.e. spins on the same position of different cells reside on the same memory bank and cannot be read simultaneously). Furthermore, the smallest lattice that can be defined is represented by one cell (one bit of each memory bank).

As the total system size is 4M spins, each memory bank consists of a number of randomly accessible memory elements, together $64K \times 1$-bit large. The hardware within the 64 memory banks has to transform a 22-bit address on the A-bus into a 31-bit data package on the S-bus. This data package is to be routed to the TP table. The position of neighbors on the S-bus depends exclusively on the position of these neighbors with regard to the central spin. The 22-bit address on the A-bus is split up in two parts. The least significant six bits define the position of the central spin within a cell (choice of the memory bank in which the central spin resides). The other 16 bits are used to select the actual cell in which the central spin resides (position within that memory bank).

The task of the additional hardware of each memory bank, all receiving the same 16-bit cell address of the central spin, is to find out whether the addressed spin is part of the local configuration. If this is the case, it must decide whether the spin is located within the same cell as the central spin, and to what line of the S-bus the orientation of the selected spin is to be sent. Considering the fact that a certain memory bank only contains spins residing on a unique position within each cell, the key to selecting the right spin (or not selecting any spin at all) of a memory bank is the use of a look-up table, the local-configuration (LC) table. This look-up table is primarily used to point out the position of the addressed spin on the S-bus. When this spin is not part of the local configuration, it is sent to the "32nd S-bus" position, which is a dead track on the memory bank hardware. This explains why the S-bus is just 31 bits wide. The hardware scheme as outlined above is shown in Figure 3.

When the lattice size is larger than one cell only, additional information must be supplied by the LC tables because certain neighbors may reside in adjacent cells in the x, y and z directions. In this case the 16-bit cell address is corrected. Zero is added to this 16-bit word when the cell address is

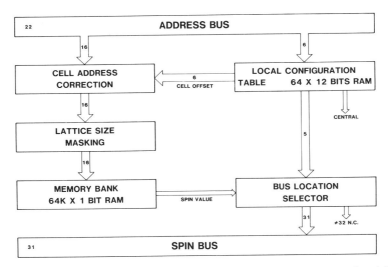

Figure 3. One of the 64 identical parts of the spin memory, each with its own neighbor-identification and decoding section.

identical, $+1$ or -1 for positive respectively negative corrections in x, y and z directions. Obviously the LC table on each memory bank needs 64 entries with five bits out for S-bus selection and six bits out for x, y and z-cell address correction.

For direct determination of the location of the central spin, an additional bit is utilized in the LC tables. This eliminates the need for decoding the S-bus line number data in order to find out on what memory bank the spin–flip command is to be executed. The data in the LC tables depend strongly on the lattice structure (2-D: triangular or square; 3-D: simple cubic, fcc or bcc) and on the interactions that have to be taken into account. For this reason random access memories (three 64×4-bit RAMs on each memory bank) are used, to be loaded by the host computer. Reading back this data from the DISP to the host computer is a standard test practice of the initialization procedure for each MC run.

The 16-bit cell address is divided in two 8-bit parts for x and y coordinates in 2-D, and in three 5-bit parts for x, y and z coordinates in 3-D systems (in 3-D the maximum lattice size is 2M spin sites). Masking out the most significant address bit in a certain direction reduces the size of the lattice in that direction by a factor two. In this way correct periodic-boundary conditions are automatically maintained because overflow of the cell address in a certain direction reverses the cell address in that direction to zero. Consequently, the size of lattices in any direction is restricted to powers of two. As a result, possible system sizes are:

$$N = 2^k \times 2^l \qquad \text{with } 3 \le k, l \le 11 \qquad \text{(2-D)},$$

$$N = 2^k \times 2^l \times 2^m \qquad \text{with } 2 \le k, l, m \le 7 \qquad \text{(3-D)}.$$

D. The Transition-Probability Table

The data in the look-up table in which the transition probabilities of Eq. (2) are stored (the so-called TP table) have a resolution of 32 bits. In order to vary the system structure, coupling constants, etc., the use of random-access memory elements combined with I/O with the host computer is imperative.

The first problem we had to cope with is the impossibility of directing a local configuration of 31 spins on the S-bus directly to the TP table (32×2^{32} bits of storage would be needed). However, the number of entries into the TP table can be reduced considerably because many spin configurations have equal energies. Since the number of plus–minus (PM) bonds of the central spin with its interacting neighbors of a certain type partly determines the energy level of a spin configuration, PROMs may be used that are programmed to generate this number; this procedure will be indicated by PM count. Whenever this is done, not the actual orientation of the neighbors but rather the result of the PM count is part of the address for the TP table. It should be noted that the spins used in the PM count cannot be used for multispin interactions. At the time the DISP was built, we decided to include elementary three- and four-spin interactions for 2-D systems only. When exclusively nearest and next-nearest neighbors are taking part in the active interactions, the number of TP-table entries for a few typical lattices is as follows:

2-D square:	2^9	(central spin and all 8 neighbors),
2-D triangular:	2^{10}	(central spin, 6 nearest neighbors and PM count of 6 next-nearest neighbors),
3-D S.C.:	2^9	(central spin, PM count of 6 nearest and PM count of 12 next-nearest neighbors),
3-D F.C.C.:	2^5	(central spin, PM count of 12 nearest neighbors),
3-D B.C.C.:	2^5	(central spin, PM count of 8 nearest neighbors).

Based on the above data, the minimum size of the TP table is determined by 2-D triangular systems; it was therefore fixed at 1024×32 bits. One can easily check that a 2048×32-bit TP table would have enabled us to use the six nearest neighbors of a simple cubic lattice directly (i.e. without PM count) as part of the TP-table address. Thus, an increase of the size of the TP table by a factor of two will open the possibility of taking into account certain multispin interactions for 3-D simple cubic systems; the corresponding additional hardware is under construction. The momentary addressing scheme of the TP table is given in Figure 4.

The 32-bit data word, which is the output of the TP table for a certain neighbor configuration, is compared directly with a random number by means of a series of cascaded magnitude comparators. The result is a spin–flip signal that is synchronized with the system clock and sent to all memory banks of the main spin memory. The spin–flip command is executed only where the LC table of a memory bank, by means of its 12th bit, indicates the presence of the central spin.

E. Lattice-Sums Updating

The lattice sums are updated at the end of each MC step in which a spin–flip command is generated. The host computer uses these sums as input for the determination of miscellaneous thermodynamic quantities. Transfer of these values to the host computer, where they are accumulated and at constant intervals stored in the background memory (i.e. on disc), is programmable by means of a parameter list, pertinent to the actual experiment; this will be discussed in Section VI.

The hardware for the updating mechanism only needs to take care of the actual change in the number of plus spins, the change in the number of PM

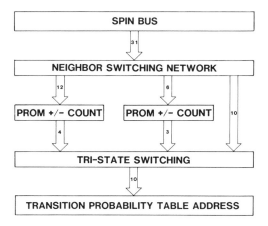

Figure 4. Data reduction scheme used for the transformation of data on the spin bus into addresses for the transition-probability table.

bonds of the central spin with its neighbors and, for multspin interactions, the change in the sum of the products of the spins involved. This means that the data on the S-bus, or rather the generated TP table address that represents the local configuration either in terms of a copy of part of the S-bus data or in terms of the already performed PM count, can be used directly for adjustment of the lattice-sum register data.

The actual hardware structure is adapted to the fact that the number of plus spins, which is equivalent to the magnetization, can change by the values -1 and $+1$ only. Therefore a series of up–down counters keeps track of this number. The change in the number of PM bonds will always be a multiple of two with a maximum of 24 for 3-D systems (12 neighbors). In this case one of the PROMs (#1 to #8 in Figure 5) translates the TP-table address into half the actual change of these lattice sums. The same principle used for keeping track of the magnetization can now be employed when the up–down counters are preceded by a 4-bit register. The 4-bit sum

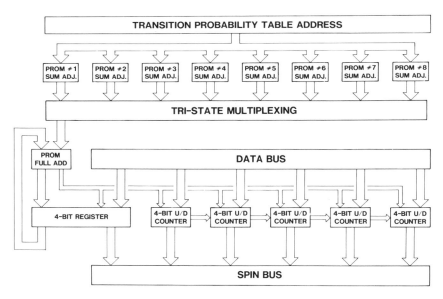

Figure 5. Lattice-sum updating section. The updating is performed by forwarding the TP-table address to a PROM. This PROM provides the quantity by which the lattice sum at hand has to be modified when a spin–flip command is issued. The D-bus is used for initialization of the lattice-sum registers, the S-bus for transferring the values of the lattice sums to the host computer.

obtained by adding the data supplied by the selected PROM to the data contained in the 4-bit register will occasionally result in overflow or under-flow, causing the counter array to add the value $+ 1$ or $- 1$ to their original contents. For this addition no adders are used but rather once more a PROM (in Figure 5: "PROM full add") that is programmed to generate the sum of the original value and the data that indicate the change. Further-more this PROM supplies one bit used for commanding the counters to change (increment or decrement) their value and one bit that tells the counters to count up or down.

When an experiment is started, the lattice-sum registers must be preset to the sums that are in force for the actual lattice stored in the main spin memory. The method employed makes use of the facility to change the values in the TP table according to one's needs. When the TP table is loaded with zero and nonzero values at locations for which the central spin is up or down respectively, the random number generator is set to produce zeros only and the main spin memory is loaded with its initial spin values; one sequential sweep through the lattice will result in turning all spins up. When in advance of this sweep the lattice-sum registers are all cleared, they will after this sweep take on values that, aside from some simple software manipulations, represent the actual lattice sums. The generated values are routed to the host computer by means of the S-bus and the modified values are sent back to the lattice-sum registers by means of the D-bus. Since the contents of the main spin memory are destroyed by the above procedure, the main spin memory must be reloaded with its initial configuration. This procedure is standard and is employed in advance of each experiment (even when the lattice sums are trivial). The same is done at the end of each experiment. The latter is not strictly necessary but enables us to check whether the experiment, as far as the lattice sums are concerned, did run correctly.

F. Monte Carlo Renormalization Group Calculations

The critical behavior of Ising models, according to Swendsen [8], can very well be studied by means of Monte Carlo Renormalization Group (MCRG) calculations. The idea behind MCRG is that real-space renor-malization transformations [9] can be formulated in terms of correlations between certain lattice sums. This means that it is not necessary to derive the renormalization transformation in coupling parameter space. It is sufficient to derive the "renormalized" block-spin configurations and to calculate the averages of the desired lattice sums and their correlations.

The time-consuming repetitive part of the MCRG algorithm can be summarized as follows:

1. Apply the MC process to an Ising system until a (sufficiently) independent configuration is obtained;
2. Calculate the lattice sums;
3. Renormalize the spin configuration and derive the renormalized lattice sums;
4. Repeat step 3 until the lattice is sufficiently small;
5. Repeat steps 1 to 4 a large number of times, thereby accumulating the (renormalized) lattice sums and their correlations.

In addition to MC simulations, the MCRG procedure is concentrated around two basic operations: block-spin transformations and the calculation of a large number of lattice sums, e.g. the magnetization, pair-correlation functions and multispin correlation functions. The structure of the DISP, outlined in the preceding section, is well suited to perform these MCRG calculations, due to the flexibility of its design, the type of periodic-boundary conditions chosen and its modularity.

1. Block-Spin Transformation   The renormalization transformation implies the substitution of blocks consisting of a number of spins by a single spin, the block spin. Here we restrict ourselves to blocks of 2×2 in 2-D or $2 \times 2 \times 2$ in 3-D systems. When we divide the lattice into such elementary blocks, a "renormalized" block spin can be calculated according to a majority rule. A random factor can be included that depends on the sum of the spins that are relevant for the local transformation. Tables 1 and 2 list the possible choices for spins that are considered to take on the values -1 or $+1$. Note that the MCRG transformation is symmetrical with respect to the situation where the number of down spins is equal to the number of up spins: up–down symmetry is conserved by the MCRG transformation.

Table 1. Transition Probabilities for 2-D Block-Spin Determination

	2-D	
	Block-Spin Probability	
Sum of 4 Spins	P_+	P_-
4	α	$1 - \alpha$
2	β	$1 - \beta$
0	$\frac{1}{2}$	$\frac{1}{2}$
-2	$1 - \beta$	β
-4	$1 - \alpha$	α

Table 2. Transition Probabilities for 3-D
Block-Spin Determination

| | 3-D | |
| | Block-Spin Probability | |
Sum of 8 Spins	P_+	P_-
8	α	$1 - \alpha$
6	β	$1 - \beta$
4	γ	$1 - \gamma$
2	δ	$1 - \delta$
0	$\frac{1}{2}$	$\frac{1}{2}$
-2	$1 - \delta$	δ
-4	$1 - \gamma$	γ
-6	$1 - \beta$	β
-8	$1 - \alpha$	α

Three factors made it possible to use the standard hardware of the DISP for block-spin transformations:

1. Within the DISP the neighbors of a spin can arbitrarily be chosen (the neighbors of the other spins follow by translational invariance);
2. The TP table may just as well contain values in which the majority rule (including the random factors α, β, γ and δ of Tables 1 and 2) is incorporated;
3. The available RNG can be used for inclusion of the random element in block-spin determination.

In practice, when all functions of the DISP are set correctly, just one sweep through the relevant part of the main spin memory will do the job; in this sweep only one spin out of each elementary block has to be visited (leap-frog sweep). As the DISP can simulate lattices that may differ in size by a factor of two in every direction from 128^3 down to 4^3 in three dimensions or from 2048^2 down to 8^2 in two dimensions, scaling down the lattice over quite a number of intermediate renormalization levels can be performed by mere repetition. Evidently, the procedure of successive block-spin transformations entirely destroys the original spin configuration, produced by the standard MC simulation. It is therefore necessary to store a copy of the original configuration before the block-spin transformations are started. Another aspect of performing successive block-spin transformations is the necessity to actually scale down the lattice within the main spin memory (by throwing all except the generated block spins away). This is achieved by a momentary storage of the block spins outside the main spin memory, followed by writing them back in a "packed" manner (see Section III.C.

All functions of the DISP described above require a number of different address counters. For block-spin transformation, only every second position in the two or three directions must be addressed. For block-spin storage (the LC tables are programmed to select all block spins within a single cell, that is, 16 block spins in 2-D or eight block spins in 3-D), just the subsequent cell addresses must be generated.

The temporary storage of the original lattice and of the intermediate block-spin lattices could in principle be achieved by using the standard I/O procedure in communication with the host computer. Since this is a time-consuming operation, two auxiliary memory arrays were built (see Figure 1): one to store the original configuration, the other to store the block spins as part of each renormalization step. The original contents of the main spin memory are saved in the auxiliary spin memory and restored after the MCRG procedures have been finished. In one sweep through the entire lattice the relevant part of the contents of the main spin memory is used to calculate the block spins, which are written into the block-spin memory. A second sweep is made in order to write the block spins back into the main spin memory. Two similar sweeps do the same at following renormalization steps.

2. Calculation of Lattice Sums   The determination of a large number of lattice sums is an important ingredient of the MCRG method. These sums can be used to calculate the critical exponents and the critical temperature.

For 3-D systems a total of 57 lattice sums is selected which pertain to correlation functions of up to eight spins. For instance, all correlation functions within a $2 \times 2 \times 2$ spin cube and all two-spin correlations within a distance of three lattice units are included. A selection criterion for higher correlation functions is used, based on the number of spins involved and on the average mutual distance of the spins; multispin correlations within a $3 \times 3 \times 3$ block that score high in the selection criterion are also taken into account. These correlation functions have to be determined at all block-spin transformation levels.

The complete local configuration for this purpose is composed of 39 spins; this number is the sum of the number of spins in a $3 \times 3 \times 3$ cube and four additional spins in each of the three directions. However, since the S-bus is only 31 bits wide, the spins for determination of all lattice sums are not simultaneously available. As a consequence, adjustment of the lattice sums during the MC process according to the method outlined in Section III.E is not possible. The calculation must now be accomplished by using three different "partial" local configurations such that by cyclic exchange of the x, y and z directions, the correlation sums can be calculated in three separate sweeps; in each sweep the local configuration needed

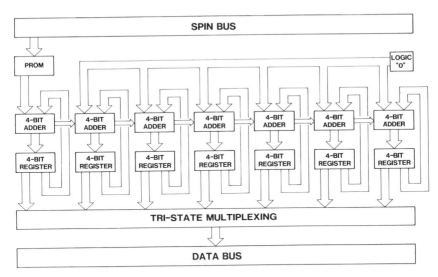

Figure 6. One of the 57 sections in which lattice sums are determined for MCRG experiments.

contains only $3 \times 3 \times 3 + 4$ spins. The contributions to the lattice sums are added in parallel in a series of hardware adder-register groups. Figure 6 shows one of the 57 sections.

G. Communication with the Host Computer

For writing to and reading from the main spin memory, single spin values are transferred in the form of 16-bit data words (which is the word size of the host computer) by means of two different hardware sections that perform a packing and an unpacking procedure.

Writing data into the main spin memory of the DISP is performed by storing a 16-bit data word into a 16-bit shift register, followed by clocking this data out of the register on a single-bit basis. Reading from the main spin memory can be done much faster when the LC tables of the memory banks are used to produce a number of spin orientations on the S-bus. Although 16 bits (which would fit into the word size of the host computer) may be sent to the S-bus simultaneously, the spins are usually ordered along the direction of the axes of the lattice (in particular for calculating spin–spin correlation functions, or producing plots of momentary spin-memory contents). This means that either eight bits (2-D) or four bits (3-D) of a single memory cell are used. These 8- and 4-bit data bundles are packed into 16-bit words by storing them sequentially in different registers that are read by the host computer from the D-bus.

The auxiliary memory and the block-spin memory are connected to the S-bus only; their organization is such that they may function as 16-bit word memories for 2-D lattices or 8-bit word memories for 3-D lattices.

IV. The Random-Number Generator

To obtain results in statistical mechanics by means of the MC method, the random numbers needed in the simulation must be of good quality. Faster simulation techniques and longer runs enable one in principle to improve the statistical accuracy of the results, but increase the demands on speed and good randomness properties in the method used for the generation of the random numbers. In the case of the DISP, speed and continuous availability allow runs in which, say, 10^{12} random numbers of 32 bits each are needed, at a rate above 10^6 per second. Under these conditions, the random-number generator should be very good.

A. Methods for Random-Number Generation

Uniformly distributed random numbers, as needed for the MC process, can be obtained either by undeterministic or by deterministic methods. Random-number generators (RNGs) that are undeterministic can be based on physical stochastic phenomena, for instance electronic noise or radioactive decay. Generators of this type may suffer from systematic errors due to the physical characteristics of the equipment used. Other limitations that prohibit their use are the irreproducibility of the generated random-number sequences and the low generation rate. Reproducibility of random-number sequences is very desirable, e.g. in order to facilitate debugging procedures, whether for MC programs in software or in hardware. A well-known deterministic method for the production of random numbers is the linear congruential method, in which the $(i + 1)^{th}$ random number R_{i+1} is calculated from the preceding random number R_i by means of

$$R_{i+1} = (aR_i + c) \bmod m, \tag{3}$$

where all quantities are integers, a, c and m being constants. The method is described in detail by Knuth [10], who for practical values of m discusses the influence of the choice made for a and c on the uniformity and other randomness properties of the numbers produced. Although by now a wide variety of combinations of a, c and m are known that produce random sequences that survive severe statistical tests, and although some general conditions for a proper choice of a and c by a given m can be formulated, the method of Eq. (3) has severe theoretical limitations. Little is known from a theoretical point of view on the correlations which must be present in sequences generated by the deterministic rule of Eq. (3); not even the behavior of the pair correlation between random numbers j positions apart in the sequence generated by Eq. (3) is known in general. Even for carefully selected combinations of a, c and m severe numerical tests are necessary, and no systematic way is known to find combinations that have improved randomness qualities.

An alternative deterministic method for the production of random numbers is based on the binary sequences generated by linear-feedback shift registers. In this method, described by Tausworthe [11], random numbers of q bits each are determined by taking subsequently q adjacent bits from the binary sequence generated by the production rule

$$a_{i+n} = (a_i + \Sigma_{j=1}^{n-1} c_j a_{i+j}) \bmod 2, \tag{4}$$

where $a_i \in \{0,1\}$ is the ith bit of the sequence, and where the coefficients c_j are either 0 or 1 (not all 0). This production rule describes the behavior of a linear-feedback shift register of n places; the values of j for which $c_j = 1$ holds define the additional feedback positions of the shift register (the first position is always included in the feedback). For further details see Golomb [12].

B. Shift-Register RNGs

Random number generators based on linear-feedback shift registers have several advantages. When the binary sequence generated by the shift register has maximum length, the bits of the sequence are uniformly distributed and the pair correlation between bits that are j positions apart in the sequence agrees (almost) with that for truly random bits, as was shown by Golomb [12]. Extensive lists of production rules for 2-bit-feedback shift registers that lead to maximum-length sequences were given by Zierler [13, 14, 15, 16] for shift registers with up to 9689 positions. Two-bit-feedback shift registers are easily realized, both in software and in hardware. For these reasons, these maximum-length binary sequences have often been used as a source for random numbers; a large amount of literature exists on the subject. Part of this literature is reviewed in [17].

For the DISP, the first RNG built was a 2-bit-feedback shift register with 127 positions. As will be discussed in Section V.C, under certain unfavorable circumstances this RNG produced results that deviated from the desired high accuracy, which was reason enough to study the problem more closely. A two-fold strategy was adopted.

First, a flexible and much more powerful RNG was built, still based on 2-bit-feedback shift registers, but for shift registers with a larger number of positions and capable of producing a great variety of maximum-length sequences. This RNG enabled us to experiment with widely different sequences, and to judge their randomness properties in practice. In view of the high accuracy that we desired, these experiments could only with great difficulty have been carried out with software RNGs. The realization in hardware is discussed in Section V.D.

Secondly, a theoretical study of the properties of these maximum-length sequences was undertaken. Since randomness is the absence of all correlations, the behavior of correlation functions of higher than second order was investigated. It turned out that among all correlation functions of third order and higher, there always exist some that show complete correlation, due to the deterministic nature of the production rule. It could be shown, however, that the number of badly behaving correlation functions of any order relative to the number of well-behaving ones of the same order vanishes asymptotically as 2^n, where n is the number of shift-register positions. This strongly supports the intuitive idea that the longer the shift register is, the better are the randomness properties of the maximum-length sequences. Since already for relatively small values like $n = 127$ only a small part of the complete maximum-length sequence will be used even for the longest MC runs conceivable, the randomness properties of small subsequences were also studied; this leads to a qualitative insight into the different behavior of different maximum-length sequences of the same length. The results of this theoretical study are given elsewhere [17]. It should be mentioned that some of these results were obtained earlier by Lindholm [18] and Fredricsson [19], whose papers however seem to have received little attention in the literature.

Our main conclusion is that under certain conditions 2-bit-feedback shift registers are indeed a very good source for random numbers. These conditions are

1. The shift-register length n should be very large compared with the number of bits q of the random numbers desired;
2. The additional feedback position j should be chosen such that a maximum-length sequence is produced, and the ratio j/n should not be equal or close to 0 or 1 or a fraction with a small denominator;
3. In addition to n being much larger than q, it is advisable that n be not equal or close to a multiple of q, the number of bits of the random numbers;
4. In general, n, j, q and l should not show simple ratios between them, not even approximately (where l indicates a typical discrete quantity of

the problem studied and of importance in the MC process, e.g. the linear dimension of the Ising lattice under investigation).

From the list provided by Zierler [13 – 16] of 2-bit-feedback maximum-length sequences that have a Mersenne prime as period, one may easily find different sequences that obey the above conditions. There seems to be no need for more involved recipes for random-number generation; in fact, a general warning against such recipes (which usually will have properties that are less well understood) seems at place. While it is true that maximum-length sequences produced by shift registers will always contain nonrandom correlations, at least a qualitative understanding of these undesirable correlations is possible. Under the conditions mentioned it is in general very unlikely that these correlations interfere with the physical correlations existing in the problem studied. If the existence of such an interference is suspected, the usual statistical tests of the RNG will not suffice; it is much better to compare different MC results for the problem under investigation obtained with maximum-length sequences with widely different values of n and j. This is where the flexibility of the hardware RNG built by us came in handy.

A final and important remark with respect to MC calculations on discrete systems like the Ising system: it is strongly advisable to select the sites to be subjected to the MC process in a random fashion (using a different RNG for the site selection), since visiting them sequentially may enhance the probability that the correlations in the RNG used for the MC process will interlock with physical correlations present in the simulated model. An example is given in Section IV.C. In fact, when the sites are visited randomly, the conditions 1 to 4 mentioned above can be considerably relaxed (although there is no need to do so) before nonrandom effects show up. In the DISP, unlike software MC programs, random site selection does not take more time than sequential site selection.

C. Results with a 127-Bit Shift-Register RNG

When the construction of the DISP was finished, its functioning was tested by comparing the results obtained for small 2-D Ising systems with nearest-neighbor interactions only with the exact results for these systems obtained by Ferdinand and Fisher [20]. The results showed small but persistent systematic deviations from the exact values. This could not be due to design errors or to incorrect functioning of the hardware, because of severe step-wise hardware tests carried out beforehand, and especially because a software emulation of the procesor (during relatively short runs) was found to run exactly parallel to the DISP. The deviations could therefore only be ascribed to the presence of hidden correlations between the random numbers produced by the 127-bit shift register originally used in the DISP for the MC process. Results of four experiments are shown in Figures 7, 8, 9, and 10, using the $n = 127$ shift register with additional feedback position $j = 63$, respectively $j = 15$ for 2-D Ising systems of 32×32 spins. In the critical region, the results obtained deviate more strongly from the exact results than is compatible with the standard deviations observed. These deviations were mainly observed when the sites of the lattice were visited sequentially; with random site selection (using the same 127-bit RNG for the site selection as for the MC process) the deviations were considerably smaller. In retrospect, the deviations are due to the rather unfortunate combination of the values adopted: $n = 127$, $q = 32$ and $j = 15$ or 63; the (almost) simple ratios between these values, also in combination with the linear dimensions of the systems we can study with the DISP (these dimensions are always a power of two), show how careless we were.

The new RNG is usually run with the following choice: $(n;j) = (9689;471)$. With this choice we never observed any unacceptable devia-

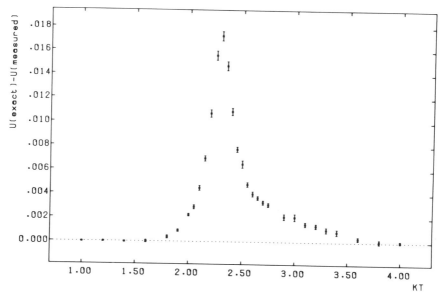

Figure 7. Deviations from the exact values of the results obtained with the DISP for the internal energy of a 32×32 Ising lattice at different temperatures. The sites are selected sequentially and the 2-bit-feedback shift-register RNG obeys the production rule $(n ; j) = (127 ; 63)$.

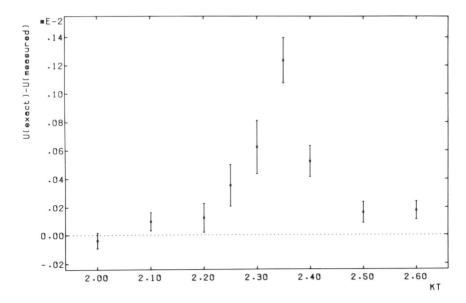

Figure 8. Deviations from the exact values of the results obtained with the DISP for the internal energy of a 32 × 32 Ising lattice at different temperatures. The sites are selected randomly and the 2-bit-feedback shift-register RNG obeys the production rule $(n ; j) = (127 ; 63)$. The deviations are one order of magnitude less compared to those in Fig. 7.

tions from known exact results or with results obtained with different choices, not even when the sites are visited sequentially. As a standard precaution, however, usually random site selection is adopted in the DISP; the old RNG is exclusively used for this purpose.

D. Hardware Design of a Flexible Shift-Register RNG

Focal points for the design of a flexible hardware linear-feedback shift register RNG for use in the DISP are 1) generation of 32-bit wide random numbers with a minimum frequency of 1.5 MHz, 2) a programmable shift-register length of at least several thousands of bits and 3) a programmable additional feedback position. The restriction to 2-bit-feedback shift registers is a necessity because of the desired flexibility and because feedback positions that lead to maximum-length sequences when n is large are known only for these shift-registers (Zierler [13 – 16]).

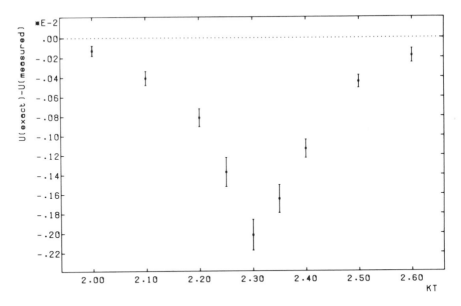

Figure 9. Deviations from the exact values of the results obtained with the DISP for the internal energy of a 32 × 32 Ising lattice at different temperatures. The sites are selected sequentially and the 2-bit-feedback shift-register RNG obeys the production rule $(n\,;j) = (127\,;15)$.

The simplest design of such an RNG involves two basic types of building blocks: shift registers and elements that perform the logic exclusive-or operation. Shift-register integrated circuits (ICs) are available in many different sizes and types. However, the requirement to create an RNG with a selectable shift-register length and also a selectable additional feedback position prohibits the use of types other than those offering instantaneous availability of all intermediate register stages within each IC. Due to the practical limitation of the number of pins per IC, the degree of integration for these shift-register elements is low, which would lead to a design beyond reasonable proportions.

With this problem in mind, a different approach has been chosen, as reflected in Figure 11. The use of random access memories (RAMs) for storage of the bit information instead of shift-register elements facilitates direct accessibility of all memory locations by means of addresses. A fixed number of bits can be accessed by a single address, depending on the interconnection and types of memories used. All data are static with respect to the position in the memory, so sequential shift operations in combination with the shift-in operation of newly generated data have to be

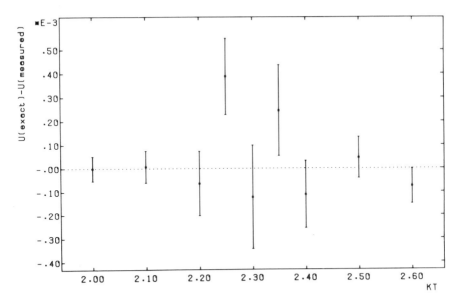

Figure 10. Deviations from the exact values of the results obtained with the DISP for the internal energy of a 32×32 Ising lattice at different temperatures. The sites are selected randomly and the 2-bit-feedback shift-register RNG obeys the production rule $(n \, ; \, j) = (127 \, ; \, 15)$. Remaining systematic errors have now drowned in the statistical deviations.

replaced by continuous modification of read and write addresses, relevant for source and destination of the successive exclusive-or operations to be performed.

RAMs are available with a high degree of integration. We use just eight 1024×4-bit RAMs which are both cheap and fast, organized as a 1024×32-bit memory array, which provides enough memory locations for the creation of RNGs with a length of 2^{15} bits.

Having in mind that 32-bit wide random numbers have to be generated, one would think that just two read and one write operations of 32 bits each are required. However, usually the length n and the additional feedback position j are not multiples of 32. Given the memory organization 1024×32, where for a certain address A $(0 < A < 1023)$ only memory bits $A \times 32$ through $A \times 32 + 31$ can be accessed simultaneously, the two 32-bit words that have to undergo modulo-two addition are each occupying part of two successive memory locations. This implies the necessity to execute four read cycles before the addition can be performed, resulting in an output of two 64-bit words. Each of these words now has a 32-bit part that is relevant

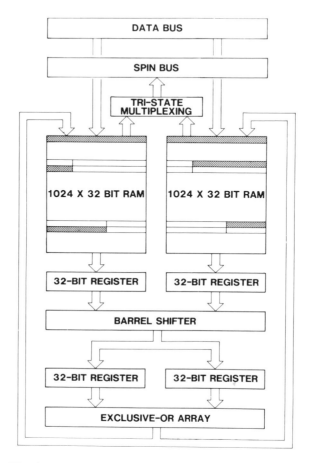

Figure 11. Hardware scheme of a 2-bit-feedback shift-register RNG with selectable length up to 32,768 bits and selectable feedback position.

for the addition. These parts are isolated by shifting the 64-bit words over a certain number of bit locations, such that the correct 32 bits of each word are fed to the inputs of the exclusive-or gates. (This static shift is performed by "barrel shifters" and is therefore instantaneous; it should not be confused with conventional shift-register elements that are operated stepwise).

The memory write action that follows the modulo-two addition can be performed in just one cycle, since the shift counts on both 64-bit words are chosen such that the destination of the 32-bit sum always matches bit locations $A \times 32$ up to $A \times 32 + 31$ for any A.

The design as outlined above implies the possibility, at no extra effort whatsoever, of generating 32-bit random numbers from 32 equal but independent shift registers, each supplying one bit at a time on a single shift basis. This corresponds precisely with the method for random-number generation proposed by Kirkpatrick and Stoll [21]. In our RNG, this situation arises automatically when both length and feedback position are multiples of 32. Then, the modulo-two sum of two bits in one column will always be entered somewhere in that same column, thus forming a shift register with a maximum length of 1024 bits. All these 32 shift registers are equal in length and have the same additional feedback position. As a result, one must be very careful in selecting seeds for each of these registers, since an incorrect choice could easily lead to overlapping random-number sequences. A more fundamental disadvantage of this scheme to generate random numbers is that the most significant bit (like all other bits) of the q-bit random number is now taken from a maximum-length sequence generated by a shift register with a length equal to $\frac{1}{32}$ of the total number of positions available.

The design as outlined above is simplified by implementation of a second memory array which is at any instant an exact replica of the basic 1024×32-bit memory array. This has the advantage that each 64-bit word can be read in one cycle only, so a total of two read cycles is needed before performing the exclusive-or operation. As a result, a net reduction of the number of integrated circuits, a decrease in hardware complexity and an improvement in speed are accomplished.

The potential speed of the RNG is ruled by the timing scheme of the DISP, in order to allow synchronous and simultaneous operation. The DISP works at a speed of nine micro-clockcycles of around 80 ns, embedded in a macro-clockcycle of 700 ns. All autonomous operations of the RNG (separated by storage registers) are executed within one microcycle. The production rate of random numbers is determined by the time needed for three memory access operations, i.e. three microcycles, adding up to around 250 ns. At the cost of a substantial number of additional ICs, the use of four memory arrays and two separate 64-bit barrel shifters, this production time could have been decreased to two microcycles at most.

Next to the building blocks shown in the RNG hardware scheme of Figure 11, the RNG hardware consists of additional elements that take care of addressing the memories, that order the counters to return to zero and that facilitate I/O with the host computer. Two 10-bit up–down counters are needed to control all memory addressing. In view of the flexibility of this RNG, communication with a host computer is imperative because length, feedback position and seed must be entered by the host computer and checked for correctness under software control. The actual random numbers that are fed to the computer section of the DISP can arbitrarily be drawn from any 32-bit word that flows through the RNG.

Tests of the RNG for correct random-number production and reliability have been performed by comparison with identical sequences generated by software programs. Due to the relative slowness of software-generated random numbers, we limited our tests to one million random numbers for a number of possible shift-register lengths and feedback positions. No discrepancies have been encountered.

V. Performance

The standard speed of the DISP is 800 ns per elementary MC step. This includes a 100 ns safety margin, since the DISP can run correctly at speeds somewhat below 700 ns. A substantial part of this time is the access time of the memory elements, in which the spin configuration is stored (300 ns maximum). The other 400 ns is the sum of the propagation delays and look-up table access times, serially performed before and after determination of the local spin configuration, excluding address generation (which takes place in advance of the MC step in which the address is needed), random-number generation (executed in parallel with the determination of the local configuration) and updating the lattice sums (carried out in parallel with the spin–flip handling).

The possibility to pipeline the processor has been considered. Due to the time needed for spin-memory access, the process can be split up into two 350 ns time slices only (including the set-up time of the pipe registers). However, since a spin–flip command imposes the necessity to access the formerly addressed spin once again, a speed improvement by a factor of two will never be reached. For example, the speedup factor due to pipe-lining, for systems around criticality, is 1.8, since the acceptance rate of spin–flips lies somewhere between 15% and 20%. This speed improvement is marginal and does not justify the extra hardware effort that would have been necessary.

A comparison of the performance of the DISP with that of general-purpose computers built around the same time cannot be adequately expressed by a single number giving the speed ratio. In particular, type and number of interactions that appear in a certain problem, and implicitly the amount of neighbors involved, will cause the computing time of a general-purpose computer to vary largely, while they do not effect the speed of the DISP. A comparison of the speed of the DISP with that of a Fortran program on a CDC 7600 for a simple cubic lattice with nearest-neighbor interaction only showed the DISP to be faster by about one order of magnitude. It can be expected, however, that utilization of machine code and other efficient programming techniques could considerably improve the performance of general-purpose computers, although recent runs on the IBM 3083 of the central Delft University computing facility indicated that the above figure still more or less holds for today's mainframes. The speed that can be reached by utilization of present supercomputers (e.g. Cray 1, Cyber 205) depends strongly on how well the MC algorithm is vectorized. We expect these machines to be not much faster than the DISP, especially when the more complicated Ising systems are simulated.

In addition, we may make a comparison between the costs involved in running the DISP with those of a mainframe. These costs, in the case of the DISP, are mainly due to the HP 1000 host computer (the use of which is shared with other users); thus, they compare favorably with the costs involved in employing a mainframe. In other words, while the DISP is continuously available for our calculations, for financial reasons a general-purpose computer of comparable speed would only be available during short periods. As a result, models with long relaxation times (some of which will be discussed in Section VII) can be investigated by means of the DISP, whereas the use of general-purpose computers would be problematic.

VI. Software

The host computer, used for initialization, data storage and data processing of experiments on the DISP, is a HP 1000 minicomputer system, which is shared with other users. It can be linked to the IBM 3083 system by means of Remote Job Entry protocol for off-line calculations that are too complex, too time-consuming and too large for execution on the HP 1000 system (in particular with respect to MCRG calculations).

A set of three programs has been developed for the control, the initialization and the execution of experiments. Furthermore, utility programs are available for the calculation of thermodynamic quantities, the plotting of distributions of magnetization, lattice sums and energy, and the processing and plotting of spin–spin correlation functions, etc.

Experiments are selected and started by a program called ICON, which reads from a disc file the parameters that define an experiment, and transfers control to the initialization program (INIT) and to the execution program (IRN). The initialization program INIT initializes look-up tables, lattice-sum registers, correlation-function registers, main spin memory, etc. The program IRN issues run commands to the DISP, keeps track of first, second, third and fourth moments of the magnetization, the energy, and of cross-products of these quantities. Optionally, IRN can store the distributions of the lattice sums and the spin–spin correlation function (along one of the axes) on disc memory. Storing the contents of the main spin memory at regular intervals, e.g. one hour, on the basis of the experiment parameter list, is standard practice. This enables one to continue experiments after a failure of the HP system due to external causes, to check the correctness of the lattice sums regularly according to the method described in section III.E, or to extend experiments when a higher statistical accuracy of the results is desired.

One of the utility programs is IFIL. This program prepares in an interactive way files in which the parameters of experiments are stored. The experiments may be split up into partial experiments that only differ with respect to the interaction constants and temperature. The run time of each of these partial experiments is determined by the desired total number of elementary MC steps. One sweep is defined as the number of these steps to give every spin in the lattice a chance to flip (when the spin addresses are randomly chosen, certain spins may not be visited within one sweep, others more than once). One cycle is the number of sweeps after which the lattice sums are sent to the host computer for further processing. This possibility is included since correlation times may be very lengthy, resulting in heavily correlated data when gathered after every single sweep. Furthermore the number of cycles must be set for storing the accumulated data, preprocessed by the host computer, in background memory. The following parameters can be specified:

1. Number assigned to the experiment (for identification purposes);
2. Lattice type (dimensionality, form of the Hamiltonian);
3. Lattice size (in x, y and z direction);
4. Interaction constants and temperature;
5. MCRG calculations (yes or no);
6. Block-spin determination constants when MCRG is specified;
7. Minimum lattice size when MCRG is specified (in x, y and z direction);
8. RNG shift-register length and additional feedback position;
9. RNG seed;
10. RNG type (single or 32 parallel independent shift registers);
11. Number of partial experiments within a complete experiment;
12. Number of sweeps per cycle;
13. Number of cycles in between storage of data on disc;
14. Total number of cycles per partial experiment;
15. Random or sequential spin visits (R or S);
16. Choice of distributions to be stored on disc;
17. Spin–spin correlation-function calculation and storage (yes or no).

Next to creating or updating files in which experiment parameters are stored, IFIL checks all parameters for consistency. Besides, IFIL updates another file which contains numbers assigned to experiments that are to be executed consecutively. This guarantees that no time is lost at night and on weekends as long as the list of experiments to be executed is not exhausted.

VII. Summary of Results

A. *The Ising Model on the Triangular Lattice*

Consider an Ising model on a 2-D triangular lattice that can be described by the Hamiltonian in Eq. (1) with arbitrary K_1 (magnetic field), K_2 (between nearest neighbors) and K_3 (acting on all elementary triangles) and with $K_4 = 0$. This parameter space includes exactly soluble models: the triangular Ising model [22] with $K_1 = K_3 = 0$, the Baxter–Wu model [23] with $K_1 = K_2 = 0$ and the hard hexagon model [24] with $K_2 \rightarrow -\infty$ while $K_1 + 6K_2 + 6K_3$ remains finite.

At the critical points of these models we investigated the susceptibility, the energy, the specific heat and their finite-size dependences. The results obtained are in good agreement with the exact theory.

Another point of interest is the phase transition between the antiferromagnetic ground states of the system. For instance, consider the K_1–K_2 plane of the parameter space in the limit $T \rightarrow 0$ ($K_2 \rightarrow -\infty$). Minimalization of the energy imposes that the lattice contains only elementary triangles with two spins up and one spin down and triangles with one spin up and two spins down. This constraint leaves so much freedom that the ground state for $K_1 = 0$ has nonzero entropy. Under these circumstances a phase transition may be induced by the external field K_1. Kinzel and Schick [25] supposed the existence of a critical point at zero temperature ($K_2 \rightarrow -\infty$) on the K_2 axis ($K_1 = 0$). Recently, Nienhuis *et al.* [26] predicted instead critical points for $K_1 \neq 0$, which separate a disordered phase for small K_1 from ordered phases at larger $|K_1|$.

The DISP was used to check this theory. It was found that the behavior of the magnetization and visual inspection of large (128×128) systems confirmed the predictions of Nienhuis *et al.* The MC experiments were performed for $K_2 = -8$. In this case the temperature is low enough to prevent temperaturelike excitations during the simulations. In order to investigate the nature of the phase transition, experiments were carried out for system sizes from 8×8 up to 512×512 spins. Figure 12 shows the susceptibility as a function of K_1 for all these system sizes. For the larger systems, the susceptibility reaches a maximum near $K_1 = 0.8$, but the data do not suggest a divergence of the susceptibility with increasing system size. The absence of such a divergence is in agreement with the theory of Nienhuis *et al.*, which predicts a transition of the Kosterlitz–Thouless type.

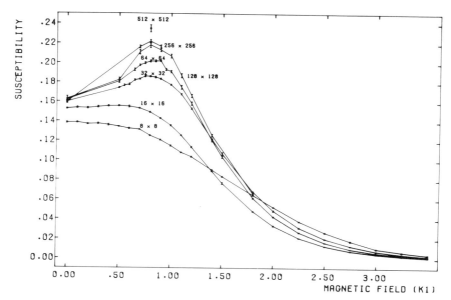

Figure 12. The susceptibility of a triangular Ising lattice as a function of K_1, measured with $K_2 = -8$ and $K_3 = 0$ for different system sizes.

More experiments are being scheduled in order to find the location of the critical points (which need not be related to the finite maxima of the susceptibility). Further details will be published elsewhere.

B. The 2-D ANNNI Model

In recent years, analytic [27] and numerical evidence has been found for a so-called floating phase in the 2-D ANNNI model. The investigations include MC studies of Selke and Fisher [28], and Barber and Selke [29]. The latter analysis pertains to the scaling behavior of the modulated susceptibility of lattices with sizes up to 88 × 8.

The Hamiltonian is given by:

$$\mathcal{H} = K_{1y} \sum_{i,j} s_{i,j} s_{i,j+1} + K_{1x} \sum_{i,j} s_{i,j} s_{i+1,j} + K_{2x} \sum_{i,j} s_{i,j} s_{i+2,j}. \tag{5}$$

The indices i and j indicate the position of the spins in the x and y direction respectively; the summations apply to all nearest-neighbor pairs in the x and y directions (terms with K_{1x} and K_{1y}) and to all next-nearest-neighbor pairs in the x direction (term with K_{2x}).

We have attempted to find additional evidence for the existence of a floating phase from the scaling behavior of the Fourier components $\chi(q)$ of the spin–spin correlation function in the x direction. To this purpose we have performed extensive MC simulations on rectangular ANNNI models which are much longer (32X) in the ANNNI direction than in the other one, with lattice sizes up to 2048×32. During these simulations, the spin–spin correlations as a function of the distance in the x direction were measured for $K_{1x} = K_{1y} > 0$ and $K_{2x} = -0.65\, K_{1x}$. Especially at low temperatures and for large system sizes, relaxation becomes very slow and very long runs are necessary. In a floating phase with wave number q, the Fourier component $\chi(n,q)$ for a system with finite size n in the y direction is expected to scale as

$$\chi(n,\, q) \approx n^{P_q}. \tag{6}$$

The exponent P_q can be estimated as

$$P_q(n) = \frac{\ln\left(\dfrac{\chi(2n,q)}{\chi(n,q)}\right)}{\ln 2}. \tag{7}$$

These estimates are plotted in Figure 13 for $q = 1.28$ and for $n = 2, 4, 8,$ and 16 as a function of kT. We observe that, for $kT \approx 1.34$, the scaling

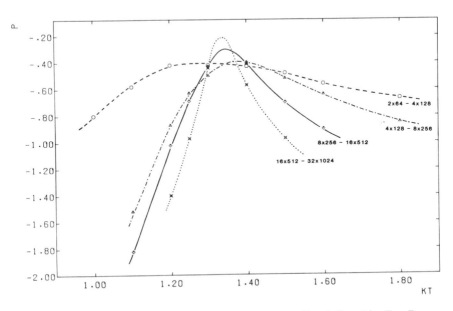

Figure 13. The ANNNI model scaling exponent P_q, defined in Eq. 7, as a function of the temperature.

relation is approximately satisfied, in accordance with the existence of a floating phase. Furthermore, on the basis of finite-size scaling one may expect that in the floating phase the scaled correlation length ξ/n would approach a constant (which may still depend on kT) when $n \to \infty$. Unfortunately we have been unable to show this behavior clearly in the temperature range $1.0 \le kT^{-1} \le 1.5$ where the floating phase is expected. Perhaps one still needs larger system sizes. We note that in the aforementioned temperature range, an approximate agreement does exist between our results for ξ/n and the anisotropic scaling laws such as have been used for the chiral clock model [30].

C. Finite Size Dependence of the Susceptibility of the Simple Cubic Ising Model

Correlation times in finite 3-D Ising models increase rapidly with system size. For large systems extremely long simulations are necessary. The longest simulations known to us are those of Barber *et al.* [31], who performed extensive MC simulations of the simple cubic Ising model by means of the Santa Barbara Ising processor [32]. The results for the susceptibility at the critical temperature showed some disturbing irregular finite-size dependence near linear system size $n = 24$. Parisi and Rapuano [33] have independently found the susceptibility of the 24^3 system at criticality by means of a software simulation. Their result was significantly different from that of Barber *et al.* [31]. Parisi and Rapuano attributed the discrepancy to the fact that different algorithms were used for the random-number generator. This suggests that the irregularity at $n = 24$ may be due to the RNG used by Barber *et al.*

In Figure 14 we show MC data by Barber *et al.*, Parisi and Rapuano, and by the DISP. It is obvious that the Parisi–Rapuano and the DISP results join smoothly and show no evidence for any irregularity near $n = 24$. It should be noted that Barber *et al.* in their paper expressed already their reservations in connection with their RNG.

D. Weak Universality in the Baxter Model

The Baxter model can be defined as an Ising model on the square lattice with next-nearest-neighbor interactions K_3 and four-spin interactions K_4. The exact solution [34] shows that the model is nonuniversal: the temperature exponent varies along the critical line in the K_3–K_4 plane. A remarkable property of the Baxter model is that the magnetic exponent [35] is constant along this line. This is called "weak universality." This invites the question if also certain dimensionless ratios of moments of the magnetization, such as $\langle m^{2k} \rangle / \langle m^2 \rangle^k$, which can be associated with ratios of critical

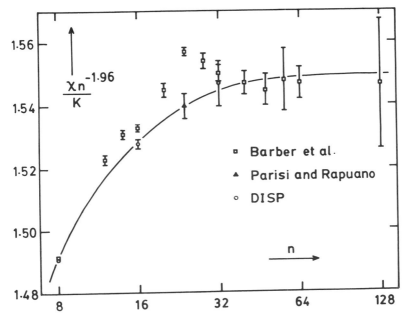

Figure 14. Combined data of Barber *et al.* [31], Parisi and Rapuano [33] and of the DISP, showing the susceptibility of finite simple-cubic Ising models at a coupling $K_2 = 0.22165$. The curve illustrates that these data are consistent with a smooth finite-size dependence of the susceptibility.

amplitudes, are constant along the critical line. In order to investigate this matter, we have carried out MC simulations of finite Baxter models on three different points of the critical line, and we sampled the magnetization distribution function. The results, when scaled properly, seem to converge smoothly with increasing system size. Typical results for 32×32 systems are shown in Figures 15, 16 and 17. They demonstrate that the magnetization profile does vary along the critical line. A more elaborate analysis on the quantity $\langle m^4 \rangle / \langle m^2 \rangle^2$, including its finite-size dependence, confirms this conclusion. Further details will be published elsewhere.

E. An Ising Model with Two- and Three-Spin Interactions

We investigate a 2-D Ising model [36] with two-spin interactions in the y direction and three-spin interactions in the x direction:

$$\mathcal{H} = K_2 \, \Sigma_{i,j} \, s_{i,j} s_{i,j+1} + K_3 \, \Sigma_{i,j} \, s_{i,j} s_{i+1,j} s_{i+2,j}. \tag{8}$$

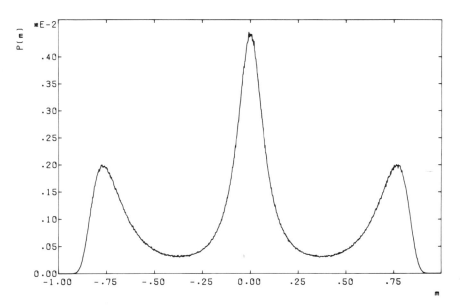

Figure 15. Histogram of the magnetization of the Baxter model with $K_3 = 0.441$ and $K_4 = 0$.

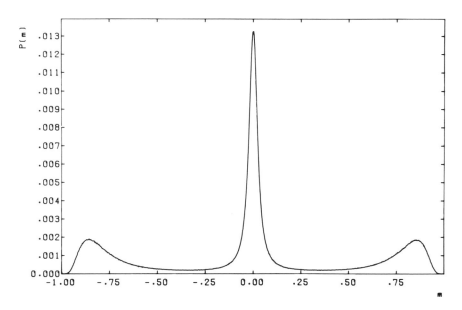

Figure 16. Histogram of the magnetization of the Baxter model with $K_3 = 0.241$ and $K_4 = 0.347$.

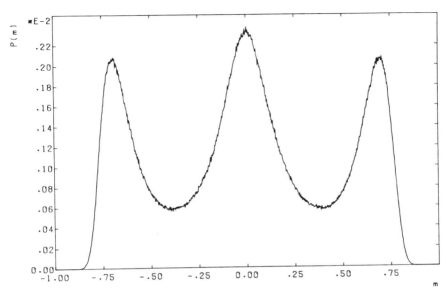

Figure 17. Histogram of the magnetization of the Baxter model with $K_3 = 0.722$ and $K_4 = -0.347$.

This model is self-dual [37]: it is expected to be critical when

$$\sinh(2K_2)\sinh(2K_3) = 1. \tag{9}$$

The model has four equivalent ground states. However, the interfaces between the associated ordered phases are not exactly equivalent. Considerable effort has been applied to verify whether the model belongs to the universality class of the four-state Potts model, e.g. by means of finite-size scaling of small systems with linear sizes L up to $L = 15$. These calculations yielded a temperature exponent $y_T \approx 4/3$, in contrast with the exactly known four-state Potts value 3/2. However, this is insufficient evidence to conclude that our model is outside the four-state Potts universality class; if it does belong to this class, then one expects anomalously slow convergence of the finite-size analysis. Usually when one estimates y_T from finite-size data with system sizes up to L, the result converges as a power series in L^{-1} when $L \to \infty$. However, for the four-state Potts and related models, the expansion parameter is $(\ln L)^{-1}$ instead. For this reason it is desirable to obtain finite-size data for much larger values of L than as usual.

Thus we have used the DISP to simulate this Isinglike model at the expected critical point $K_2 = K_3 = \frac{1}{2} \ln(1 + \sqrt{2})$, for system sizes $L = 8$,

16, . . . ,128. Very long simulations (3×10^8 sweeps for the largest system size) were performed in order to obtain good statistical accuracy.

Figure 18 shows estimates $y'_T (L)$ obtained from the MC specific heat results for system sizes up to L, as a function of $(\ln L)^{-2}$. On the basis of a renormalization group description, $y'_T (L)$ is expected to behave linearly on this scale for sufficiently large L. Although considerable curvature is still present for the largest L values, it is clear that these data strongly support the value $y_T = \frac{3}{2}$. This confirms that the present model is indeed in the four-state Potts universality class.

The model discussed above is a special case of the following Hamiltonian with two-spin and n-spin interactions:

$$\mathcal{H} = \Sigma_{i,j}(K_2 s_{i,j} s_{i,j+1} + K_n \Pi_{p=0}^{n-1} s_{i+p,j}).$$ (10)

For $n = 2$ we recover the 2-D Ising model and for $n = 3$ the model described above. These models are self-dual for all n; the expected critical

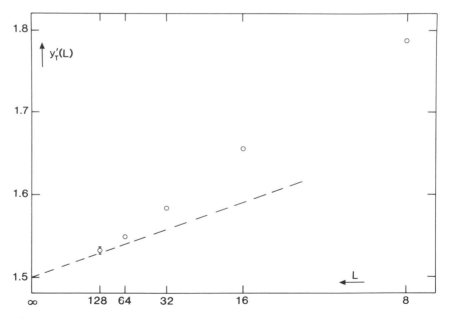

Figure 18. Estimates $y'_T (L)$ of the temperature exponent y_T of the $n = 3$ model as a function of L on a $(1/\ln L)^{-2}$ scale. As explained in the text, linear behavior may be expected for large L. The dashed line represents a plausible extrapolation leading to $y_T = \frac{3}{2}$. Except for the largest value of L, the numerical uncertainties do not exceed the size of the data points.

point does not depend on n. We have also simulated the $n = 4$ model. This model is known to undergo a first-order transition at the self-dual point. Systems that are not too small remain very long in the same phase during MC simulations at the transition point. Typical configurations of a 512×512 system at the transition temperature are shown in Figures 19 and 20. More details of this work and adequate references to previous work are given in [38].

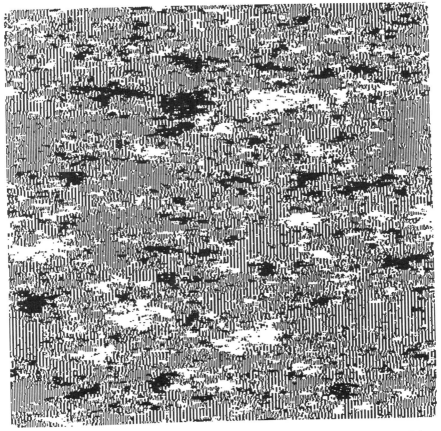

Figure 19. The $n = 4$ model with linear size $L = 512$ at the transition point. This configuration was obtained after 1.5×10^5 sweeps, starting from a disordered (random) configuration. No transition to an ordered phase was observed: the simulation time to observe such a transition grows very rapidly with system size.

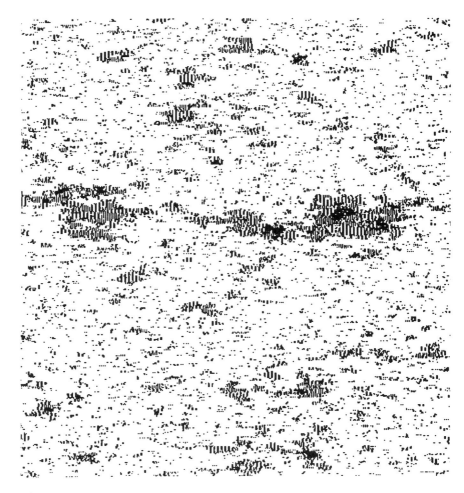

Figure 20. The $n = 4$ model with linear size $L = 512$ at the transition point. This configuration was obtained after 5×10^4 sweeps, starting from an ordered (all spins up) phase. Although small patches corresponding with other ordered phases appear, the background is stable over long simulations.

F. The Square Ising Model with Crossing Bonds

We have also investigated the ferromagnetic critical line of the simple quadratic Ising model with nearest-neighbor couplings K_2 and next-nearest-neighbor couplings K_3:

$$\mathcal{H} = \Sigma_{i,j}(K_2 s_{i,j}(s_{i+1,j} + s_{i,j+1}) + K_3 s_{i,j}(s_{i+1,j+1} + s_{i+1,j-1})). \quad (11)$$

For K_3 not too large the location of the ferromagnetic critical line ($K_2 > 0$) is well known: it can be accurately determined by numerical methods such as series expansion and finite-size scaling. Besides, the critical points for $K_2 = 0$ and $K_3 = 0$ are known exactly from Onsager's exact solution. Unfortunately, for $K_2 \gtrsim 2$, numerical methods become increasingly inaccurate, so that the phase diagram was not well known in that region of the K_2–K_3 plane. Also MC results rapidly become less accurate when K_2 increases; this method alone is inadequate to reach the large K_2 limit.

However, help is available from the renormalization group theory. This theory predicts that, for large K_2, the critical line behaves asymptotically as $\epsilon_c(K_2) \simeq \alpha\, e^{-K_2}$ where α is an unknown constant and $\epsilon = 2K_2 + 4K_3$.

Thus we have two different sources of information about the location of the ferromagnetic critical line: firstly, numerical information restricted to sufficiently small K_2, and secondly a renormalization group prediction containing an unknown parameter and applying only to sufficiently large

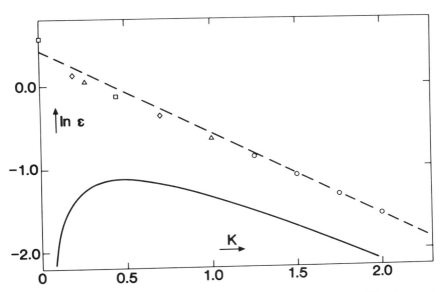

Figure 21. Plot of the critical points $\ln \epsilon$ versus K_2 as defined in the text. The data points include, in addition to those obtained during the present Monte Carlo simulations ($\bigcirc$), the series expansion results of Oitmaa [40] ($\triangle$), Onsager's [41] exact critical coupling ($\square$) and finite size scaling results ($\diamond$) obtained by Nightingale and Blöte [42]. For large K_2, the renormalization trajectories satisfy $\ln \epsilon = -K_2 +$ constant. The full curve represents a so-called disorder solution [39]: the system is known to be paramagnetic on this line.

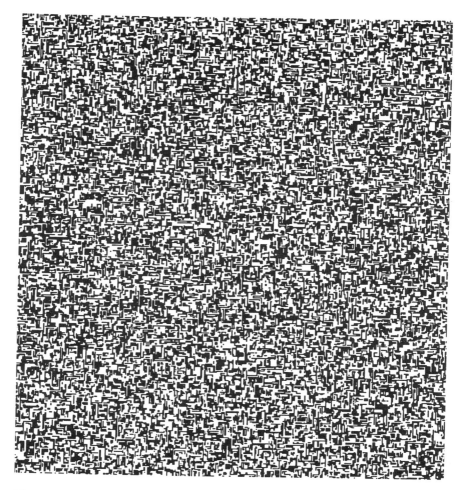

Figure 22. Spin configuration on a 512×512 lattice with a nearest neighbor coupling $K_2 = 1.2$ and a next-nearest coupling $K_3 = -0.6$. This picture was taken after a simulation of 10^4 sweeps. Apart from a change of scale, it bears some similarity to Figs. 23 and 24.

values of K_2. If sufficient overlap between the two ranges of K_2 exists, we can determine α, and therewith the whole critical line.

Therefore we have used the DISP to determine the critical line up to as large values of K_2 as practical, i.e. $K_2 \leq 2.0$. The method we used relies on the finite-size scaling behavior of the second and fourth moments of the magnetization distribution, which is easily determined during MC simula-

Figure 23. Spin configuration on a 512×512 lattice with a nearest-neighbor coupling $K_2 = 2.0$ and a next-nearest-neighbor coupling $K_3 = -1.0$. This picture was taken after a simulation of 5×10^4 sweeps. Apart from a change of scale, it bears some similarity to Figs. 22 and 24.

tions. At criticality, scaling predicts that $\langle m^2 \rangle^2 / \langle m^4 \rangle$ is a nontrivial constant independent of the system size L, at least for sufficiently large L. For fixed values K_2, we have determined K_3 such that this scaling behavior was obeyed. The results are shown in Figure 21 in terms of $\ln \epsilon$ versus K_2. Statistical errors do not exceed the size of the data points. The total simulation time necessary to reach this accuracy was about five weeks. We

276   A. Hoogland, A. Compagner, and H. W. J. Blöte

Figure 24. Spin configuration of a 512×512 lattice with a nearest-neighbor coupling $K_2 = 2.8$ and a next-nearest neighbor coupling $K_3 = -1.4$. This picture was taken after a simulation of 2 times 10^4 sweeps. Apart from a change of scale, it bears some similarity to Figs. 22 and 23.

observe that there exists indeed a range $1.5 \lesssim K_2 \lesssim 2.0$ where the numerical results follow a renormalization trajectory as predicted for large K_2 (dashed line). On the basis of these data, we conclude that $\alpha = 1.64 \pm 0.04$. The critical line has the line $K_2 = -2K_3$ as an asymptote. Typical spin configurations of 512×512 systems are shown in Figures 22, 23 and 24 for three points on the asymptote. These figures clearly exhibit signs of scale covariance, which is predicted by the renormalization group theory for $K_2 \to \infty$: the physical length scale is proportional to e^{K_2}. More details and references are given in [39].

VIII. Current Activities

A. Additional Hardware Features of the DISP

1. A 64K × 32-bit TP Look-Up Table   Because of the limited size of the TP table (i.e. the number of entries), the Hamiltonians that can be realized in simulations of 3-D Ising systems may contain only interactions between nearest neighbors and, depending on the type of 3-D lattice simulated, next-nearest neighbors (see Section III.D).

The simulation of cubic systems with multispin interactions requires a TP table larger than the one described in Section III.D which has 1K × 32-bit locations. To study more elaborate Hamiltonians in 2-D and 3-D systems, including for instance a 3-D simple cubic system with a local configuration of 27 spins (central spin plus 6 nearest, 12 next-nearest and 8 third-nearest neighbors), we decided to build a TP table of 64K × 32 bits. This is sufficiently large to allow even breaking down the lattice sums in the x, y and z directions. The latter implies the necessity to have more than four lattice-sum registers available, as will be discussed in the next section.

2. Extension of the Number of Lattice-Sum Registers   Due to the expansion of the TP table, the number of lattice-sum registers in which the MC results are collected must be increased to eight, in order to study efficiently the more complicated Hamiltonians that now can be studied. Likewise, the amount of different adjustment sets, depending on the chosen local configuration and containing the actual adjustments of the lattice sums when a spin–flip is invoked, expand to a level where preprogramming these in PROMs (#1 to #8 in Figure 5) is not practical. Instead, each new lattice-sum register (the old ones will be replaced) will have a RAM available in which the adjustments that pertain to a particular lattice sum will be stored by the host computer in the initialization phase of a simulation.

The hardware implementation of the new lattice-sum registers will be similar to those for the determination of the correlation functions in MCRG experiments (as shown in Figure 6). However, the updating mechanism will be quite different since the MCRG lattice-sums are calculated by making a sequential sweep through the lattice, whereas the eight new lattice-sum registers have to be updated each time a spin–flip takes place.

3. Spin–Spin Correlation Function Hardware   For many Ising models the spin–spin correlation function as a function of the spin–spin distance is an important quantity, but its determination by the host computer is a time-consuming affair. In many cases this implies a substantial slowing down of the MC experiment. For this reason a hardware device is being built that performs the necessary calculations on a number of rows sampled from the lattice in one particular direction, while the MC process is continuing. This device is equipped with a 256K RAM and will be able to calculate the spin–spin correlation function using all rows for lattices with up to 256K spins. For larger lattices the number of rows used in the calculation of the correlation function must be reduced in order to have the number of spins fit within the 256K memory. In all cases the total calculation time is less than the time needed for making one MC sweep through the lattice.

The correlator will be especially useful when the lattice size in the direction of the correlation function is large. This was the case during our simulations of the 2-D ANNNI model (Section VII.B), and such a correlator, if available, would have speeded up the calculations considerably. Another obvious possibility to utilize the correlator is for the zero-temperature triangular Ising model, in order to find out whether or not the spin–spin correlation function decays algebraically.

B. Profile of the Second-Generation DISP

The greatly increased performance and higher integration level of newly developed ICs present a challenge to build a "second-generation" Ising system processor that is at least a factor of 100 faster than the DISP while having basically the same structure. This structure has the advantages set out in Section III: simultaneous determination of up to 30 neighbors, no influence of the actual amount of neighbors on the speed per MC step, extremely simple implementation of MCRG procedures and the possibility to select spins at random. Along these lines, we are at present designing the DISP-2.

The same cell structure outlined in Section III will be preserved. Therefore, the memory-bank structure is not redesigned, except for the lattice-size masking facility that will be able now to allow linear lattice sizes of multiples of eight (2-D) or four (3-D).

The use of memory chips with access times of around 20 ns will allow us to pipeline the operations to be performed down to time-slices as small as 30 ns. When eight MC steps are effectuated in parallel, the speed per elementary spin update will be around 4 ns. This time includes the execution of spin–flips, since the arrangement of the spin memory in the pipeline and its access mechanism allow for both spin retrieval and spin–flip within one pipestroke. Special features (i.e., extension of the spin memory and a rearrangement of the neighbor determination section) will result in a reduction of the number of S-bus lines (for eight parallel sections one would need already $8 \times 31 = 248$ lines) by a factor of two. This would make the implementation of 16 parallel sections feasible, each containing its own look-up table, comparator and random-number generator. The resulting speed will then be 2 ns for each MC step. This figure is the theoretically attainable speed when all operations of the MC process can be squeezed into pipestrokes of 30 ns or less, requiring that capacitive cross-talk and undesirable effects in loading conditions are avoided.

Major efforts will be needed in preserving flexibility and in keeping down the size of eight spin–flip decision sections. The incorporation of gate arrays in several stages of the design is imperative, not only because of the size reduction but also because of the very high speed of these "semi-custom-design" chips. The random-number generator may serve as an example: in principle, it is possible to incorporate into a single chip a two-bit feedback shift-register with a length of 9689 bits and all possible feedback positions for which a maximum length sequence is generated.

We expect to start building the DISP-2 by the end of 1988.

Note added in proof (June 1988): Presently, we also consider alternative possibilities concerning the cell structure for the DISP-2 mentioned in Section VIII B.

Acknowledgments

We acknowledge helpful discussions with Prof. B. P. Th. Veltman, Dr. W. Selke and Dr. A. F. Bakker. The assistance is acknowledged also of N. Karssemeyer, J. Spaa, B. Selman, J. W. Schilperoort, P. A. M. Cornelissen, J. H. Croockewit, J. A. de Bruin, A. L. van Willigen and J. P. L. van Amen, who as students were involved during various stages of the project.

One of us (H. B.) acknowledges useful suggestions from, and exchange of information with, Prof. J. M. J. van Leeuwen, Prof. H. J. Hilhorst, Prof. R. H. Swendsen, Prof. D. Wallace, Dr. A. Bruce and Dr. P. Bak, as well as support from the FOM foundation and NATO grant #198/84.

References

1. Hilhorst, H. J., Bakker, A. F., Bruin, C., Compagner, A., and Hoogland, A. (1984). *J. Stat. Phys.* **34**, 987.
2. Hoogland, A., Spaa, J., Selman, B., and Compagner, A. (1983). *J. Comp. Phys.* **51**, 250.
3. Bakker, A. F., Bruin, C., van Dieren, F., and Hilhorst, H. J. (1982). *Phys. Lett.* **93A**, 67.
4. Vogelij, H. N. J., van Leeuwen, C., and Veltman, B. P. Th. (1981). *Springer Series in Synergetics,* Vol. 9, p. 97.

5.   Bakker, A. F. (1984). Thesis, Delft.
6.   Yang, C. P. (1963). *Proc. Symp. Appl. Math.* **15**, 351.
7.   Fosdick, L. D. (1959). *Phys. Rev.* **116**, 565.
8.   Swendsen, R. H. (1979). *Phys. Rev. Lett.* **42**, 859.
9.   Niemeyer, Th., and van Leeuwen, J. M. J. (1976). In *Phase Transitions and Critical Phenomena* (C. Domb and M. S. Green, eds.) Vol. 6, p. 425. Academic Press, London.
10. Knuth, D. (1969). *The Art of Computer Programming,* Vol. 2, 82. Addison-Wesley, Reading, Mass.
11. Tausworthe, R. C. (1965). *Math. Comp.* **19**, 201.
12. Golomb, S. W. (1967). *Shift Register Sequences.* Holden-Day, San Francisco, Calif.
13. Zierler, N., and Brillhart, J. (1968). *Inform. and Control.* **13**, 541.
14. Zierler, N., and Brillhart, J. (1969). *Inform. and Control.* **14**, 566.
15. Zierler, N. (1969). *Inform. and Control.* **15**, 67.
16. Zierler, N. (1970). *Inform. and Control.* **16**, 502.
17. Compagner, A., and Hoogland, A. "Maximum-Length Sequences, Cellular Automata and Random Numbers". (1987). *J. Comp. Phys.* **71**, 391.
18. Lindholm, J. H. (1968). *IEEE Trans. Inform. Theory.* **14**, 569.
19. Fredricsson, S. A. (1975). *IEEE Trans. Inform. Theory.* **21**, 115.
20. Ferdinand, A. E., and Fisher, M. E. (1969). *Phys. Rev.* **185**, 832.
21. Kirkpatrick, S., and Stoll, E. P. (1981). *J. Comp. Phys.* **40**, 517.
22. Houtappel, R. M. F. (1950). *Physica.* **16**, 425.
23. Baxter, R. J., and Wu, F. Y. (1974). *Phys. Rev. Lett.* **31**, 1294.
24. Baxter, R. J. (1980). *J. Phys. A.* **13**, L61.
25. Kinzel, W., and Schick, M. (1981). *Phys. Rev.* **B23**, 3435.
26. Nienhuis, B., Hilhorst, H. J., and Blöte, H. W. J. (1984). *J. Phys.* **A17**, 3559.
27. Villain, J., and Bak, P. (1981). *J. Physique.* **42**, 657.
28. Selke, W., and Fisher, M. E. (1980). *Z. Phys.* **B40**, 71.
29. Barber, M. N., and Selke, W. (1982). *J. Phys.* **A15**, L617.
30. Duxbury, P. M., Yeomans, J., and Beale, P. D. (1984). *J. Phys.* **A17**, L179.
31. Barber, M. N., Pearson, R. B., Toussaint, D., and Richardson, J. L. (1983). Univ. Calif. preprint, #NSF-ITP-83-144.
32. Pearson, R. B., Richardson, J. L., and Toussaint, D. (1983). *J. Comp. Phys.* **51**, 241.
33. Parisi, G., and Rapuano, F. (March 1985). CERN preprint, #CERN-TH.4141/85.
34. Baxter, R. J. (1971). *Phys. Rev. Lett.* **26**, 832.
35. Barber, M. N., and Baxter, R. J. (1973). *J. Phys.* **C6**, 2913.
36. Debierre, J. M., and Turban, L. (1983). *J. Phys.* **A16**, 3571.
37. Gruber, C., Hintermann, A., and Merlini, D. (1977). *Group Analysis of Classical Lattice Systems,* p. 25. Springer, Berlin, New York.
38. Blöte, H. W. J., Compagner, A., Cornelissen, P. A. M., Hoogland, A., Mallezie, F., and Vanderzande, C. (1986). *Physica.* **139A**, 395.
39. Blöte, H. W. J., Compagner, A., and Hoogland, A. (1987). *Physica.* **141A**, 375.
40. Oitmaa, J. (1981). *J. Phys.* **A14**, 1159.
41. Onsager, L. (1944). *Phys. Rev.* **65**, 117.
42. Nightingale, M. P., and Blöte, H. W. J. (1982). *J. Phys.* **A15**, L33.

Index

A

ALU (arithmetic logic unit), 56, 105, 114, 209
Amdahl's law, 147
AMETEK, 14
array processors, 137
assembly language, 45, 63
asynchronously, 9

B

bandwidth, 9
bus, 168, 206, 238

C

"C," 31
chess, 35
CHiP, 81
CMOS, 85
communication, 33, 74, 86, 169, 249
complex system, 22
conjugate gradient, 72
connection, 28, 83
cosmic cube, 3, 10, 33
CRAY–1, 64
CRAY X–MP, 93
crystalline operating system, 33
CUBIX, 33

D

decomposition, 52, 149
disks, 140
domain decomposition, 19, 34
DRAM, 55

E

efficiency, 28
Ethernet, 16

F

Feynman path integral formulation, 43
finite–element machine, 80
finite–element method, 68, 101
floating point arithmetic, 45
Fourier transforms, 159
FPS–164, 137

G

Gauss–Seidel method, 126
geometry, 67
grain size, 24, 51, 173
granules, 35
graphics, 67
grid, 46

H

host, 16, 34, 54

HP 1000, 192, 237
hypercube, 1, 8, 19, 29, 80

I
IBM, 137
ILLIAC IV, 102
inner product, 79
INTEL
  8086/8087, 3
  8088, 86
  80286, 55, 108
  8203, 222
  microprocessor, 116
interconnect, 115

L
latency, 33, 81, 171
leapfrog, 186
linked–list method, 188
load balance, 34, 147
look–up table, 238, 274
loops, 144
loose synchronization, 33

M
matrix, 35
matrix multiplication, 63
MAX board, 141
memory, 24, 47, 56, 168
mesh, 75
MFLOPS, 93, 123, 133
MIMD, 24, 46, 104, 141
MISD machine, 103
molecular dynamics, 150, 183
Monte Carlo, 43, 53, 146
multitasking, 35

N
NCUBE, 14
NEC μPD70108, 85
neural networks, 8
nodes, 46, 55, 103, 121
numerical integration, 43

O
operating system, 33
optimizer, 63
overhead, 92

P
parallelism, 68
pattern recognition, 22
performance, 93, 146, 225

pipeline, 50, 106
pipeline registers, 201
portable, 34, 141
precision, 46
processors
  control, 207
  floating point, 50
  Motorola 68020, 14
  vector, 57
PROM, 194

Q
quantum chromodynamics (QCD), 2, 40f

R
RAM, 50, 55, 86, 140, 195, 241, 256, 276
RAM/ROM, 108
random number generator, 250
random numbers, 52
reconfigurable, 76
  dynamically, 105

S
shared memory, 9, 32
shift/delay unit, 125
shift register, 255
SIMD machine, 24, 52, 102
SISD machine, 102
spectral methods, 101
speedup factor, 28, 148
startup, 92
SURF cube system, 9
switch, 50, 107
switching networks, 114
symbolic manipulation program, 2
synchronization, 48, 148

T
throughput, 33
transmission rates, 170
TRW 1022, 55

U
UNIX, 2, 122

V
VAX, 2, 12, 54, 103
VAX 8200, 122
VLSI, 2

W
wave equation, 159
WEITEK, 14
word length, 193

Computational Techniques

Edited by Berni J. Alder and Sidney Fernbach

Garry Rodrigue, editor, *Parallel Computations*

Michael P. Ekstrom, editor, *Digital Image Processing Techniques*

Jeremiah U. Brackbill and Bruce I. Cohen, editors, *Multiple Time Scales*

Bruce A. Bolt, editor, *Seismic Strong Motion Synthetics*

Berni J. Alder, editor, *Special Purpose Computers*